PLYWOOD PROJECTS

35 EASY-TO-BUILD PROJECTS FOR YOUR HOME, YOUR SHOP AND THE OUTDOORS

BY PAUL AND MARYA BUTLER

Rodale Press, Emmaus, Pennsylvania

Printed in the United States of America on acid-free ⊗,
recycled paper ♻

Editor in Chief: William Gottlieb
Senior Managing Editor: Margaret Lydic Balitas
Editor: David Schiff
Editorial/Administrative Assistant: Stacy A. Brobst

Cover and Book Design: Jerry O'Brien
Photography: Paul Butler
Illustrations: Marya Butler

If you have any questions or comments concerning this book,
please write:
> Rodale Press
> Book Reader Service
> 33 East Minor Street
> Emmaus, PA 18098

Library of Congress Cataloging-in-Publication Data

Butler, Paul.
    Plywood projects : 35 easy-to-build projects for your
  home, your shop, and the outdoors / Paul and Marya Butler.
        p.   cm.
    Includes bibliographical references.
    ISBN 0–87857–952–4 hardcover
    ISBN 0–87857–958–3 paperback
    1. Plywood craft.   2. Cabinet-work.   3. Woodwork.
I. Butler, Marya.   II. Title.
  TT191.B88   1991
  684.1′04—dc20   90–19575
                                                        CIP

Distributed in the book trade by St. Martin's Press

2 4 6 8 10 9 7 5 3 1   hardcover

2 4 6 8 10 9 7 5 3 1   paperback

CONTENTS

Acknowledgments vii

Chapter One   Plywood: Combining the Best
of Man and Nature 1

Chapter Two   Tools and Techniques.................... 11

Chapter Three   Shelving and Storage Projects........ 25

Partition Shelves............................. 27
Magazine Cabinet 33
Hanging File 39
Sliding Shelves.. 44
Blanket Chest 48
Wedged Shelves 53
Banker's Box Cabinet.................................. 58
Security Gun Cabinet 63
Coat Racks.. 69
Wall Bins... 74
Closet Organizer.. 79
Accessory Shelves.. 85
Mug and Spice Rack 90
Kitchen Knife Rack 96
Recycling Bins 99

Chapter Four   Indoor Tables 105

Trestle Table... 107
Dropleaf Table 117
Bed and Breakfast Tray 122

Chapter Five   Plywood and Epoxy Projects 127

Mahogany Picnic Table 139
Camp Box 149
Hexagon Hot Tub 155
Rowing Dory.. 165
Camper Cap.. 187
Fireplace Bench 214

Chapter Six   More Outdoor Projects 219

    Folding Picnic Table 221
    Solar Shower 227
    Patio Box.. 233
    Boat or Garden Cart................................... 237
    Floating Bait Tank 240
    Camp Rocker.. 246
    Shooting Bench 249

Chapter Seven   Around the Shop........................ 257

    Woodworking Bench................................... 259
    Tool Caddy 267
    Tool Bench/Sawhorse 271
    Tool Strip 274

Chapter Eight   And Just for Fun! 277

    Rocking Moose 279
    Flower Press... 291

Sources 295

ACKNOWLEDGMENTS

We had a lot of help with this book from start to finish. Bill Hylton of Rodale Press pointed out ideas for organization and content, and David Schiff then took over the heavy work. David was patient enough to let me rant and rave about details from time to time and get it out of my system so we could move on. Best of all, he has a sense of humor. May his projects always turn out well.

Maryann Olson of the American Plywood Association helped get the whole project rolling. She provided encouragement, technical support, and expert information regarding softwood and overlay plywood.

Bill Powell of States Industries provided support and education regarding various types of hardwood plywood. Bill was a pleasure to work with, even when his schedule got hectic. His voice on the phone was always a calming, organizing influence.

Jim Derck, Jim Watson, and Jan and Meade Gougeon of Gougeon Brothers supplied ideas and information regarding the proper and innovative use of epoxy. I've been relying on these guys for almost 20 years for advice, ideas, and technical information.

Also, I would like to thank Tony "The Greek" Zografides of Newport Mantel Company and the notorious McCullouch brothers at McCullouchs Cabinet shop in Newport Beach. They put up with me while this book was in the formative stage.

Finally, I would like to thank my partner, Marya, for, among many other things, her design work and illustrations. Without her talents and her role as a sounding board and confidante, this book just wouldn't have happened. She did it all while being mother to our seven-year-old daughter and while training for the triathlons.

Paul Butler

CHAPTER ONE

PLYWOOD: COMBINING THE BEST OF MAN AND NATURE

In the projects that follow, we will explore the many uses of a special, hybrid material. This material, known as plywood, marries many of the best characteristics of solid wood with the advantages of a regular, man-made panel. It's a marriage that allows the home woodworker to efficiently complete projects that otherwise would be difficult or impossible.

Solid wood is a wonderful and beautiful material. It is strong, pleasing to the touch, and responsive to tools, with grain patterns that never cease to fascinate. But solid wood has a mind of its own. Most significantly, solid wood is very hydroscopic—moisture always moves through it, which causes it to expand and contract, twist, bow, and cup in response to humidity changes. This movement is much more pronounced across the grain than with the grain. The amount of expansion and contraction you can expect changes with conditions and with each species, but in all cases the effect is cumulative. That is, the wider you make something—a table top for example—the more its width will change and the trickier the design problem becomes.

The other difficulty with solid wood is that it doesn't grow in convenient shapes and sizes. To make a table top of solid wood, you would have to glue up several planks to get the width you need. You also would need to run the planks through a thickness planer. Even if you bought planed stock, you still would need to joint the edges and then glue them up using numerous clamps. After the glue dried, you would have squeezed out glue to remove and lots of scraping and/or sanding to do.

Plywood Makes It Possible

These problems disappear if you make that same table top from a sheet of high-quality plywood. The hydroscopic problem is solved because plywood consists of an odd number of layers, with the grain direction alternated from one layer to the next. As a result, each layer counteracts the movement of the next layer to it. This means you don't have to design around wood movement. And rarely would you want to make that table top bigger than a standard 4 × 8 sheet of plywood. So instead of all that planing, jointing, gluing, clamping, scraping, and sanding to create a surface that might split or warp anyway, all you need to do is cut a sheet of plywood to size and do a little finish sanding. That's why the only power tools you will need to complete most of the projects in this book are a table saw and a drill, and sometimes a router, jigsaw, or circular saw.

Plywood's alternating layers offer a couple of other advantages. One is that, unlike solid wood, you can screw or nail into plywood close to the edges without worrying about splitting the wood. Another advantage is that plywood has substantial strength across the grain of the face veneers as well as along the grain. Solid wood is much weaker along the grain—a fact we use to our advantage when we split firewood or cedar shake shingles. Plywood's strength is that when you build something with it, you can often orient the face veneers in whatever way you find most aesthetically pleasing or that creates the least waste.

Howard Hughes dramatically demonstrated plywood's great strength-to-weight ratio when he built the *Spruce Goose*, an enormous plywood airplane.

Modern glues used for plywood are stronger than the wood they hold together. The result is a material that is stronger pound per pound than steel. Howard Hughes put plywood's excellent strength-to-weight ratio to work when he built his *Spruce Goose* airplane of plywood and glue.

Plywood's strength, stability, and regularity can work in harmony with other modern materials such as epoxy and fiberglass sheathing to produce structures that are very stiff, abrasion-resistant, and water proof. As a result, you can make outdoor projects that you might not otherwise think of building from plywood. A picnic table, rowing dory, camper cap for your truck, and hot tub are projects you'll find in chapter five of this book, which is devoted to epoxy projects. Chapter five will give us a chance to share a lot of what we have learned over many years of building plywood and epoxy boats.

Problems with Plywood

All of the great features of plywood are not without their price. Most of the projects in this book use hardwood plywood that is almost always more expensive per board foot than solid hardwood of the same species. Another problem is that a 4 × 8 sheet can be unwieldy to handle and cut in the home shop. Often you will need to cut pieces to approximate size with a portable circular saw before making final cuts on the table saw. For large final pieces, you may even have to make finish cuts with a straightedge-guided circular saw. There are other problems, too. The 4 × 8

sheet often leaves you with more waste than if you were working with smaller pieces of solid wood. The face veneers of hardwood plywood are only about $\frac{1}{30}$ inch thick and require special care when cutting and handling. Face veneers tend to splinter when cut, especially across the grain, so it's a good idea to score your cuts with a sharp utility knife or cover your cut line with masking tape. And be careful when you move this material around; you can't sand out gouges, dents, or stains.

The face of a piece of plywood looks just like solid wood, but plywood reveals its true nature at every edge. The multiple plies of good quality plywood panels can be used to make an attractive design; an approach we take in many of the projects in this book. Otherwise, you'll have to cover exposed edges with wood.

Another disadvantage is that your selection of plywood with hardwood face veneers usually is limited to the three or four most popular species stocked by most lumberyards—birch, mahogany, oak, and perhaps maple or cherry. If you are willing to pay more for a special order or are lucky enough to have a friend in a production cabinet shop who'll let you piggyback on an order, you'll have access to a dozen or so of the most common hardwood veneers.

Finally, hardwood plywood panels often vary by $\frac{1}{64}$ to $\frac{1}{32}$ inch from their stated dimension. In most cases, they are smaller not bigger than stated. This often occurs because the plywood was manufactured abroad to metric measurements. But even plywood from domestic mills can vary in size. You can adjust jigs, measurements, and cuts to compensate, but it's a good idea to buy all your plywood for a project at the same time.

Anatomy of a Plywood Sheet

Choosing a face veneer is only the first step in selecting a plywood sheet that's best for the project you have in mind. There are several types and many grades of plywood available. Before we get into a detailed discussion of types and grades, however, let's take a look at the anatomy of plywood and how it is manufactured.

Originally, veneer meant a thin decorative layer of valuable wood laminated onto less expensive wood. But in talking about plywood, all of the layers are made up of veneers. As mentioned, all plywood is made up from an odd number of layers, or plies. Sometimes a layer consists of two or more veneers, or plies, glued together with their grain patterns running parallel.

So, while a plywood panel always has an odd number of layers, it may have an even number of veneers.

The outer veneers are called *face veneers*, although when one side of the panel is a better grade than the other, the inferior side may be referred to as the *back veneer*. The grain of the face veneers always runs the length of the sheet. A hardwood plywood panel is identified by the species of the face veneer. Thus, a panel of oak plywood may have inner plies of other hardwoods or even softwoods. In hardwood panels, the face veneer is usually the thinnest ply. The face veneers must be the same thickness on both sides of the panel.

Some plywood panels, usually the thinner sheets such as the ¼ inch or ⅜ inch that are often used for cabinet backs, simply consist of three layers. The middle layer is called the *core* and is usually thicker than the outer layers.

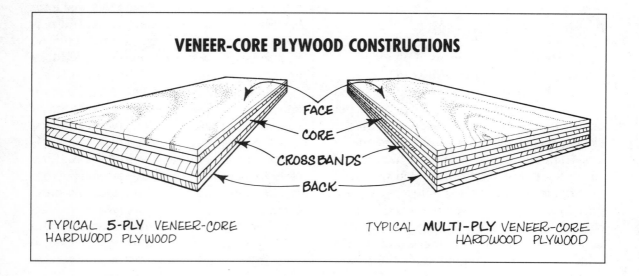

VENEER-CORE PLYWOOD CONSTRUCTIONS

FACE
CORE
CROSSBANDS
BACK

TYPICAL **5-PLY** VENEER-CORE HARDWOOD PLYWOOD

TYPICAL **MULTI-PLY** VENEER-CORE HARDWOOD PLYWOOD

If the plywood has five or more layers, the plies between each face and the center are known as *crossbands*. The crossbands don't have to be the same species or the same thickness as the face veneers or the core or even each other. But for every crossband on one side of the core, there must be one of the same species and thickness on the other side. This is to ensure a balanced, stable panel.

Four types of cores are used to make plywood. All softwood plywood and most hardwood plywood have a veneer core. This is the only type of sheet used in the projects in this book. Typically, the core will be thicker than the other plies, but this is not always the case. A subcategory of veneer core known as *multi-ply veneer core* is a very high-quality product with seven or more plies. Usually the core ply of multi-ply is the same thickness as the crossbands. Multi-ply is extremely stable and its voidless edges can be strikingly attractive when left exposed. Several projects in this book use an American-made multi-ply called Appleply. A readily available European version of multi-ply is commonly known as baltic birch.

The remaining three core types are used only for hardwood plywood. They are *lumber core, particleboard core*, and *fiberboard core*. In lumber core, the core is relatively thick and consists of short, narrow strips of lumber that have been edge-glued together. It's not quite as strong as veneer core, but is used in some applications where an exposed edge is required. Particleboard and fiberboard cores are thick. These cores are much weaker than veneer or lumber cores. They provide an inexpensive alternative when strength is not important.

How Plywood Is Made

The plywood industry is divided into two categories: softwood and hardwood. Approximately 80 percent of the softwood plywood sold in North America is produced by mills that belong to the American Plywood Association (APA). These mills voluntarily grade their plywood according to standards the APA has established in cooperation with the National Bureau of Standards, a part of the U.S. Department of Commerce. No law says the mills have to follow APA standards, but most softwood plywood sheets sold in the United States bear an APA stamp that tells you everything you need to know to put the sheet to good use. Softwood plywood is used mostly for structural, nondecorative purposes such as house sheathing and floor underlayment. Although most of the projects in this book use hardwood plywood, some use special types of softwood plywood, specifically siding for the solar shower, and marine plywood, high density overlay (HDO), and medium density overlay (MDO) plywood. You'll learn more about these materials in the grading section of this chapter.

Many hardwood plywood mills in the United States grade their plywood according to standards set by the Hardwood Plywood Manufacturers Association (HPMA). But hardwood plywood grading is less standardized and controlled than softwood plywood grading. You need to ask your supplier if the panels you are purchasing are HPMA-certified because they may not be stamped. Plenty of good-quality hardwood plywood made in this country and abroad is not HPMA graded, so it's important to know something about the construction of plywood so you can judge the quality of the panels for yourself.

The process of manufacturing plywood is a complicated one that varies from mill to mill and application to application. In this book, we'll stick to the basics as they relate to how you will eventually use the plywood.

Virtually all softwood plywood veneers and 80 to 90 percent of all hardwood plywood veneers are cut on a rotary lathe. The bark is removed and the log is wetted and heated to make the wood fibers less brittle. The log is secured in the center of each end of the lathe and rotated against a knife to produce a continuous sheet of veneer. The process looks like a giant roll of paper towel being unwound. In most species, rotary cutting produces a bold, variegated grain pattern. It's the simplest, most efficient method of producing veneer because it usually covers a panel in one piece. Rotary cutting is used for all softwood plywoods where grain pattern is not as important as structural concerns. When high-quality hardwood logs are used, rotary cutting also produces very attractive grain patterns that are suitable for face veneers in most decorative applications.

Sometimes hardwood plywood face veneers aren't rotary cut. The veneers must be flat cut because they are to be matched. A matched plywood face can be very at-

tractive, much like a matched set of glued up boards. Architects can create dazzling effects by special ordering whole sets of panels that have been matched to each other in various ways. But short of expensive special orders, hardwood plywood usually comes book matched, slip matched, or random matched. Matching is usually done for grading purposes. Specifically, Premium Grade A, the top plywood face veneer grade, can be either one nearly flawless piece of veneer, or two or more carefully matched pieces. By investing in the labor and equipment required for matching, a mill can produce top-grade veneers from smaller, more flawed logs.

There are two ways to flat cut a log for matching. One way is slicing. Most slicers consist of a stationary knife. The flitch, or segment of the log to be cut, is mounted on a log bed that passes up and down against the knife. One slice of veneer is produced on each downward stroke of the log bed. The second method is called stay log cutting and is done on a rotary lathe. In this process, the log is mounted on the lathe off-center so that it pulls away from the blade halfway through each revolution, instead of slicing off a continuous veneer.

After the veneers are cut, they are sorted and dried. Veneers that will not be on the face of the panel are generally of lower quality and may end up getting numerous repairs. Defects such as wormholes and knots may be cut out and patched. Sometimes, parts of two sheets are taped or even stitched together with thread to make one good layer of veneer. Face veneers also get some repairs, depending on what is allowed by the grade. The veneers

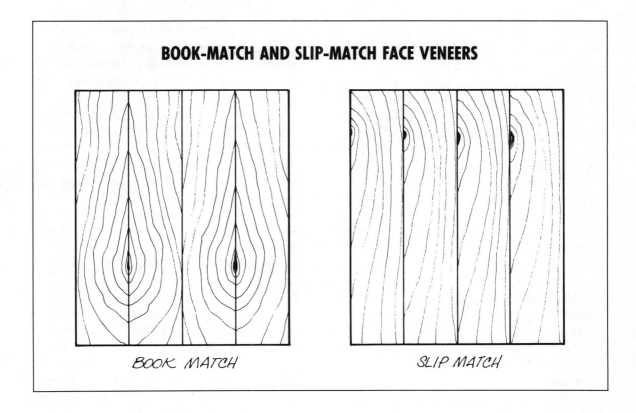

BOOK-MATCH AND SLIP-MATCH FACE VENEERS

BOOK MATCH   *SLIP MATCH*

then are bonded together with glue, usually in combination with heat. The type of glue used depends on the intended use of the panel and whether it will be used indoors or outdoors. The panels then are trimmed to final length and width and may be sanded depending again on intended use. Some panels are touch sanded. Just the high spots are sanded to make the panel a uniform thickness. High-quality hardwood plywood gets careful sanding. Some types of plywood get further decorative finishes such as the grooves in Textured 1-11 exterior siding. Plywood that will be used for interior paneling often gets stained and varnished.

Plywood Grading

As mentioned before, there are separate grading systems for hardwood and softwood plywood. Let's begin with hardwood, since that's the type used in most of the projects in this book.

We noted above that hardwood plywood panels are identified by their face veneers and that the inner plies may be one or more species of hardwood or even softwood. To further complicate matters, some decorative panels graded under the HPMA don't even have hardwood plywood face veneers! Pine plywood paneling is a common example. And remember, even HPMA-graded panels may not be stamped. If there is a stamp, it will appear on the edge so as not to mar the face veneers.

The first question addressed by the hardwood plywood grading system is whether the panel will be used inside or outdoors. The suitability of a panel for exterior use is determined mostly by the glue, although there are other considerations as well. The important thing to know is that hardwood plywood panels are categorized into the following four types:

Technical Type uses a fully waterproof glue and can withstand permanent exposure to the weather.

Type I also uses a fully waterproof glue, but due to other characteristics is not recommended for continuous exposure to moisture.

Type II uses water-resistant glue. It's a high-quality plywood intended only for interior use.

Type III uses a glue that is only moisture resistant. Not much Type III plywood is manufactured, so you're not likely to encounter it.

In addition to being graded by type, both face veneers of each panel are graded according to appearance. For example, if you are building a cabinet that will have a natural finish on the outside and be painted inside, you can use a panel graded top quality A on one face and lesser quality B on the other face. For the back of the cabinet, you might use a panel with a B side and a Sound Grade 2 side. The B side would be painted and the lesser Grade 2 side would never be seen. The hardwood plywood grades and their criteria include:

A Grade veneer must be smooth, tightly cut and full length. The face veneer, even when it consists of more than one piece, must have edges that appear parallel and are edge matched. Edge joints also must be tight.

B Grade veneer must be smooth, tight, and full length. The face veneer, even when it consists of more than one piece, must have tight edge joints. Slip or book matched Grade B veneers are available if specified by the buyer.

Sound Grade 2 veneer must be free from open defects. Matching for grain or color is not required.

Industrial Grade 3 and *Backing Grade 4* grades allow many defects and are not suitable for projects in this book.

Specialty Grade (SP) includes veneers that possess characteristics unlike any of those described in the other grades. Characteristics are agreed upon between the buyer and seller. Species such as wormy chestnut, bird's-eye maple, and English brown oak, which have unusual decorative features, are considered specialty grade. Wall paneling often falls into this category.

Softwood Plywood Grading

Softwood plywood also is categorized by its veneer quality and by how much exposure to the elements it is designed to withstand. Again, the glue used is the most important, but not only factor used to determine a panel's exposure rating. Here are descriptions of the four categories:

Exterior panels have a fully waterproof bond and are designed to withstand permanent exposure to the weather or to moisture. All plywood sidings have exterior ratings, including the T1-11 used for the solar shower in this book. Other APA siding textures are available, including channel groove, reverse board and batten, kerfed rough sawn, brushed, and striated.

Exposure 1 panels use the same fully waterproof glue as Exterior grade and are designed for applications where long construction delays may be expected before protection is provided, or where high moisture conditions may be expected in service. Although the glue is waterproof, other compositional factors may affect its performance. Exposure 1 panels should not be used for projects that will be permanently exposed to the weather.

Interior Type or Exposure 2 panels are made with a water-resistant glue. This grade is recommended for use where only moderate delays are expected before the panel will be protected from moisture.

Softwood plywood panels that may be used in an application where appearance is a consideration are given appearance grades for each face. N and A are the highest grade; D the lowest. But lots of plywood is selected for purely structural purposes in which appearance is of no concern. So, instead of the appearance grade, the plywood is graded according to its intended use such as sheathing, siding, or underlayment. Appearance is important in all the projects in this book. Here are the criteria for softwood plywood appearance grades:

N Grade is a special premium grade that is intended for a natural finish. N Grade is produced by a limited number of manufacturers and usually is available only on special order.

A Grade is smooth and can be painted. Not more than 18 neatly made repairs are permitted. The repairs must be parallel to the grain. Wood or synthetic repairs are permitted. A Grade may be used for a natural finish in less demanding applications.

B Grade requires a solid surface. Shims, circular repair plus, and tight knots up to 1 inch across the grain are permitted. Some minor splits are permitted. Wood or synthetic repairs are permitted.

C Plugged Grade is an improved C Grade veneer with splits limited to ⅛ inch in width and knotholes and borer holes limited to ¼ to ½ inch. Some broken grain is allowed. Wood or synthetic repairs are permitted.

C Grade allows tight knots up to 1½ inches in diameter and knotholes up to 1 inch across the grain. Some knotholes up to 1½ inches are permitted if the total width of the knots and knotholes is within specified limits. Synthetic or wood repairs are allowed. Discoloration and sanding defects that do not impair strength are permitted. Limited splits are allowed. Stitching is permitted.

D Grade permits knots and knotholes up to 2½ inches wide across the grain. Knotholes can be ½ inch larger within specified limits. Limited splits are allowed. Stitching is permitted. D Grade is limited to Interior, Exposure 1, and Exposure 2 panels.

Specialty Panels

There are several types of APA specialty panels. This book uses three of them—high density overlay (HDO), medium density overlay (MDO), and Marine. All three of these are made only in Exterior Grade, so they are great for outdoor projects. As you'll see, there's often good reason to use them inside, too.

HDO and MDO panels combine the structural advantages of exterior plywood with a resin treated fiber overlay that can stand up to rough duty. In the projects in this book, we use panels that have overlay on both sides, but you can order panels with the HDO or MDO on one side only.

HDO is the toughest of the two. The resin is impregnated into the fiber surface with heat and pressure to produce a surface that is very smooth, almost like plastic laminate. HDO usually comes in a natural, semiopaque color, although other colors such as black, brown, or olive drab are also available. The surface is designed to be used without further finishing. It's extremely resistant to abrasions and waterproof. As a result, it's often used for such punishing applications as concrete forms and industrial tanks. Because it is so tough and smooth, it's easy to clean. HDO is perfect for countertops, workbench tops, or other surfaces that will be exposed to a lot of abuse, moisture, or dirt. For example, the partition shelves project is made of HDO because we use it to house plants in our greenhouse where it is constantly exposed to water and soil.

MDO has a softer, resin-treated fiber overlay that is designed with just the right tooth, or surface, for rapid, even paint application without presanding or any other preparation. This makes it a convenient material for interior projects that will be painted. Coated with a good exterior primer and paint, MDO is excellent for outdoor projects, too. Because it is easy to paint and is durable, MDO is often used for road signs.

As of this writing, the biggest drawback to HDO and MDO is that both materials can be difficult to obtain in some parts of the country, especially in small quantities needed for projects in this book. Many lumberyards don't stock HDO and MDO and it's not worth their while to order just a few panels. For this reason, wherever HDO or MDO is used for a project in this book, we offer an alternative type of plywood.

Marine plywood, as the name suggests, is designed to be ideal for boat hulls and other marine applications. It is made only of Douglas fir or western larch. It has solid jointed cores and highly restrictive limitations on core gaps and face repairs. Obviously, if plywood is made to stand up to the ocean, it'll stand up to use in backyard projects. But you might want to use it indoors, too. For one thing, it has high-quality face veneers. For another, you won't find gaps in the inside plies when you cut pieces from it. This makes it an excellent material for projects that will leave the plywood edges exposed.

TOOLS
AND
TECHNIQUES

Most of the tools and techniques used in plywood projects are the same or similar to the ones you'd use for any woodworking project. But, as discussed in the first chapter, plywood does have some special advantages and disadvantages. In this chapter, we will share the tricks and techniques that will help you achieve excellent results with plywood.

Some of the techniques we'll discuss in this chapter are included because they arise frequently in the projects. For example, several projects use slots, so we'll talk about the best way to make them. At the end of the chapter, you'll find a section on finishes.

Tools

You can build every project in this book with only three portable power tools—a jigsaw, a circular saw, and a drill. Add a router to the list and you'll greatly increase your efficiency. A table saw or radial arm saw will, of course, help ensure square, true cuts, but if you don't want to invest in one, you can use a straightedge-guided circular saw and invest more time and patience instead. And we often find a use for our band saw, but only because

some operations are a little easier on a band saw than with a jigsaw. Let's take a closer look at the power and hand tools you'll need to complete these plywood projects.

Jigsaw

You'll find that the jigsaw gets used more often than any other power tool for most of the projects in this book. In fact, the jigsaw can stand in for a circular saw in many of the projects. A circular saw, or better yet a table saw, is handier for cutting most pieces to overall dimensions, but many of the projects have radiused corners that require a jigsaw. We also use the jigsaw for slots and notches. If you don't own a jigsaw, we recommend that you invest in a good one. It just doesn't make sense to attack a $60.00 sheet of hardwood plywood with a $39.95 jigsaw.

Most good jigsaws are variable speed or have two speeds. Slower speeds reduce vibration and give you more control around tight curves. Orbital action is a feature that increases the versatility of a jigsaw. It thrusts the blade forward on the cutting stroke. Equipped with a large-toothed blade and set for maximum orbital action, a good jigsaw can slice through almost 3 inches of plywood or solid wood. Set for little or no orbital action and equipped with a sharp fine-toothed blade, a jigsaw can cut across plywood without splintering even the most delicate face veneer. To further protect face veneers, good jigsaws come with inserts or reversible shoes that press down close to the blade as you cut. Some top-quality saws even have little blowers that clear the blade area of sawdust. This is a nice feature, but you can always blow the dust away yourself.

Running a good jigsaw with cheap blades is like driving a Porsche with bald tires. We almost always start a new project with new blades. For fine cutting, which includes most of the cutting in this book, use hollow-ground or taper-ground blades with at least ten teeth per inch. The hollow or taper shape means that only the teeth contact the wood, not the body of the blade. This reduces friction and heat and allows the saw to work more efficiently.

Circular Saw

Even if you do have a table saw or radial arm saw, you'll probably find it more convenient to cut panels to rough size with a portable circular saw instead of trying to wrestle full sheets through a stationary saw. If you are buying a circular saw just for woodworking and not for carpentry, you needn't buy the most expensive circular saw on the market. In fact, the most expensive worm-drive saws are designed for house-framing contractors. These heavy saws are more awkward for finer work than the less expensive, lighter duty saws. The

cheapest circular saw will easily cut through any plywood. The only disadvantage to a really cheap circular saw is that it will be more difficult to adjust and to keep adjusted. You'll have to be careful not to knock it around. General purpose circular saws take 7¼-inch blades. This will work fine for any plywood cutting task.

More important than the saw is the blade you put in it. For plywood and other finish work, use a hollow-ground, carbide-tipped blade with teeth set at an alternate top bevel.

Drill and Screwdriver

Surveys show that the variable speed, reversible power drill is probably the most commonly owned power tool in the American home. Just chuck in a 25-cent Phillips-head or flat bit and the tool becomes a power screwdriver.

Although the drill will do a great job of zipping screws in and out, you still may want to invest in a battery-powered screwdriver. Then you can use the drill for pre-drilling and the driver for inserting screws without switching bits. Screwdrivers are slower than a drill, but that can be an advantage because it reduces the chance of stripping the screw head.

But when it comes to very exact control over screw tightening or removing tough screws, there's still no substitute for granddad's old bit and brace.

Router

Routers come in a wide array of sizes, powers, and types. Some routers have plunge bases that are great for making mortises. However, a fixed-base router is all you need for projects in this book. If you are shopping for a router, we recommend that you look for one with at least 1 horsepower, which is enough for most woodworking jobs. We also recommend that you buy a router that takes bits with ½-inch-diameter shanks, instead of only ¼-inch-diameter shanks. A ½-inch shank is more stable. And since routers that can take ½-inch bits come with an adapter for ¼-inch bits, you can use a wider selection of bits.

Rasp, File, and Surform

A rasp may bring to mind a sort of Fred Flintstone type of woodworking, but when working with plywood you will nevertheless find a number of uses for a fine rasp, no matter how exacting a craftsman you may be. A rasp, file, or Surform tool can be very handy for breaking or creating a slight round over, or for chamfering an edge to protect face veneer and create a surface that will hold paint. The Surform tool comes in various lengths and has a replaceable cutter that resembles and works like a cheese grater. The Surform tool works great when you have a lot of material to remove.

Scraper and Plane

We use a flat-hand cabinet scraper to remove dust and bubbles when finishing. The scraper is also handy for removing a thin shaving from face veneer or moldings. The scraper is virtually unaffected by con-fused grain and there is little danger of lifting grain as with a plane. The scraper can be sharpened in moments by clamping it deeply into a vise and filing straight across the top. This produces two sharp edges on each side that are ideal for smoothing cured epoxy.

A sharp block plane should never be out of reach when making any woodworking project. Designed to cut across the end grain as well as with the grain, the block plane is particularly useful for plywood work when you have to cut through the grain both ways at every plywood edge.

Table Saw

Table saws can cost as little as $150.00 or as much as $2,000.00. Many woodworkers consider the table saw to be the most essential stationary tool in their shops. Less expensive table saws are *motorized*, meaning the arbor that turns the blade is connected directly to the motor. Better saws have separate motors that run a belt that turns the arbor. This system is quieter, vibrates less, and keeps the motor away from the sawdust coming off the blade. However, you can do excellent work with a good-quality motorized saw. It's a matter of how much you want to spend and what projects you intend to make with the saw.

We do recommend that you buy a saw with at least 1 horsepower. And, for plywood work, make sure you get a saw that lets you set the fence at least 24 inches from the blade. This will allow you to rip to the middle of a panel. As with the circular saw, use a hollow-ground, carbide-tipped blade with teeth set at an alternate top bevel.

Orbital Pad Sander

The orbital pad sander is one of those tools you can do without. But once you buy one, you'll get lots of use out of it. Nothing beats it for sanding tight spots or getting into corners, and it's great for making slight round overs. Be careful when using the pad sander. It can leave swirl-shaped marks that only become obvious after you apply a clear glossy finish. To avoid this, start with a grit no coarser than #80. Progress through #120, #180, and, for a very fine surface, #220. Resand lightly by hand with the finest grit you used in the pad sander to remove any swirls.

Cutting Slots

If you have only one or two slots to cut, the jigsaw is the tool for the job. You can mark out and cut a slot in just a few minutes. But when there are several identical slots to cut, we find it pays to set up a jig for the router.

In this book, we use slots most frequently for joinery, particularly knockdown joinery. Sometimes the slots are open on one end to receive shelves, such as in the magazine cabinet. Or the slots might be closed, such as the mortises in the legs of the trestle table or the wedge slots in the stretcher tenons. We occasionally use closed slots as hand holds as well.

You'll have to invest some time and care to make an accurate template for the slots and you'll still have to rough-cut with a jigsaw, but if you have more than two or three identical slots to cut, the job will go faster overall if you cut with a router. A router equipped with a ½-inch-diameter flush-trimming or pattern bit will make a cleaner slot with more perfectly squared edges, so you'll need the rasp and file only to break the edges.

The flush-trimming and pattern bits are both roller-bearing-guided straight bits. The flush-trimming bit, most often used to trim plastic laminate flush with the substrate, has the roller-bearing at the bottom of the bit. This works fine for template routing, except that the template must be on the bottom where you can't see it. The pattern bit, designed specifically for working with templates, has the roller bearing on top. This makes it easier to use because you can keep your eye on the bearing surface. In addition, most pattern bits are designed to plunge. So if you have a plunge router, you can make closed slots without drilling a starter hole.

Make your template large enough so that you can clamp it to the workpiece without the clamps getting in the way of the router. Use a piece of high-quality ½-inch-thick plywood. Marine grade or multi-ply is ideal because there will be no voids. If you discover any voids in the laminates within the slot, fill them with wood putty. If the roller-bearing dips into a void, it will ruin the slots. Hardboard, such as Masonite, makes an excellent template and doesn't have any voids. Sand away any saw marks.

Cutting Slots with a Router

Use the jig to draw your slots. Remove the jig and rough cut the slots with a jigsaw. This may seem like extra work, but the

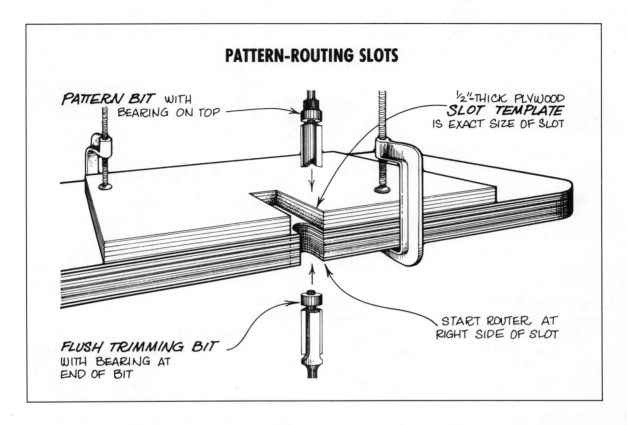

PATTERN-ROUTING SLOTS

PATTERN BIT WITH BEARING ON TOP

½"-THICK PLYWOOD *SLOT TEMPLATE* IS EXACT SIZE OF SLOT

START ROUTER AT RIGHT SIDE OF SLOT

FLUSH TRIMMING BIT WITH BEARING AT END OF BIT

bit you are using is designed to trim material not cut through it. You can make quick work of the jigsaw cuts by staying ⅟₁₆ to ⅛ inch within the layout lines.

Set the bit depth so the bearing rides on the template. Clamp or screw the template and workpiece to a stable surface. If it's an open slot, the open part should be facing you. Begin routing the slot at the right side, as *Pattern-Routing Slots* indicates, and rout around the back and the left side of the slot in one pass. This way the rotation of the bit works with you to hold the bearing firmly against the template.

When you are done routing, the corners of the slot will be rounded. In most

cases, you'll need to square them with a jigsaw. The sliding shelves project is an exception because the shelves are rounded over to fit the round slots.

Most often, you'll be making multiple slots in the sides of a cabinet to receive shelves. In this case, the set of slots in one side needs to be an exact mirror image of the set of slots in the other side. Use your template to make all of the slots in one side. Then clamp the inside face of the routed piece to the inside face of the other side and use it as a template to rout the second set of slots. If there is any variation in the spacing of the slots in one side, it will be duplicated in the other side. When you are done using your template, drill a hole in one corner and hang it on a nail in your shop. You are bound to find a use for it again.

Cutting Slots with a Jigsaw

Joinery slots rely on friction to hold the pieces together, so they work best when they are really snug. To lay out joinery slots that will be cut with a jigsaw, we use a scrap of the material the slot will receive. That is, if we are making a slot for a ½-inch-thick shelf, we use a scrap of ½-inch-thick plywood. Put the scrap in position on its edge. Lay out the cut lines by scoring with a sharp utility knife. Besides giving you a very fine, accurate cut line, scoring the top veneer will prevent splintering.

If you cut a slot with a jigsaw, it probably will need to be cleaned up with a rasp or file and sandpaper. If you use a rasp or file in a slot, work carefully from both sides. The important thing is not to let the teeth of the tool catch on the face veneer as you move the tool out of the slot because the unsupported face veneer will splinter. If we are cutting a slot for a hand hold or a wedge, we lay it out by measurement because these slots don't have to be as accurate. Hand holds usually are rounded on the ends. We lay out these radii with a compass.

Jigsaws are capable of making plunge cuts for closed slots such as a hand hold or mortise. But it's not always easy to keep the blade from bouncing out of the layout line. So to eliminate any chance of marring the veneer outside the slot, we always drill a starter hole for the blade. Make the hole just a little smaller than the width of the slot.

After cutting and fine-tuning a slot, we break all the edges to protect the veneer from splintering. This is done by making two or three angled passes on the edges of the slot with a file or fine-toothed rasp.

Sawing and Drilling Plywood

Sawing and drilling plywood requires a little more care than sawing or drilling solid wood. This is especially true of the thin face veneers of hardwood plywood. Maple face veneer, for example, is particularly prone to splintering when sawed or drilled.

The key to protecting face veneers is to use a hollow-ground, carbide-tipped blade with teeth set at an alternate top bevel. Make sure the blade is sharp. There are no special drill bits for plywood, but again sharpness is key. Spade bits dull quickly, but you can sharpen them easily by clamping them in a vise and running a flat file across the cutting edge. Run the file at an angle, along the original bevel of the edge. We routinely give spade bits a few strokes with the file before drilling through thick plywood.

The blade or bit is more likely to splinter face veneer as it plunges out of the wood than on its way in. If the appearance of one face of your workpiece is more important than the other face, cut with the show face up when using a table saw, radial arm saw, or hand saw. The show face should be down when using a circular saw.

A jigsaw cuts on the upstroke, so will tend to splinter more at the top of the cut.

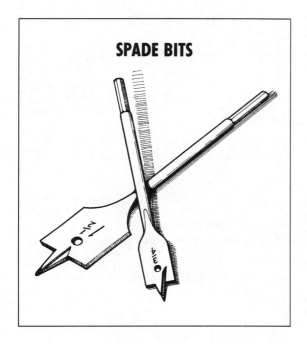

SPADE BITS

However, jigsaw blades always wander slightly out of square so you'll usually want to mark and cut the show face so that the most accurate cut will be on the show side.

If you still have problems with splintering face veneers, here are a couple of tricks you can try. Lay a metal straightedge along your layout line and score it with a sharp utility knife. Press hard and make a few passes with the knife until you are completely through the face veneer. Now the veneer fibers are already severed so they can't splinter when you saw. Another method is to put masking tape along the area to be cut and then make your cut line on the masking tape. You can put the tape on both sides of the cut. The tape will hold the veneer fibers in place as you cut.

When drilling, you can alleviate the splitting problem by putting a piece of scrap underneath the hole so the veneer fibers are supported as the drill bit exits. You can also use a piece of masking tape underneath or even on top.

Cutting Plywood with a Circular Saw

To cut a large piece of plywood accurately and safely with a circular saw, the piece must be properly supported on both sides of the cut. When making crosscuts we accomplish this by laying two 2 × 4s across two sawhorses and then laying the plywood on the 2 × 4s. For ripping the length of the sheet, we add a third 2 × 4 directly under the cut so both sides of the cut are supported. Set the depth of cut about ⅛ inch deeper than the thickness of the plywood.

Another method is to use a sacrificial sheet of plywood, Masonite, or particleboard. Simply lay the sacrificial sheet on the ground and put your workpiece on top. Set your depth of cut so that it cuts through the workpiece and into the sacrificial piece. Then climb aboard and make your cut. This method works particularly well for thin, floppy plywood because it supports the entire sheet.

If you make final cuts with a circular saw, it's important to guide the saw with a straightedge, which can be just a straight piece of plywood or solid wood. This can be a bit time consuming. First, align the blade to your layout line and make sure the saw base is square to the work. Then align the straightedge to the base and clamp it down. You can speed the job and ensure

A STRAIGHTEDGE GUIDE FOR THE CIRCULAR SAW

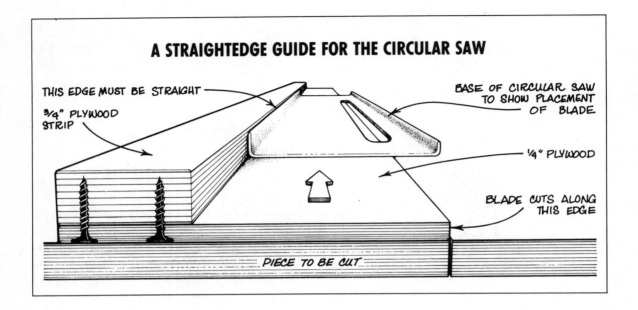

THIS EDGE MUST BE STRAIGHT

¾" PLYWOOD STRIP

BASE OF CIRCULAR SAW TO SHOW PLACEMENT OF BLADE

¼" PLYWOOD

BLADE CUTS ALONG THIS EDGE

PIECE TO BE CUT

accuracy by making a simple jig like the one shown in *A Straightedge Guide for the Circular Saw.* This jig has a base of ¼-inch plywood with a guide of ¾-inch plywood screwed to one edge. Leave the base wide. After the jig is assembled, run the saw along the guide to trim the base to width. Now you have a jig that's customized to your saw. All you need to do is align the edge to the cut line on the workpiece. You can make the jig even easier to use by making a T on one end. Just screw another piece of ¾-inch plywood to the bottom of the base, perpendicular to the guide. Now the jig will automatically align your work piece for a right-angle cut. You can make the jig any length and, in fact, may want to make several. But 5 feet is a good all-purpose length that will let you cut the width of a full sheet of plywood in one pass or the length of a sheet in two overlapping passes.

Laying Out Curves

To help lay out the curved portions of projects, we often provide a grid. Because of size changes that occur during book production, the squares in the grids may vary in size from project to project. But that doesn't matter because when you lay out grids on your project, one square always equals 1 or 2 inches. Draw the grid with very light pencil marks on the plywood parts and then make reference marks on the squares. In some cases, you'll want to measure the squares in the book where layout lines cross grid lines and then use a scale ruler to transfer these measurements to the grid on the plywood. But in most cases, the curves are decorative and you can just estimate the points. You may want to connect the points freehand or use the batten method described below. It depends a lot on your freehand drawing ability.

Sometimes, usually for gentle curves such as the rockers on the moose and the sheer of the rowing dory, we skip the grids and provide measurements from definite points. This method is faster than the grid. It uses a framing square and a tape measure to lay out the reference points. Again, you can connect the dots by drawing a freehand line or you can use the batten method. Even if you do draw well, we recommend the batten for rockers. It's important that rocker curves be perfectly fair.

Making and Using a Flexible Layout Batten

Most people find it difficult to freehand an unwavering, curved line. To help draw long gradual curves, we use a thin strip of clear, straight-grained stock about ¼ inch wide by ¼ or ½ inch thick. Knots and other irregularities will distort the curve. Determining the width of the rip is a matter of trial and error. It must be thin enough to bend easily to the curve, but thick enough so that it doesn't have wows that will distort the curve. Start with the

thickest rip you think might make the bend. Rip it thinner as necessary until it is just flexible enough. We usually end up with a batten about ⅜ to ½ inch thick, but sometimes for tight curves we have to rip down to ¼ × ¼ inch. If there is a hard spot in the batten that resists bending more than the rest of the batten, you can make a few passes along the hard spot with a hand plane until it assumes the correct shape. The same thing can be done on the ends of the batten if they are too stiff.

Lay out the reference points on the stock. Drive tacks into the reference points and flex the curve along them. (Boat builders use heavy lead weights called spline weights or ducks to hold the batten, but finish nails will work almost as well.) Have a helper hold the batten in position while you draw the curve. Or you can tack nails into the stock on either side of the batten, as necessary, to hold it in position. The idea is to let the batten assume a fair curve, without irregularities. Eyeball the batten from different positions, adjust as necessary, and when it is finally just right, draw the curve with a pencil or ballpoint pen.

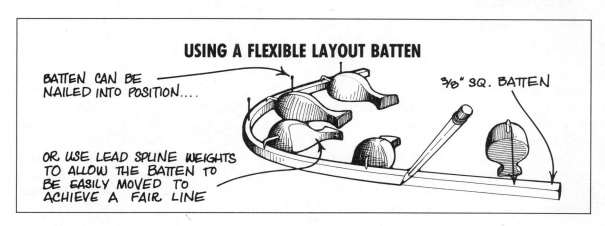

USING A FLEXIBLE LAYOUT BATTEN

BATTEN CAN BE NAILED INTO POSITION....

⅜" SQ. BATTEN

OR USE LEAD SPLINE WEIGHTS TO ALLOW THE BATTEN TO BE EASILY MOVED TO ACHIEVE A FAIR LINE

Fastening

Screws work great in plywood, especially through the face. Because of the alternating laminations, plywood won't split like solid wood, so you can screw quite close to the edge. If appearance isn't important, such as a cabinet back, you can screw without predrilling if you use drywall screws.

In fact, we find ourselves using drywall screws with increasing frequency. Besides being self-tapping, they go in quickly, don't break easily, and their Phillips head fits snugly into the proper-sized driver. Recognizing that these screws get used for a lot more than drywall, some manufacturers call them all purpose screws or bugle head screws because of the shape of the head. They come in lengths from ½ to 4 inches.

Because they are so quick and easy to insert and remove, we often use drywall screws where clamps won't reach when gluing up a project or to hold jigs or guides in place where a clamp would get in the way. This is especially handy for projects that will get coated with epoxy. We take the screws out and then sand and seal with epoxy. You can't tell the screws were ever there.

If you want to use drywall-type screws outdoors, make sure they are galvanized. Interior drywall screws will rust and streak your project unless they are sealed well with a plug or epoxy.

We also find plenty of use for conventional Phillips-head and square-drive screws, especially if we'll be predrilling anyway. Or sometimes we need something heftier than drywall screws, which don't come any wider than #8. The square-drive screws, sometimes called Robertson screws, are great because they don't strip the screw head as Phillips-head screws sometimes will under the high speed of a power drill. Robertson screws are widely available in Canada where they were invented, but in this country they usually are available only through mail order. (See "Sources," page 295.)

Predrilling, Countersinking, and Counterboring

If you are screwing solid wood close to the edge or are screwing into a narrow piece such as a cleat, you need to predrill to prevent the wood from splitting. If you are screwing anywhere into hardwood, you will need to predrill so that you don't strip, bend, or break the screw. Even with plywood, you'll often want to predrill and countersink or counterbore so that the screw sits in a neat hole on the surface instead of crushing into the veneer.

If you want the screw head to be flush with the surface, you need to predrill with a countersink. If you want the screw below the surface so it can be covered with a plug or putty, then you need to predrill with a counterbore as shown in *Countersink and Counterbore*.

There are several types of pilot bits that predrill and countersink or counterbore in one operation. We use Fuller tapered bits with adjustable countersink/counterbore collars. For a countersink, drill just to where the bottom of the collar stops getting wider. Go deeper for a counterbore. As with most pilot bits that countersink

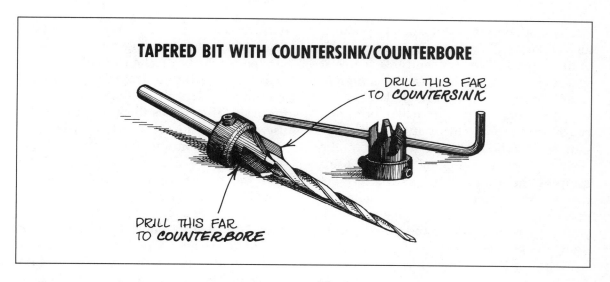

TAPERED BIT WITH COUNTERSINK/COUNTERBORE

DRILL THIS FAR
TO *COUNTERSINK*

DRILL THIS FAR
TO *COUNTERBORE*

and counterbore, you'll need to use a bit and collar that are sized for the screw you are using. If the bit is too big, the screw may not hold. If it is too small, you may break the screw or split the wood, especially when driving into hardwood.

Plugs

You can buy plugs in little cellophane wrappers at the hardware store. We don't like these plugs because they often have the end grain running lengthwise like a dowel. Then the plug is obvious because

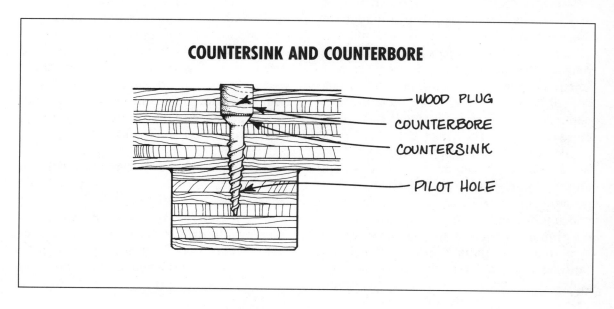

COUNTERSINK AND COUNTERBORE

WOOD PLUG
COUNTERBORE
COUNTERSINK

PILOT HOLE

you've got end grain stuck in face grain. It also makes it difficult to shave them flush with a chisel. The problem gets worse if you stain the project because the end grain absorbs more stain and gets darker.

We much prefer to make our own plugs with a plug cutter. If you are plugging solid wood, save a scrap from the project. If you are plugging plywood, use a scrap of the same species as the face veneer. Align the grain in the plug to the grain in the face. You can shave it flush with a chisel in seconds and you'll hardly know the plug is there.

Sanding Plywood

One of the nice things about high-quality plywood is that it doesn't need much sanding. If you plan to paint your project or coat it with epoxy, the only sanding the plywood may need is to remove saw marks from the exposed edges. We usually start with #60 grit sandpaper on the edges to quickly remove saw marks. Then we sand all surfaces with #80 and/or #100 grit for varnish or oil. For a nicely polished oil finish, we sand between coats with #400 or #600 grit wet or dry sandpaper. These very fine grits actually polish more than they sand.

When sanding plywood, follow the same cardinal rule as for solid wood—sand only with the grain. This is particularly important for hardwood plywood because you might sand through the thin face veneer before you get all the scratches out.

An orbital palm sander and a hand sanding block are our choice for sanding hardwood plywood face veneers. But for edges and other sanding jobs, we prefer sandpaper disks attached to circular foam pads chucked into a drill. The foam pads are more resilient than other sanding pads for drills. This makes them much easier to use without causing swirls and gouges. They come in various sizes. We find that diameters of 4 or 5 inches work well for most woodworking tasks. (See "Sources," page 295.)

The sandpaper is applied to the pad with adhesive available from the source provided or from paint stores. You can also buy precut pads with adhesive already applied. The pads are available with a small stud for chucking into a hand drill and come threaded for various types of sanders/polishers.

Repairing Voids

Even top grades of plywood will have small voids in the interior plys, unless you buy marine or multi-ply. Inferior grades will have larger voids. If you run your hand over the panel, you can sometimes hear the void as a change in pitch. If you hear a large void, you may want to plan your cutting strategy so that you don't cut through it and won't have to repair it.

Because of its structural properties, epoxy makes the best filler for voids. You can thicken the epoxy with commercially available filler (see "Epoxy as a Glue," page 131). Or you can use sanding dust as a filler, by adding dust from the same species as the face veneer. In situations where the strength of the plywood is important, we have gone so far as to set the piece on edge and pour unthickened epoxy into a void until it is filled.

If you aren't working with epoxy and you are filling just for appearance or to give a piloted router bit a smooth path, then any wood filler such as Plastic Wood will work fine.

Breaking Edges

Throughout the projects, we routinely cut a small chamfer or round on all unprotected plywood edges. This is commonly known as breaking the edge. Doing this makes the edges more appealing to the eye and the hand, but that's not the only reason to break edges. This step also protects the face veneers from chipping and provides a better surface for finish to adhere to. That's why we break edges that will not show. The only edges we don't break are those that are joined to another piece.

To create a slightly rounded edge, we use sandpaper. For a chamfer, as shown in *Breaking Edges*, we use a block plane or file. The block plane produces a smooth, finished chamfer when used on an edge that's parallel to the grain of the face veneer. But when used across the grain of the face ve-

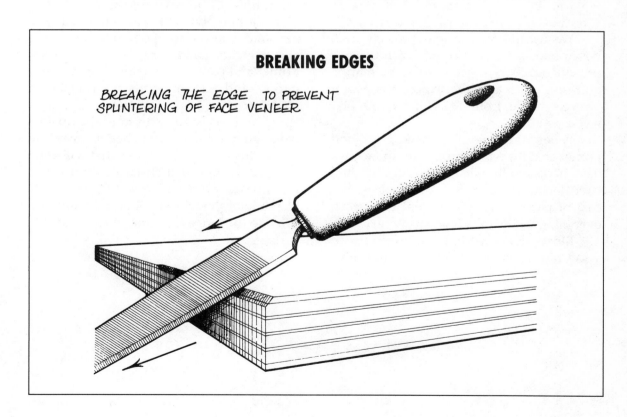

BREAKING EDGES

BREAKING THE EDGE TO PREVENT SPLINTERING OF FACE VENEER

neer, it may splinter the veneer. So, we use a file for cross-grain chamfers. Most of the time, a filed chamfer requires some sanding.

Applying Finish

Penetrating oils such as Watco Danish Oil, tung oil, or boiled linseed oil are our favorite finishes for hardwood plywood that will be used indoors. We like these oils for plywood for the same reasons we like them for solid wood. Oil finishes provide a low luster finish that shows off the grain of the wood. It is easy to apply and can be renewed by applying more oil. If an area gets damaged, you can sand and re-oil it.

We use oil for outdoor projects, too. Watco makes an exterior oil finish that we use on outdoor projects made of marine plywood or to coat the exposed edges of projects made from MDO or HDO plywood.

Penetrating oil also makes a good primer coat for paint or varnish. In fact, we have occasionally oiled a project and then later decided to give it a new look with a coat of paint. Before you paint or varnish over oil, give the oil a few days to dry.

Most often, we apply oil finishes with a soft rag, especially the second and third coats that get rubbed in well. Heat can build up in oily rags and cause a fire, so make sure you dunk the oily rags in water and dispose of them properly. You can also use a foam brush, paint brush, or, for large areas, a roller.

We often coat outdoor projects with two or three applications of epoxy. Epoxy is great for outdoor projects, but it always needs a final finish with a paint or varnish that includes a sunscreen. Epoxy is a great undercoat for paint or varnish, but you can't epoxy over paint or varnish. Epoxy can be applied only on bare wood. See "Epoxy as a Coating," page 132, for more about finishing epoxy projects.

Painting plywood is the same as painting solid wood. Use a good interior primer and paint for inside projects, and exterior primer and paint for exterior projects. Both interior and exterior paints are available in an oil or latex base. The latex is easier to apply and easier to clean up. Latex paints have gotten better and better over the years. But for wood surfaces that will get a lot of wear, such as shelves, we think a coat of oil-based primer followed by two coats of semigloss or glossy oil-based paint will provide the longest-lasting, most washable surface.

CHAPTER THREE
SHELVING
AND STORAGE
PROJECTS

PARTITION SHELVES

We started out designing a room divider for our home office/studio. We wanted it to be freestanding and to have lots of storage space on both sides for books, files, reference and art materials, and a few potted plants.

We decided to use high density overlay (HDO) plywood because the tough, smooth surface, which is similar to plastic laminate, is easy to wipe clean—perfect for the office environment.

As we built the divider, it occurred to us that this unit also would work great in our attached greenhouse because the HDO is impervious to soil and water. We ended up filling the shelves with greenhouse supplies and potted plants. The unit would work equally well on a patio, or in a sewing

PARTITION SHELVES EXPLODED VIEW

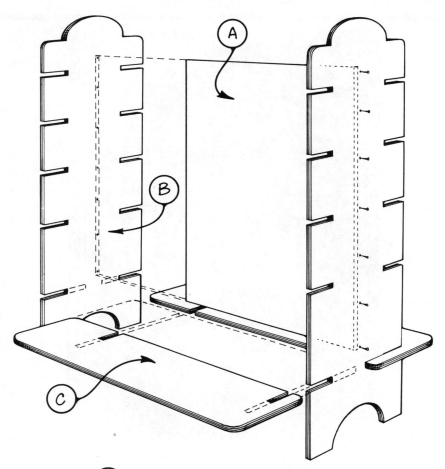

(A) PARTITION · 1 PC. 36" × 48"

(B) SIDES · 2 PCS. 24" × 72"

(C) SHELVES · 8 PCS. 16" × 36"

ALL PIECES ARE ¾" PLYWOOD

TOP, FRONT, AND SIDE VIEWS

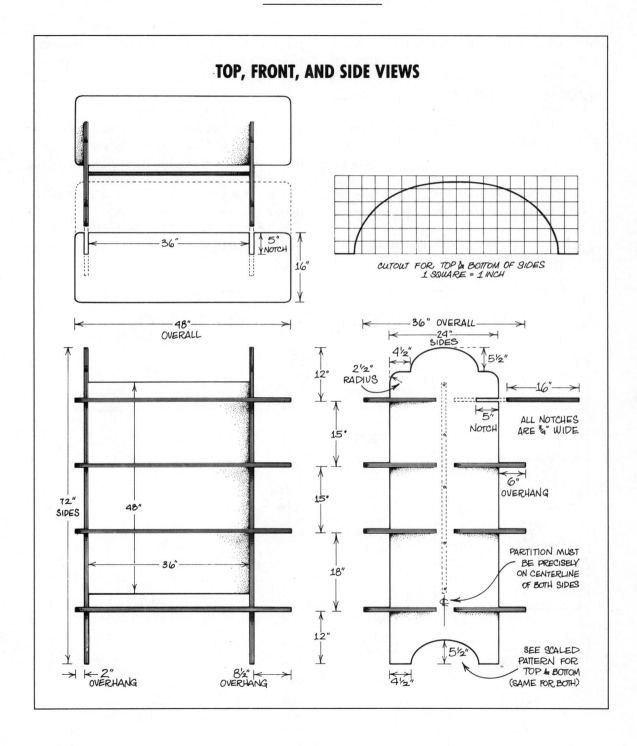

36"

5" NOTCH

16"

CUTOUT FOR TOP & BOTTOM OF SIDES
1 SQUARE = 1 INCH

48" OVERALL

12"

2½" RADIUS

4½"

5½"

16"

5" NOTCH

ALL NOTCHES ARE ¾" WIDE

36" OVERALL

24" SIDES

15°

15°

6" OVERHANG

72" SIDES

48"

36"

18"

PARTITION MUST BE PRECISELY ON CENTERLINE OF BOTH SIDES

12"

2" OVERHANG

8½" OVERHANG

4½"

5½"

SEE SCALED PATTERN FOR TOP & BOTTOM (SAME FOR BOTH)

room, library, or any place where lots of shelf storage would be handy. And of course, you don't have to use HDO. Another tough, waterproof approach is to use painted medium density overlay (MDO) plywood. Or, you might want to select a hardwood plywood that fits with your decor. The unit has a scalloped top and matching bottom cutout design that suggests art deco. A pastel paint job would make the unit fit right into that style of decor.

We cantilevered the shelves 8½ inches past one side because we wanted a space for houseplants that would be separate from books and files. If this design doesn't suit your needs, you can make the unit symmetrical by changing the position of the slots in the shelves and making the partition wider. In any case, the shelves provide nearly 40 square feet of space, enough for hundreds of books. The unit is heavy, strong, and stable.

We designed the unit to make efficient use of three sheets of plywood. The unit is 23⅞ inches wide. The shelves are 15⅞ inches wide to allow for material lost to saw kerfs.

CUTTING DIAGRAM FOR THREE 4 × 8 PLYWOOD PANELS

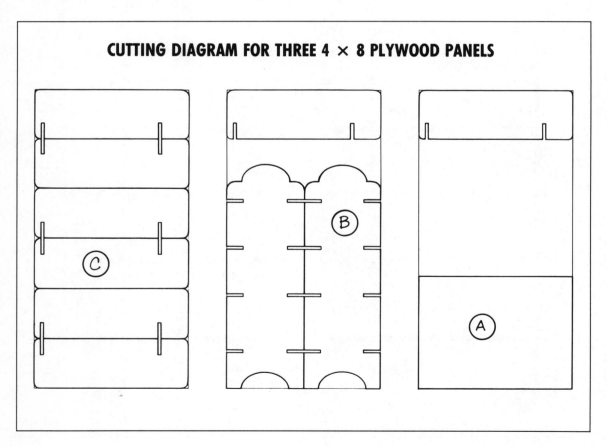

1. CUT THE PARTS. On the table saw, cut the sides, shelves, and partition to their overall dimensions. Lay out the curves as shown and cut them with a jigsaw.

TIP ▶

To cut the sides safely and accurately, begin by crosscutting a plywood panel to 72 inches. Then strike a line exactly down the center of the length of the panel. Cut down the middle of the line with a portable circular saw. Next, set your table saw fence for a 23⅞-inch rip. With the factory edge against the fence, rip the two pieces to the final dimension.

2. CUT THE SLOTS. Lay out the slots on one side and one shelf. Pay special attention when marking and cutting the slot locations in the shelves. Keep them square to the edge and the proper distance apart. If they're inaccurate, the shelves will bind when installed. If you force the shelving to fit one side because of a slight inaccuracy, it will affect the fit on the other side of the unit. Cut along the layout line with the jigsaw by cutting the line in two. Use a scrap of your shelf stock to check that the slots have proper clearance. The fit should be snug, but not so tight that you won't be able to assemble and disassemble the unit without pounding on it. If necessary, true up the cut with a file. Now use the one side and one shelf as templates to rout the other side and shelves as explained in "Cutting Slots with a Router," page 14. Square the ends of the slots with the jigsaw after using the router. Check for fit. Then bevel each sharp edge slightly by making two or three passes with a block plane and a fine-toothed combination rasp or a ½-inch-wide file for tight corners.

3. ASSEMBLE THE SIDES TO THE CENTER DIVIDER. Assemble the side to the partition with 2½-inch #12 Phillips-head wood screws spaced 9 inches apart. Begin by marking the exact vertical centerline on the inside of both side pieces. Drill ⅛-inch holes through the centerline. These tiny holes will locate the pilot screw holes you will drill from the outside of the sides. To locate the partition during assembly, draw a vertical line exactly parallel and ⅜ inch to one side of the centerline.

Because the parts are big and the unit isn't completely stable until the shelves are installed, you'll need a helper for assembly. Have the helper hold the parts together while you drill pilots and counter-sinks and insert the screws. Wax the screw threads. To avoid stripping the screws, tighten them with a conventional screw-driver, not a brace or power drill. This way you'll be able to disassemble the unit for moving or storage.

---

4. TEST FIT THE SHELVES. The shelves do not butt into the partition. We left a little space in case you want to run electrical wires or to facilitate drainage if the unit is used in a greenhouse. Place the screwed-together unit upright on a flat level surface and install both bottom shelves. Then work your way up, alternating sides to avoid racking the unit. If you want, you can leave a shelf out for larger plants.

Don't force anything. If a shelf binds as you insert it, use a file or rasp inside the slots to relieve the pressure. If the shelves end up slightly loose, wait until the finish is applied and then put a dab of silicone sealant into the loose slot and on the underside of the shelf where it won't be seen. When you disassemble the unit, you may have to break the seal by slipping a thin, flexible putty knife into the slot.

---

5. APPLY FINISH. Disassemble the unit to make finishing easier. If you use HDO, the only finish you need is two or three coats of Watco exterior oil applied to the edges. A disposable sponge brush works great for this. Apply a first coat and let it soak in overnight before applying a sec-ond coat. After a final coat, sand the edges smooth and flush with #80 grit sandpaper and wipe dry with a clean cotton rag. Use a mild soap to remove any oil from the HDO surface. You can apply furniture wax to the HDO if you want. If you built the unit from hardwood plywood, you can use Watco on the entire piece or you may varnish or paint it.

MAGAZINE CABINET

Our home office was becoming inundated with stacks of magazines, newsletters, illustrations, photos, brochures, tool catalogs, and every other kind of reference material. To get at that one magazine we wanted, if we could find it, we ran the risk of causing an avalanche. We had to tame the paper beast.

This shelving unit, built of birch plywood, has proven to be the answer. Whether you work from a home office or just can't bear to part with those *National Geographics*, we think this magazine rack will help you get organized. Imagine! Instead of letting those back issues get buried deeper every month, they'll be easily accessible on a designated shelf.

Part of the problem with periodicals is

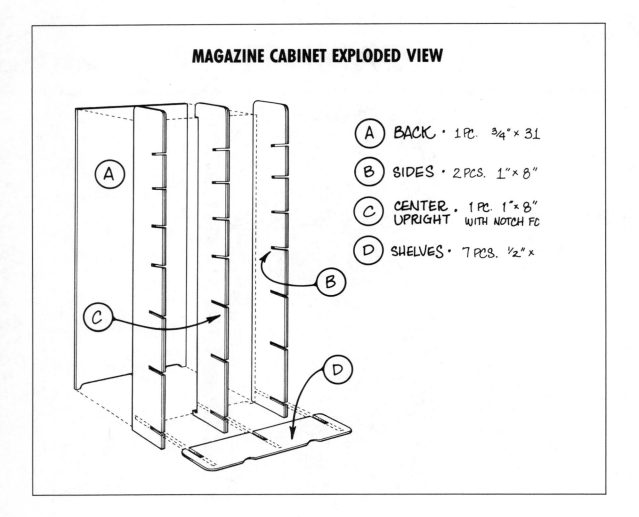

MAGAZINE CABINET EXPLODED VIEW

(A) BACK · 1 PC. ¾" × 31

(B) SIDES · 2 PCS. 1" × 8"

(C) CENTER · 1 PC. 1" × 8"
UPRIGHT   WITH NOTCH FC

(D) SHELVES · 7 PCS. ½" ×

that they come in various sizes ranging from 6 × 9-inch back issues of *Organic Gardening* to *Life* magazine's large format. We designed this cabinet to accommodate them all, either standing up or lying down. The top four shelves are slanted toward the back, so you can stack materials without having them slide to the floor.

When the cabinet is full, the load can add up to a few hundred pounds of paper.

So we made the back and sides of hefty 1-inch-thick hardwood plywood. As a bonus, the vertical edges are thick enough to accommodate adhesive labels, which we often use to label our stacks.

The cabinet is as slim and as tall as practical so it can stand against a wall and not take up too much room in a small office.

TOP, FRONT, AND SIDE VIEWS

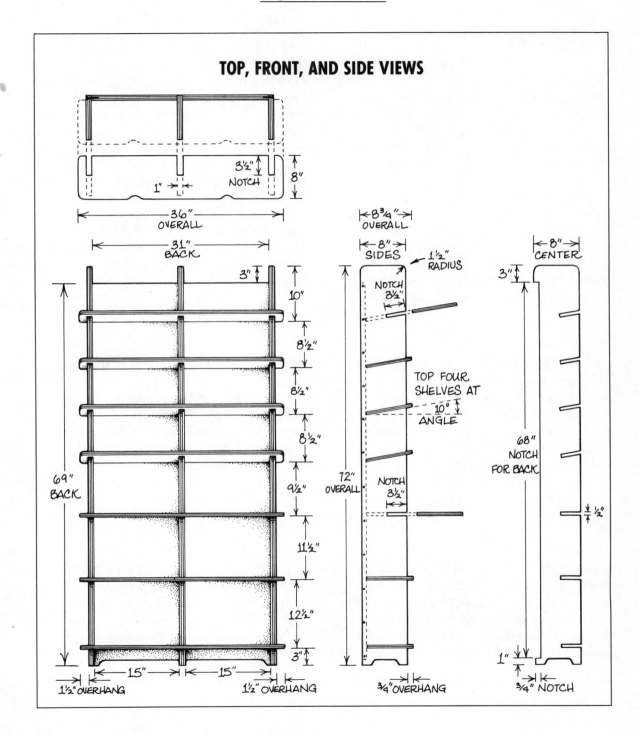

3½" NOTCH

1"

8"

36" OVERALL

31" BACK

3"

10"

8½"

8½"

8½"

9½"

11½"

12½"

3"

69" BACK

15"

15"

1½" OVERHANG

1½" OVERHANG

8¾" OVERALL

8" SIDES

1½" RADIUS

NOTCH 3½"

TOP FOUR SHELVES AT 10° ANGLE

72" OVERALL

NOTCH 3½"

¾" OVERHANG

8" CENTER

3"

68" NOTCH FOR BACK

½"

1"

¾" NOTCH

1. **CUT THE PIECES.** Plan your cuts to use the best face veneers for the areas that show—the outside of the sides and the bottoms of the top four shelves. On the table saw, cut all pieces to their overall dimensions. Then draw 1½-inch radii on the top corners of one side and one shelf. Cut them out and use them as a pattern for the other pieces.

The cutouts on the bottom of the sides and centerpiece are optional. If you plan to place the cabinet on carpeting, you may wish to leave the bottoms flat for more bearing surface. But if the unit is to be placed on a hard floor, the cutouts will add stability and look good. Lay out the cutout on your pattern side and cut it out with a jigsaw. The indentations at the front of each shelf are optional, too. They make it easier to pull publications off the shelves. The shelf indentations are 1 inch deep. Lay out one on one shelf using a 2-inch radius jar lid.

Use a file to slightly chamfer all edges and to clean up the jigsaw cuts. When you are satisfied with your pattern pieces, cut the remaining side, centerpiece, and shelves with a router as described in "Cutting Slots with a Router," page 14. Then slightly chamfer the edges of the remaining pieces.

2. **NOTCH THE BACK OF THE CENTERPIECE.** The centerpiece has a long vertical cutout to receive the back. The most accurate way to make this cutout is with a stopped cut on the table saw. Mark both ends of the cutout. Set the table saw for a 7-inch-wide rip. Crank the blade up to just over 1 inch. Position the piece against the fence and over the stock, then carefully lower it into the spinning blade. Make sure the blade enters far enough into the cutout so that it does not over cut the cutout on the side against the table. For the same reason, stop a few inches before the other end of the cutout. Turn off the saw and wait for the blade to stop before lifting the work from the table. Finish the cut on both ends with a backsaw or jigsaw.

3. **MAKE THE SHELF NOTCHES IN THE UPRIGHTS.** Lay out each notch on the center upright and cut them with a jigsaw. Test the width of the notches with a scrap of ½-inch plywood and fine-tune them if necessary with a rasp, file, and/or sandpaper. When you are satisfied with the notches, use the center upright as a pattern to rout the notches in the outside uprights. After routing, bevel the edges of the notches slightly with a rasp or file.

4. SAND THE PIECES. It's easier to sand the pieces before assembling the unit. Smooth the faces and then smooth and round the edges with #80 grit sandpaper. If you'll be painting your unit, sanding with #80 grit is enough. For an oil finish, you may want to move on to a #120 grit or even a #220 grit paper.

---

5. ASSEMBLE THE SIDES TO THE BACK. Because the 1-inch-thick plywood gives screws plenty to bite into, the uprights are attached to the back with a simple screwed butt joint as illustrated in *Top, Front, and Side Views.* Begin by attaching the sides to the back. Predrill through the sides for screw holes every 6 inches. Counterbore if you want to plug the screw holes.

 TIP

If you anticipate disassembling the shelving unit in the future, rub wax on the threads before inserting screws. The screws will be easier to insert and withdraw.

---

6. ASSEMBLE THE CENTER UPRIGHT TO THE BACK. On the back, mark the exact centerline of the center upright and drill pilot holes along it. Draw a light pencil line ½ inch off the centerline to help you align the center upright when you attach it to the back. Have someone hold the center upright in position, or clamp it in place, while you screw through the back.

---

7. FIT THE SHELVES. Begin at the bottom. Don't force the shelves. It's usually a simple matter to relieve any pressure with a few strokes of a file, rasp, or block plane on the shelf notches. There is a small gap behind each shelf as a route for electrical wires. Number the shelves on the back edges to ease reassembly, if you take the unit apart.

8. APPLY FINISH. We finished our cabinet with oil. Birch plywood also is an excellent base for paint. If you are undecided about a finish, you can oil the cabinet now and paint it later.

 TIP

For handy reference, glue pads of bulletin board cork to each side of the cabinet. Then you can pin notes to the sides and list the contents, title, month, and year of the magazines in each compartment.

HANGING
FILE

No matter how large our home office desk is, it never seems to be big enough to keep our papers organized. Here is the ultimate solution, a filing tray with seven shelves. This unit makes it easy to separate the outgoing from the incoming and the urgent from the trivial. You can devote shelves to now, later, someday, and, if you want to be truly realistic about it, you might even label one never.

This versatile unit can sit right on your desk or, to save even more desk space, it can be mounted on the wall. You can easily modify the basic file pattern for more or fewer shelves, or make it wider and/or deeper to accommodate legal-size papers

HANGING FILE EXPLODED VIEW

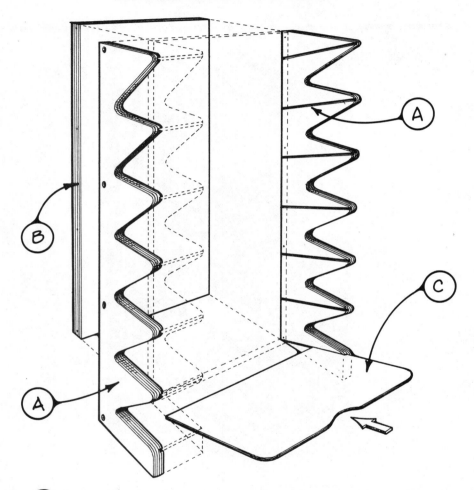

(A) SIDES · ¾" PLYWOOD · CUT FROM 1 PC. 11" x 35"
(SEE PATTERN)

(B) BACK · ¾" PLYWOOD · 12" x 32½"

(C) SHELVES · ¼" AA MARINE PLYWOOD · 7 PCS. 9½" x 12¾"
(ROUND CORNERS ON ONE SIDE)

CUTTING DIAGRAM

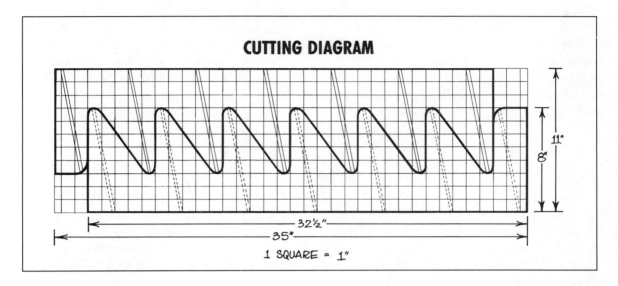

11"

8"

32½"

35"

1 SQUARE = 1"

and folders. For a finishing touch, you can purchase brass label holders at office supply stores. Whatever final form your file takes, it'll be a lot easier to build than a larger desk.

We made the tray sides and back from ¾-inch-thick high density overlay (HDO) plywood and the shelves of ¼-inch AA Marine Grade plywood. You could, of course, substitute AA Marine Grade plywood or hardwood plywood for the sides and back. Softwood plywood, other than Marine or HDO, is not a good choice for this project because you'll end up with voids in the exposed edges. You can glue the tray together or assemble it without glue so it can be knocked-down for travel or storage.

1. CUT THE SIDES AND BACK. As shown in the *Cutting Diagram*, the right and left sides can be made at the same time in one careful, start-to-finish cut. Start by laying out the section shown in the grid, using a quarter coin for the radius as indicated. Lay out the rest of the cut with a square, a bevel gauge, and the quarter. Make the cut with a thin, fine-cutting blade in the jigsaw. The blade probably will burn the tight turns a bit, but they can easily be cleaned up with a piece of sandpaper wrapped over a wood rasp. Of course, making the two pieces in one cut leaves no margin for error. If you are not confident of your jigsawing skills, you might want to lay out the two pieces separately and make two cuts.

Now cut the back according to the dimensions listed.

2. MARK OUT THE GROOVES. The plywood shelves slide into grooves on the sides of the file. Mark them out at an angle of 11 degrees off the back, as shown in the *Cutting Diagram,* so that gravity will hold the shelves and their contents firmly in place.

To ensure that each groove lines up with its mate on the other side, use the pattern to mark out the grooves for one side. Then stack the two sides together and mark the edges of the second side at the front and back of each groove. Now use a ruler to connect the marks and lay out the grooves on the inside of the second side.

---

3. CUT THE GROOVES. The grooves should be slightly wider than the shelves so that the shelves slide easily in and out, particularly if the file may be disassembled. Rout the grooves with a ¼-inch, straight bit using a straightedge to guide the router. Router bits are precise while plywood is usually a bit scant of the nominal thickness, so the shelves should slide easily. If they don't, sand the edges of the shelves with #60 grit sandpaper. The grooves should be ⅜ inch deep, or one-half the thickness of the sides.

---

4. CHAMFER THE EDGES. After cutting out the back and sides and routing the shelf grooves, chamfer the edges slightly on all components. Take special care with HDO edges since they are sharp enough to cut your hand. Slightly chamfer the straight edges with a block plane. Sand or chamfer the curves. Finally, sand carefully with #100 grit paper.

---

5. MAKE THE SHELVES. Cut seven shelf blanks to the dimensions listed. Now carefully align and stack the blanks. Clamp the stack to your bench so that the long sides overhang by a couple of inches. Put a wide, wood-cutting blade in your jigsaw to prevent the blade from wandering, and round the overhanging corners. As the *Exploded View* shows, you can also cut an indent into the front edge for grasping papers from the tray. Unclamp the shelves and use sandpaper and a block plane to round-over all but the back edge.

6. **ASSEMBLE THE FILE.** Predrill and countersink for 1½-inch-long #6 wood screws every 9 inches to attach the sides to the back. If you choose to make a knock-down tray, leave out the plugs on the sides. Coat the screws with wax to make them easy to insert and withdraw.

7. **APPLY FINISH.** One of the things we like about HDO plywood is that the surface needs no finishing. Just apply some tung oil, Watco Danish Oil, or varnish to the exposed plies of the HDO edges and use the same finish on the marine ply shelves. This creates a nice contrast between the HDO sides and the oiled plywood shelves. If you do paint the HDO surface, sand it first with #80 grit sandpaper. Otherwise, it will be too smooth to accept paint. If you use marine or hardwood plywood for the whole unit, you can oil, varnish, or paint it.

SLIDING SHELVES

Here's a handy knockdown shelving unit that's perfect for a college student or someone who lives in a small apartment. Built from a single sheet of plywood, it consists of two sides, a back, and four shelves that slide easily in and out for versatility and easy assembly and disassembly.

We built our unit from ¾-inch maple Appleply, a high-quality multi-ply made by States Industries. A similar product that is available in many lumberyards is called baltic birch.

The shelves are twice as long as the case is wide. They can be aligned with

SLIDING SHELVES EXPLODED VIEW

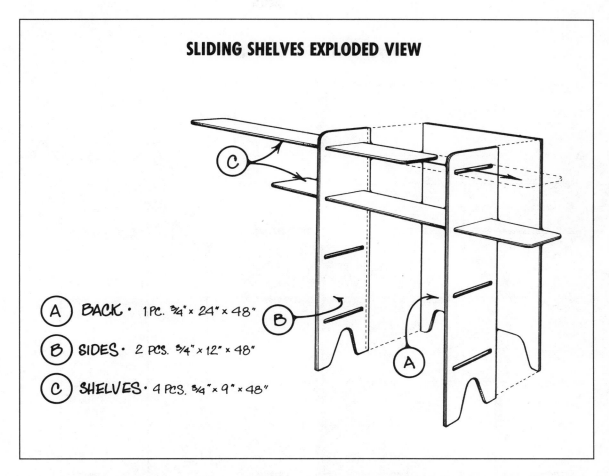

A BACK · 1 PC. ¾" x 24" x 48"

B SIDES · 2 PCS. ¾" x 12" x 48"

C SHELVES · 4 PCS. ¾" x 9" x 48"

equal overhangs of about a foot on each side or alternated as desired for potted plants. You can cantilever the shelves to one side, but make sure you have enough weight between the sides to keep the unit from tipping. You might even add more slots and shelves.

1. CUT THE PARTS TO DIMENSIONS LISTED. Cut the sheet of plywood in half across the width and then rip the back, sides, and shelves. It is important that the rip cuts be square so that the sides align to the back and the shelves slide easily. Cut the radius on the shelves with a jigsaw.

TOP, FRONT, AND SIDE VIEWS

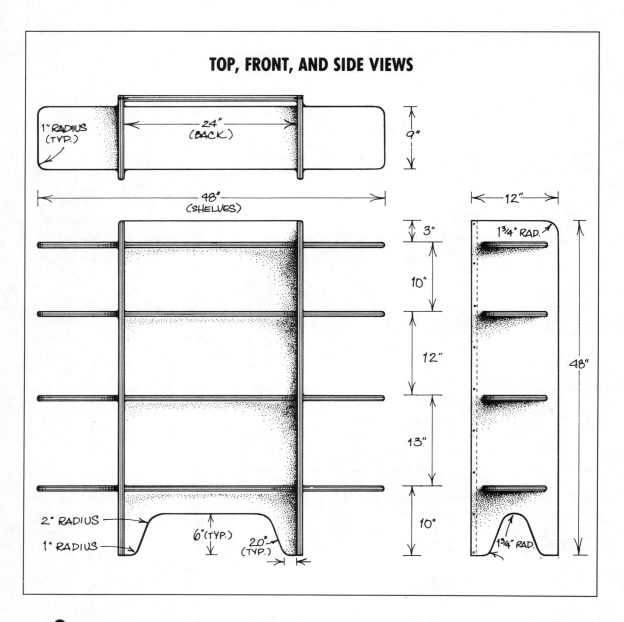

2. SHAPE THE SIDES AND SHELVES. With a jigsaw, cut the indentation that forms the legs in the back. Also cut the radius at the top front of the sides and at the corners of the shelves.

3. **ROUT THE SHELVES AND SLOTS.** Round-over both sides of each shelf edge with a ¼-inch round-over bit in the router. This will allow the shelves to fit perfectly into the rounded ends of the slots and eliminate edges that could chip and splinter

when the shelves are moved in or out.

Use a template and a ½-inch piloted bit as described in "Cutting Slots with a Router," page 14, to cut ¾-inch-wide slots in the sides. Leave the corners of the slots rounded to match the shelves.

4. **ASSEMBLE THE CASE.** Predrill, countersink, and screw the back into the rear edges of the sides with waxed 2-inch #10

Phillips-head wood screws every 6 inches. The wax will make it easier to disassemble the unit.

5. **APPLY FINISH.** We gave our unit a natural finish. Begin by removing any sawmarks from the edges with #60 grit sandpaper. Then carefully sand all the

parts with #100 grit, moving on to finer grits if you like. Apply at least two coats of oil finish, then two coats of varnish.

TIP ▶ Our young daughter found it great fun to slide the shelves in and out of the cabinet. So we locked them in place by stapling a pad of ⅛-thick plywood to the bottom of each shelf, against the sides.

BLANKET CHEST

Here's a blanket chest that combines the updated look of high-quality multi-ply with the traditional aroma and advantages of cedar. It's made from ¾-inch Appleply and the bottom is lined with a ¼-inch-thick cedar plywood panel. Both the Appleply and the cedar paneling are made by States Industries. Many lumberyards carry a European-made multi-ply commonly called baltic birch.

The cedar panel dresses up the inside of the chest. The biggest advantage to cedar in a blanket chest is that people love the aroma, but moths won't go near it. To renew the scent, give the cedar panel a very light sanding once or twice a year.

BLANKET CHEST EXPLODED VIEW

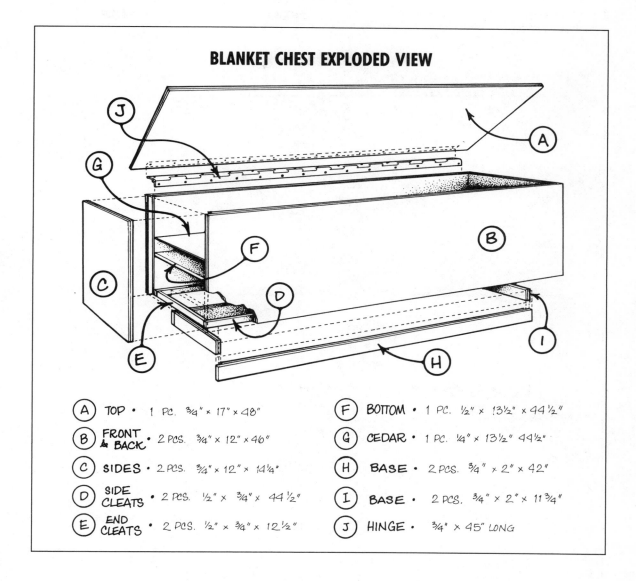

(A) TOP • 1 PC. 3/4" × 17" × 48"

(B) FRONT & BACK • 2 PCS. 3/4" × 12" × 46"

(C) SIDES • 2 PCS. 3/4" × 12" × 14 1/4"

(D) SIDE CLEATS • 2 PCS. 1/2" × 3/4" × 44 1/2"

(E) END CLEATS • 2 PCS. 1/2" × 3/4" × 12 1/2"

(F) BOTTOM • 1 PC. 1/2" × 13 1/2" × 44 1/2"

(G) CEDAR • 1 PC. 1/4" × 13 1/2" 44 1/2"

(H) BASE • 2 PCS. 3/4" × 2" × 42"

(I) BASE • 2 PCS. 3/4" × 2" × 11 3/4"

(J) HINGE • 3/4" × 45" LONG

1. CUT THE TOP, SIDES, AND ENDS. Cut the sides, tops, and ends to the dimensions in the materials list. You can cut the bottom and the cedar to rough size, but don't trim them to their final dimensions until the sides and ends are assembled so you can cut them to fit.

TOP, FRONT, AND SIDE VIEWS

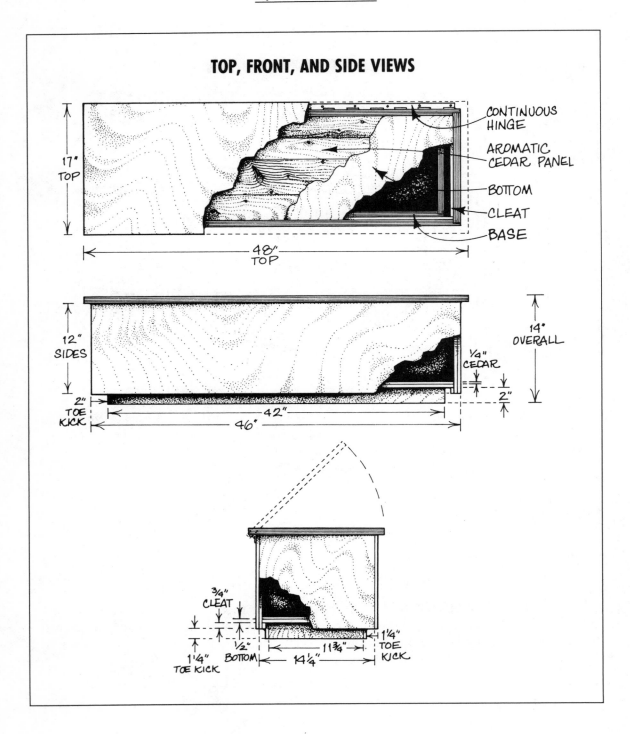

17"
TOP

CONTINUOUS HINGE

AROMATIC CEDAR PANEL

BOTTOM

CLEAT

BASE

48"
TOP

12"
SIDES

14"
OVERALL

1/4"
CEDAR

2"

2"
TOE KICK

42"

46"

3/4"
CLEAT

1 1/4"
TOE KICK

1/2"
BOTTOM

11 3/4"

14 1/4"

1 1/4"
TOE KICK

2. RABBET THE FRONT AND BACK. The ends of the front and back are rabbeted to receive the sides. Make the rabbets with a ⅜-inch piloted rabbeting bit by making two passes to cut ¾ inch deep.

TIP ▶

Rabbeting an edge can be a tricky balancing act. In this case, the router base has only a ¾-inch edge to ride on. To provide more base, clamp the front and back of the chest together so that all edges are perfectly flush. Secure the clamped-together pieces in your bench vise with the edge to be rabbeted facing up. Cut the rabbet, routing from left to right and being careful not to let the pilot bearing run off the right end. Turn the clamped-together pieces around in the vise and cut the next rabbet. Flip the pieces over and repeat the process on the remaining two ends.

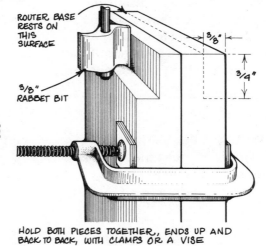

ROUTER BASE RESTS ON THIS SURFACE

⅜"

¾"

⅜" RABBET BIT

RABBETING AN EDGE

HOLD BOTH PIECES TOGETHER, ENDS UP AND BACK TO BACK, WITH CLAMPS OR A VISE

3. ASSEMBLE THE SIDES AND ENDS. Put yellow glue in the rabbets and assemble the chest with long clamps. Check all corners with a framing square and adjust the clamps until the chest is perfectly square. Remove glue that squeezes out with a damp sponge or rag.

4. INSTALL THE CLEATS. Cut the cleats to fit. It's not important that they butt each other at the corners, so it won't matter if they are a little short. Predrill them for 1-inch drywall screws and make sure the tops of the cleats are flush to the bottom of the chest. Apply glue to the cleats and screw them into place.

5. CUT AND INSTALL THE BOTTOM. Measure the inside of the chest and cut the bottom to fit. While you are setting the table saw fence for the bottom, cut the cedar panel to the same dimensions. To avoid getting glue on the inside of the chest, put glue only on the cleats and install the bottom. Predrill and countersink to attach the bottom with 1¼-inch drywall screws.

6. RABBET, ASSEMBLE, AND INSTALL THE BASE. Rip and cut the base, sides, and ends to width. Rabbet the front and back base pieces as you did the front and back of the chest. Put glue on the top edge of the base and position and center the chest on the base. Predrill and countersink to screw through the bottom into the base with 1-inch drywall screws.

7. INSTALL THE CEDAR PANEL. You can lay the panel in the chest so that it is easy to remove for sanding or replacing. To keep the panel from warping, however, you will have to glue the panel in place.

8. INSTALL THE TOP. Position the top on the chest with a 1-inch overhang all around. Put the hinge in position and screw it in place with two screws in each leaf. Check for alignment and install the remaining screws.

9. APPLY FINISH. Sand the entire chest. Break the edges slightly so they will hold finish. The chest is finished with oil followed by two coats of spar varnish with sunscreen. We added a little stain to the oil to darken the maple veneer.

WEDGED
SHELVES

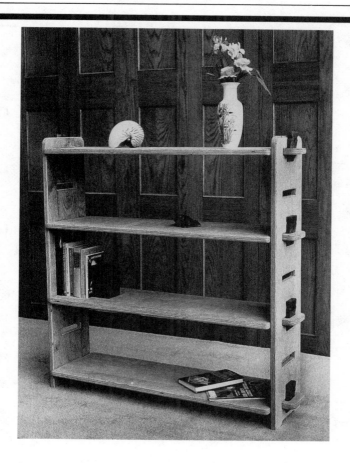

Everybody's shelving needs are different and everybody always needs more shelves. With that in mind, we offer this simple, flexible shelving unit that easily can be expanded as your needs grow. It's wide enough to hold a television, video cassette player, and stereo components. It is held together with wedges.

You might choose to build a unit to the size shown here. But more likely, you have a specific wall in mind and you'll size your unit to fit your space. Notice that there are more slots in the sides than there are shelves. This is to allow you to extend the unit later by adding more shelves and another upright. Just slip the tab ends of the new shelves into the empty slots and wedge them in place.

WEDGED SHELVES EXPLODED VIEW

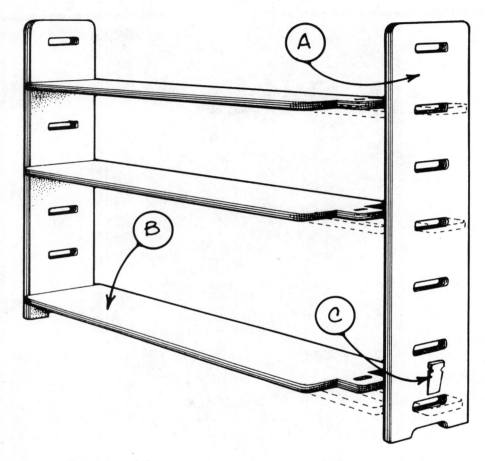

(A) PLYWOOD SIDES • 2 PCS. 1"× 12"× 48"

(B) PLYWOOD SHELVES • 2-7 PCS. 1"× 14"× 48"

(C) HARDWOOD WEDGES • 4-14 PCS. ¾"× 2"× 5"

TOP, FRONT, AND SIDE VIEWS

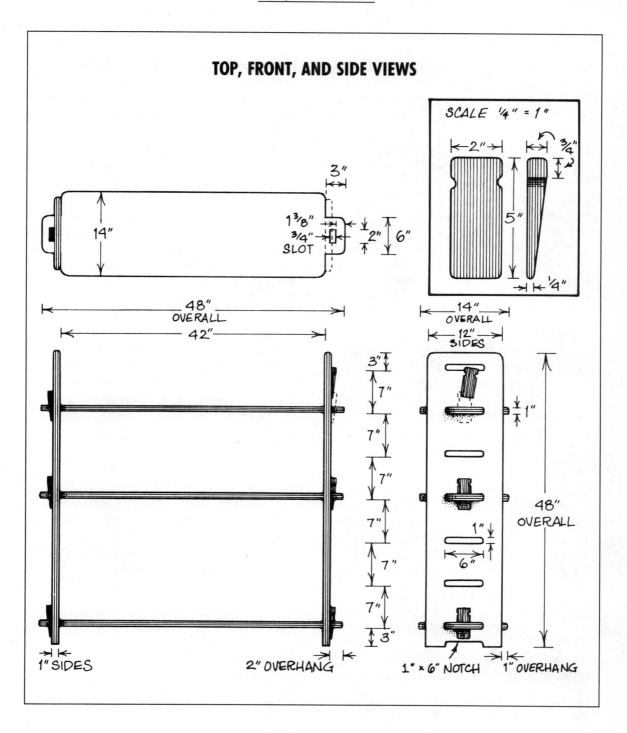

When you design your own unit, keep in mind that the 1-inch hardwood plywood we used can span no more than 4 feet. If you'll be spanning no more than 3 feet, you can use ¾-inch plywood. So, for example, if you've got a 5-foot wall to cover, you might use three uprights with 30-inch shelves and build the whole thing of ¾-inch plywood. Whatever thickness you choose, make sure you use high-quality hardwood plywood so the edges will be attractive.

We made our uprights 11⅞ inches wide and 47⅞ inches long to allow for material lost to saw kerfs and still use a plywood panel efficiently, but you can change those dimensions. We made our shelves 14 inches wide. You could make them up to 15¾ inches wide and still get three pieces out of the width of one sheet. For the VCR and small television we had in mind, 14 inches was wide enough.

Our unit is made of birch plywood. We used walnut for the wedges to add some contrast. Naturally, you can use any hardwood you like for the wedges and any hardwood plywood for the unit. However you choose to adapt this design, it's easy to see that this add-on, knockdown system is perfect for people on the move.

1. CUT THE PIECES. On the table saw, cut all pieces to their overall dimensions. Lay out the shelf tabs and then use a standard 4-inch diameter coffee can to draw a 2-inch radius on all corners except at the bottom of the uprights. Make these cuts with a jigsaw. Cut two small legs in the bottom of the uprights, as shown in the side view. Rout all edges, except the bottom of the uprights and the shoulders of the shelf tabs, with a ¼-inch round-over bit.

2. CUT SLOTS IN THE UPRIGHTS. We cut slots on 6-inch centers for the shelves. You can make them closer as long as you leave enough room to get the wedges in and out. You also can space the shelves further apart. Cut the slots with a template and a ½-inch bit in the router as described in "Cutting Slots with a Router," page 14. Leave the corners of the slots rounded to fit the rounded edges of the shelves.

3. CUT SLOTS IN THE SHELF TABS. Cut the wedge slots in the shelf tabs with a jigsaw as described in "Cutting Slots with a Jigsaw," page 16.

4. MAKE THE WEDGES. Cut the wedges to the profile shown. Make the wedges so that they tighten the unit when inserted about halfway. If necessary, adjust the fit with a few strokes of the rasp inside the slot.

Cut a small finger grip on each edge of the top of the wedges as illustrated. To make the finger grip, cut a small V with a backsaw at the proper location, then clamp the wedge onto a workbench and use a round or oval rasp to open up and shape the cut. Soak the wedges overnight in a penetrating oil such as boiled linseed or tung oil. After the wedges have soaked, wipe them off and wet sand them with #400 grit sandpaper. Wipe and polish the wedges until they are dry again.

TIP ▶ A convenient way to soak wedges or other small pieces in oil is to make an aluminum foil trough that's just a little bigger than the piece to be soaked. When the soaking is done you can pour the oil back into the can.

5. APPLY FINISH. We finished our unit with a couple of coats of oil. Birch plywood, which we used, also is an excellent choice if you plan to paint your unit. Birch is cheaper than other hardwood plywoods and its less-pronounced grain makes a smooth painting surface.

BANKER'S BOX CABINET

This cabinet will enhance the usefulness of those cardboard banker's boxes, also called data or archive boxes, that are sized to hold standard files.

Banker's boxes can be stacked two or three high, but it's inconvenient to move them around every time you want to get into the box underneath. With this cabinet, you can pull out any box you want. The top can act as a handy desk or the cabinet can provide a sturdy support to let you stack a second cabinet on top of it.

Our cabinet is made of ¾-inch-thick, high density overlay (HDO) plywood because we wanted the hard-wearing surface and did not want to have to apply paint or any other finish. Alternately, you can use medium density overlay (MDO), ABX, or Marine Grade softwood plywood or hardwood plywood.

BANKER'S BOX EXPLODED VIEW

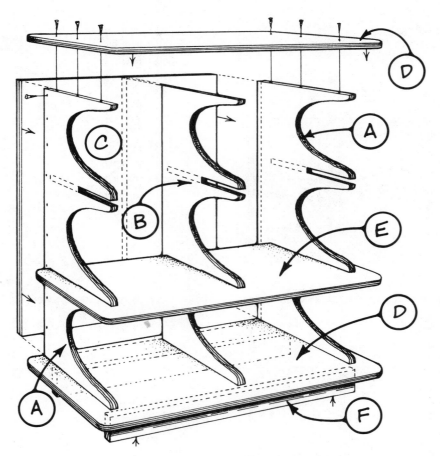

(A) SIDES • 2 PCS. 16" × 37½"

(B) CENTER • 1 PC. 15¼" × 37½"

(C) BACK • 1 PC. 30½" × 37½"

(D) TOP & BOTTOM • 2 PCS. 18" × 36"

(E) SHELVES • 2 PCS. 15" × 36"

(F) TIMBER SUPPORTS • 2 PCS. 32" LONG (2×4 CUT TO LENGTH)

TOP, FRONT, AND SIDE VIEWS

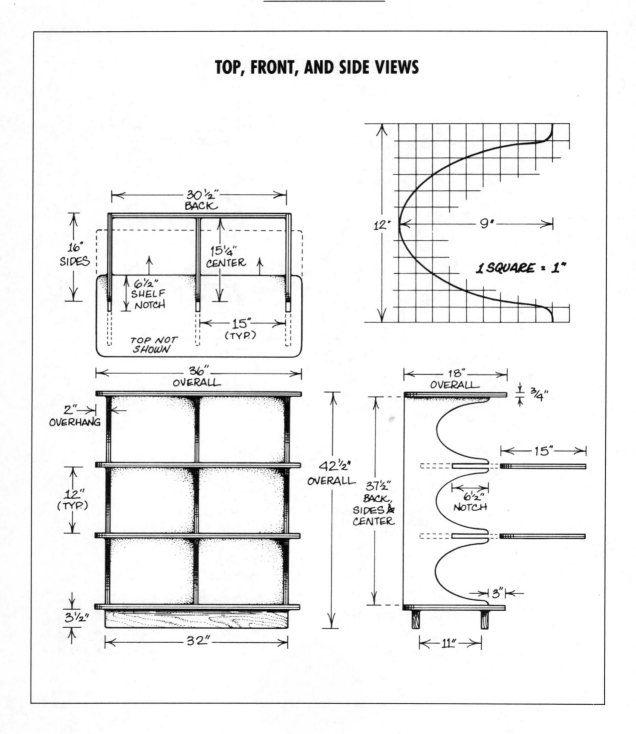

1. CUT THE PIECES. Cut all of the pieces to overall dimensions on the table saw. Note that the center upright is ¾ inch narrower than the side uprights to allow for the thickness of the back.

Lay out and cut the curves and slots in one of the uprights with a jigsaw. Be careful to make the slots accurately. This will be a pattern, so any mistakes will be transferred to the other parts. Do the same with one shelf. Use a standard 1-pound coffee can to lay out the 2-inch radii at the corners of the shelf. Sand the curves smooth.

Use these two pieces as patterns to cut the remaining uprights and shelves as described in "Cutting Slots with a Router," page 14. Chamfer all edges on the shelves and uprights by making two or three passes with a block plane and using a file on the corners and slots. Do not chamfer the back piece.

TIP ▶

If you find it difficult to draw the curves on the front of the banker's box, make the pattern on heavy paper or cardboard. Then tape the pattern to the plywood so you can stand back and see how it looks before cutting. When you like the pattern, use it to cut all the curves on one side. Then use that side as a pattern for the other. This way, even if your pattern deviates from the shape we've provided, at least each curve will be identical. That's the most important element for an attractive cabinet.

2. ASSEMBLE THE SIDES TO THE BACK. Lay the back on a flat surface and assemble the center upright, sides, and shelves around it. If the shelves don't slide easily into position, fine-tune them with a rasp. Clamp the sides in position against the back. If you don't have long enough clamps, a helper can hold the pieces in place. Pre-drill and countersink through the sides and into the back for 1½-inch drywall screws every 4 to 6 inches. Counterbore if you want to plug the holes. Space the screws neatly at regular intervals since they will show.

3. ATTACH THE CENTER UPRIGHT TO THE BACK. Stand the unit up and check that the center upright is square to the back. Mark the top edge of the back where it meets the middle of the center upright. Extend this line down the back. Predrill and countersink for 1½-inch drywall screws every 4 to 6 inches along the line.

---

4. ATTACH THE TOP AND BOTTOM. The shelves will help hold the sides in alignment while you attach the top and bottom. Predrill and countersink or counterbore for screws every 4 to 6 inches, again taking care to make an attractive, regular pattern. Insert the screws.

---

5. ATTACH SOLID WOOD SUPPORTS TO THE BOTTOM. These two pieces of 2 × 4 hold the unit off the ground. Attach each support with four screws through the bottom.

---

6. APPLY FINISH. If your unit is built of HDO, apply some oil to the exposed edges. Otherwise, the cabinet may be painted or oiled. You can paint the solid wood supports, oil them, or leave them natural.

SECURITY GUN CABINET

This display and storage cabinet for guns can be customized in a variety of useful ways. It may be made slightly longer to accommodate special guns or it may be made wider to increase capacity. Temporary or permanent shelves or compartments may be added as required to hold hand guns, reloading gear, or ammunition. The inside of the cabinet is lined with black velvet.

The cabinet is built of 1-inch-thick marine plywood, which is thick enough to let you cut a ½-inch groove for the sliding

SECURITY GUN CABINET EXPLODED VIEW

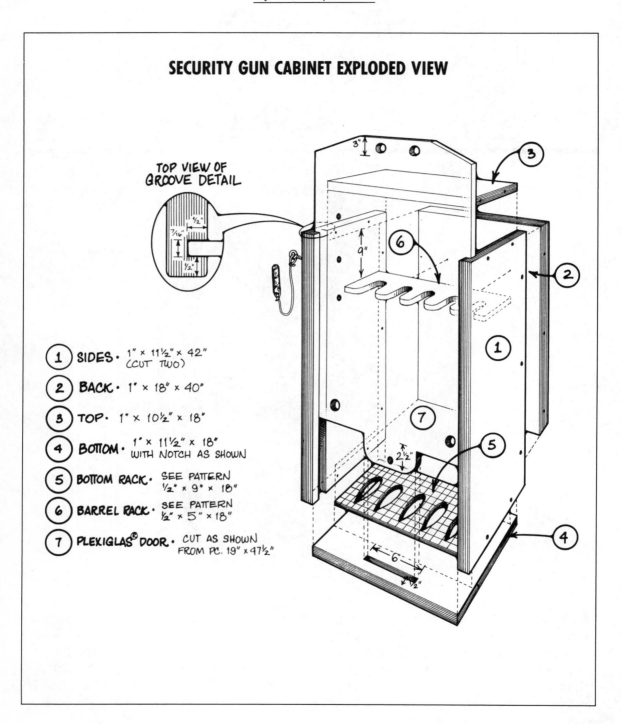

TOP VIEW OF
GROOVE DETAIL

1 SIDES · 1" × 11½" × 42"
(CUT TWO)

2 BACK · 1" × 18" × 40"

3 TOP · 1" × 10½" × 18"

4 BOTTOM · 1" × 11½" × 18"
WITH NOTCH AS SHOWN

5 BOTTOM RACK · SEE PATTERN
½" × 9" × 18"

6 BARREL RACK · SEE PATTERN
½" × 5" × 18"

7 PLEXIGLAS® DOOR · CUT AS SHOWN
FROM PC. 19" × 47½"

**SECURITY GUN CABINET
BOTTOM RACK AND
BARREL RACK PATTERNS**

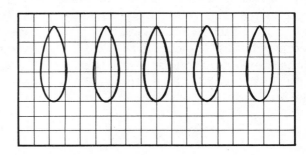

1 SQUARE = 1 INCH

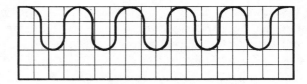

door without weakening the sides of the cabinet. This sturdy cabinet weighs almost 40 pounds. The $\frac{5}{16} \times 3\frac{1}{2}$-inch lag bolts that hold the cabinet to the wall and the 3-inch #14 wood screws that hold the cabinet together make it very tight. Complete security is provided by a lock inserted through a ½-inch tab of Lexan that fits into a slot in the cabinet bottom. The tough, resilient nature of Lexan makes this tab extremely difficult to break.

---

1. DETERMINE THE REQUIRED SIZE. To determine the size cabinet you need, lay out your guns as you plan to store them in the cabinet. Leave enough room between rifles to easily remove them from the cabinet. The grid provided should work for the butts of most guns.

---

2. CUT THE PARTS TO SIZE. After marking out the size cabinet required, cut out the two sides, back, top, and bottom. A table saw makes quick, accurate cuts. Remember the top is smaller than the bottom to accommodate the sliding door.

---

3. **CUT THE SLIDING DOOR GROOVES.** After the five plywood pieces are cut to size, cut the sliding door groove into the inside front edge of both side pieces to the dimensions shown. You can use a variety of tools, but it's easiest to cut the grooves with a dado blade on the table saw or a straight bit in the router. If you use a router, guide the router with a full-length straightedge clamped to the cabinet side. Drill a starter hole and use a jigsaw to cut the slot in the bottom piece to accept the Lexan lock tab.

4. **DO A TRIAL FITTING.** After the groove is cut, test fit all the parts. Clamp the cabinet together. Then predrill and counterbore for 3-inch #14 Phillips-head wood screws spaced 6 to 9 inches apart. Also predrill a counterbore for the screws. Use Phillips or square-drive Robertson-head screws, not slotted screws that strip easily and require almost exact driver alignment. Take care to predrill pilot holes straight into the center of the back piece to prevent it from splitting out as the screws are tightened. A tapered drill bit will provide the best fit for the screws. Make sure you have the correct diameter wood plugs for the countersinks. It's usually worthwhile to drill a sample hole and countersink in scrap wood so you can test fit a screw and wood plug. Remember to keep the countersinks shallow enough so the plugs stick out a bit. They can be sanded flush later.

Tighten the screws and check for a proper fit. Then disassemble the cabinet. Sand all the pieces with the grain. Slightly round the corners with #80 or #100 grit sandpaper. Final sanding will come after the cabinet is assembled.

5. **ASSEMBLE THE CABINET.** Work on a flat surface to help keep everything square. Hold everything in alignment with clamps and screw the cabinet together. Glue is optional since the large size and number of fastenings provide considerable strength. Glue will substantially reinforce the cabinet frame, however, and make it even tighter. Predrill and counterbore for 3-inch #14 wood screws. Put a little wax on the threads of each screw to facilitate final tightening. Insert the screws and plugs, then sand the plugs flush. (See "Predrilling, Countersinking, and Counterboring," page 20). Give the outside of the cabinet a final light sanding before finishing with oil, paint, or varnish.

6. CUT THE BUTT AND BARREL RACKS. The butt and barrel rack patterns that worked best for our selection of rifles and shotguns are shown in the plans. It should work for most guns. Cut both pieces from ½-inch plywood. Round-over the top and bottom edges of the barrel and butt racks with sandpaper or a ¼-inch round-over bit in the router. Don't install the racks yet.

---

7. INSTALL THE VELVET. Cut the velvet to cover the entire inside of the cabinet, except for the bottom where it should cover just an inch or so of the perimeter. You can attach the velvet with staples, tacks, glue, or rubber cement. Cut velvet to cover the butt rack. Don't cut out the slots, just leave the velvet a bit loose so the butts are cradled in the slots. Attach the velvet to the butt rack.

---

8. INSTALL THE RACKS. Predrill and counterbore for the screws that will hold the racks in place. Drill slowly so you can stop if the velvet starts to wrap around the drill bit. Install plugs.

---

9. CUT AND INSTALL THE SLIDING DOOR. The sliding front door of the cabinet is ⅜-inch-thick Lexan, the same tough material used for aircraft windows and canopies. Other types of acrylic sheet with a wide range of quality, scratch resistance, toughness, and price are also available from local glass and plastic supply shops. Further information on specific types of acrylic sheet is available from local suppliers. A clear or lightly smoked sheet displays the guns to best advantage. A dark, smoked Lexan obscures the contents of the cabinet.

Cut the acrylic sheet with a fine-toothed blade in a jigsaw, table saw, or band saw. You can trim the edges with a sharp block plane or router. The acrylic sheet comes with an adhesive paper on both sides to prevent scratching during shipping. Leave the adhesive paper on and lay out the pattern for the door directly on the paper. The paper will protect the plastic during cutting and drilling. Some brands of acrylic come with a grid of 1-inch squares printed on the adhesive paper cover to help you draw your pattern.

After cutting the door to size, check that the door slides easily up and down in the grooves in the cabinet sides and that the tab fits through the slot in the bottom.

Cut a hole in this tab big enough for the lock you'll use.

You may wish to drill some 1¼-inch-diameter finger holes in the Lexan door, as shown, to help lift and lower the door. You can create stops to hold the door open at convenient positions by drilling 5/16-inch-diameter dowel holes as illustrated. Insert a dowel into one of these holes and rest it on top of the cabinet to hold the door open. The number and location of these holes depends on what is convenient for you. It's best to insert the door and hold it open at convenient spots to mark for the stop holes. You can keep dowels, or a pencil of the right size, inside the cabinet or attached to a lanyard, which in turn is attached to the side of the cabinet with a screw eye.

10. ATTACH THE CABINET TO THE WALL.

For safety and security, it is important to attach the heavy cabinet solidly to a wall stud or other framing member. Make sure there is enough overhead room to open the cabinet door. Predrill for four to six 5/16 × 3-inch lag bolts.

COAT
RACKS

We can't bear to throw away scraps of hardwood plywood. After all, the stuff isn't cheap! So we designed a couple of coat racks to let you put those scraps to good use. Both of these coat racks are simple to build and can be completed in just a few hours. They are both good projects for the novice woodworker.

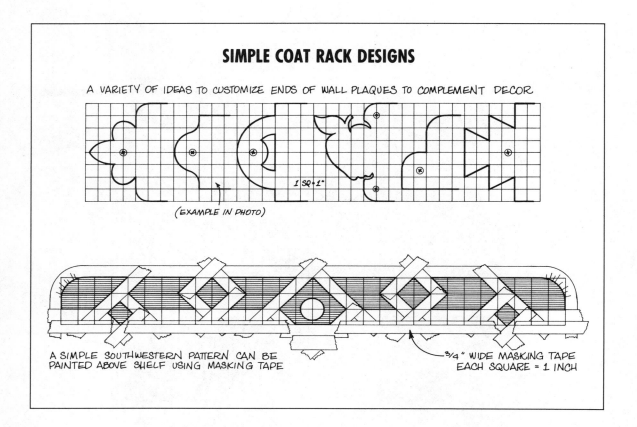

SIMPLE COAT RACK DESIGNS

A VARIETY OF IDEAS TO CUSTOMIZE ENDS OF WALL PLAQUES TO COMPLEMENT DECOR

1 SQ = 1"

(EXAMPLE IN PHOTO)

A SIMPLE SOUTHWESTERN PATTERN CAN BE PAINTED ABOVE SHELF USING MASKING TAPE

3/4" WIDE MASKING TAPE EACH SQUARE = 1 INCH

Simple Coat Rack

This first coat rack is about as simple as a woodworking project can get. It's just one piece of plywood with five brass hooks. The fun part is cutting details on the ends. The illustration shows six ideas. You also can design your own.

You can make the rack as long as you want and add or subtract hooks. It's a good idea to leave about 8 inches between hooks and to make the rack at least 6 inches wide. To mount on stud walls, plan the length so that screws at each end will go through a stud.

1. CUT THE RACK TO OVERALL DIMENSIONS. On the table saw, rip to width and then cut the ends square.

2. **LAY OUT AND CUT THE END DETAILS.** You can skip this step if you want to leave the ends square or just add a router detail. Otherwise, lightly draw in pencil a grid of 1-inch squares as illustrated. Use the grids to draw your pattern and then make your cuts with a jigsaw.

3. **FINISH THE EDGES.** If your end detail doesn't have angles that are too tight for a router, you can add a router detail such as an ogee, bead, or round over. Otherwise, you can just round the edges slightly with sandpaper. If you have left the ends square, you could cut a 45-degree chamfer with the router or a hand plane.

4. **APPLY FINISH AND INSTALL THE HOOKS.** Sand the plywood edges as necessary. We chose a light walnut stain. Use any stain you like. Or skip the stain and give the rack a light coat of oil. You could also paint it a color that coordinates with your decor. Screw the brass hooks into the plywood.

5. **MOUNT THE RACK.** If you are mounting into studs, you can use brass, flathead wood screws and leave them exposed, or you can counterbore and plug the screw heads.

Coat and Hat Rack Shelf

This shelf has southwestern flair that would be right at home in a stucco hacienda. We liked the alder face veneer of the scrap we had on hand, so we finished ours with a light coat of oil. If you really want to emphasize the southwestern style, you can paint yours with a bold geometric design, as described in step 4.

1. **CUT THE BACK AND SHELF.** Rip the back and shelf to width and then crosscut them to overall length. Note that the shelf is 48 inches long, so you can make it from the end of a panel without crosscutting. Use a compass to lay out all the rounded corners and then make the cuts with a jig saw. Cut a snug notch in the shelf to fit around the back.

COAT AND HAT RACK EXPLODED VIEW

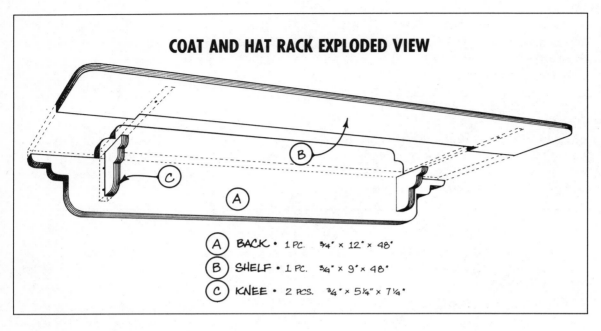

(A) BACK • 1 PC. ¾" × 12" × 48"
(B) SHELF • 1 PC. ¾" × 9" × 48"
(C) KNEE • 2 PCS. ¾" × 5¼" × 7¼"

COAT AND HAT RACK, TOP, FRONT, AND SIDE VIEWS

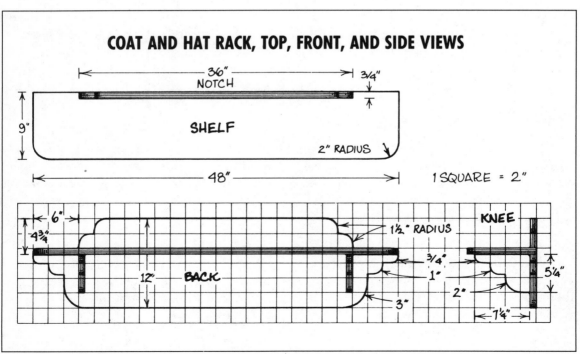

2. **CUT THE SUPPORT BRACKETS.** Cut two 5 × 7-inch blanks for the brackets. Lay out the curves on one with a compass and cut them with a jigsaw. Then use it as a template for the other. Cut the other bracket.

3. **SAND THE RACK.** Sand a slight round on all the edges that will be exposed. You don't need to sand the face veneers if you are going to use paint, but you might want to sand them for an oil finish.

4. **ADD OPTIONAL GEOMETRIC DESIGN.** If you want to add a southwestern-style paint job to the back above the shelf, now is the time to do it. Mark off the design with masking tape as illustrated. Brush or roll on paint. When the paint has dried, remove the tape.

5. **ASSEMBLE THE RACK.** Put yellow glue on the joint between the shelf and back and assemble these parts. Clamp the pieces together or run a few 1½-inch #10 Phillips-head wood screws through the back to act as a clamp until the glue cures. Glue and screw the brackets under the shelf. Predrill for two 1½-inch #10 Phillips-head wood screws through the back into each bracket.

6. **FINISH THE RACK.** Stain, oil, or paint the rack.

7. **INSTALL THE HOOKS.** We used four two-part plastic hooks because we think they blend better than brass would with the style of this rack. The first part is screwed to the rack and the second part is screwed to the first. You'll find a wide variety of plastic and metal hooks at home-supply centers, hardware stores, and lumberyards.

WALL
BINS

Get organized quickly with this easily constructed, versatile wall bin project. The unit shown here uses exactly one sheet of plywood, excluding the backing strip, which could be made of scrap plywood or solid wood.

The unit can be mounted on the wall with either the long or short dimension running horizontally. You could even hang it diagonally, perhaps to store skeins of yarn or bottles of wine. The 1-foot-deep cubby holes will hold a wide variety of

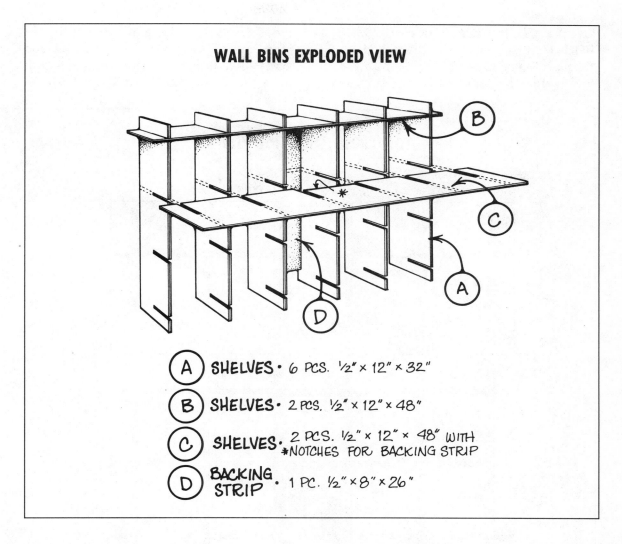

WALL BINS EXPLODED VIEW

(A) SHELVES • 6 PCS. ½" × 12" × 32"

(B) SHELVES • 2 PCS. ½" × 12" × 48"

(C) SHELVES • 2 PCS. ½" × 12" × 48" WITH *NOTCHES FOR BACKING STRIP

(D) BACKING STRIP • 1 PC. ½" × 8" × 26"

items: toys, clothes, shoes, tools, linens, or towels, to name a few. It's easy to see how you could expand this unit, even doubling its size by using 8-foot instead of 4-foot rips of plywood for the long shelves. If you do increase the size, add one or two more backing strips. They are needed to keep the unit from racking and for additional places to attach the bin to the wall.

The plywood you choose for this unit depends on the use you have in mind. For storage in the shop, garage, or wine cellar, BB Interior Grade with a couple of coats of paint would be an inexpensive choice. For a finer, painted surface, use birch or maple plywood. Or put a natural finish on a high-quality hardwood plywood to create a deluxe model.

1. CUT THE PIECES TO THE DIMENSIONS LISTED. First run the sheet of plywood through the table saw and cut it into 1-foot-wide strips. You can cut the plywood into 8-foot-long strips and then cut the strips in half. Or, you can cut the plywood across the grain into 4-foot strips, depending on how you want the face grain ar-

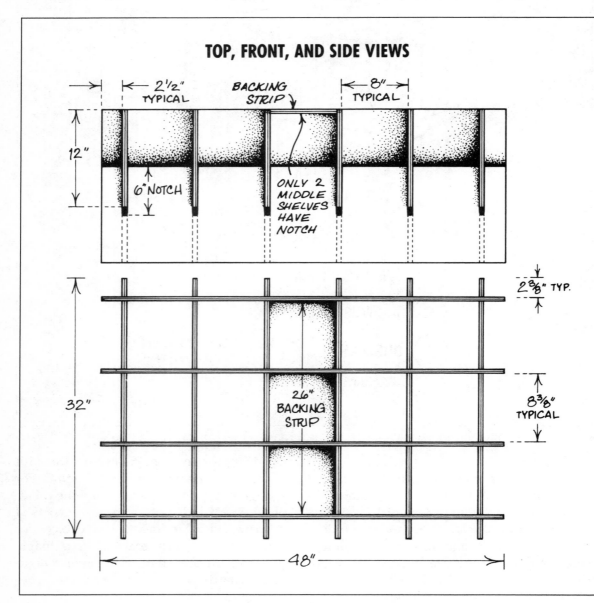

TOP, FRONT, AND SIDE VIEWS

ranged. This is a consideration only if you plan to use a natural finish on the plywood surface.

After cutting the entire sheet into 8-foot strips, cut two of the strips in half to make four 4-foot-long strips. Then cut the remaining two strips in thirds to make six 32-inch long strips. Clean up the edges as necessary with a block plane and sandpaper. Cut a tiny chamfer on all edges to protect the face veneer.

2. CUT THE SLOTS. Cut ½-inch-wide slots with a template and a router as described in "Cutting Slots with a Router," page 14. Use the template to cut all the slots in one long shelf and then use that piece as a pattern to lay out the other long shelves. Mark the left end of the pattern shelf and the shelves you cut out with it. Repeat for the short shelves. Keeping the pieces oriented this way will compensate for any uneven spacing you may have built into the shelves.

3. FIT AND CUT THE BACKING STRIP. Assemble the unit with the back facing up on a flat level surface. Check that it is square and measure for the backing strip, so you can compensate for any deviations from the listed dimensions. As *Top, Front, and Side Views* shows, four of the shelves will have to be notched so that they set flush with the back of the unit. Put the backing strip in position and mark the four shelves for the beginning and end of each notch. Disassemble the unit. Lay the backing strip on a flat surface. Set each shelf next

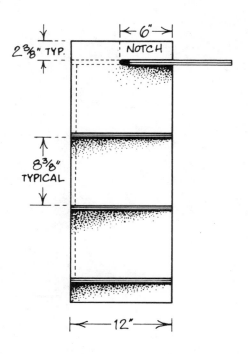

to it and scribe them for the depth of the notches. Cut out the notches with a jigsaw. Reassemble the unit. The backing strip should fit snugly into the notches and stiffen the unit.

Put yellow glue in the notches and on the edges of the backing strip. Screw the strip into the notches with 1½-inch wood screws and clamp it between the shelves running along its length.

Drill the attachment screw holes in the corners of the backing strip. We used four 2-inch #12 Phillips-head wood screws to hold the bin onto the studs in the wall.

---

4. **APPLY FINISH.** Sand off all sharp edges. If the bin will be used around children, you may want to cut a small radius on exposed corners. The bin is ready for an oil, paint, or varnish finish.

CLOSET
ORGANIZER

Most closets are just the standard full-width pole with a single shelf above. This project is designed to make that same space more efficient for organizing and storing clothes, shoes, sports equipment, and other gear normally kept in closets. It's designed for a large closet that has folding or sliding doors for easy access.

The key to organizing a closet is to provide lots of various size shelf space. That's what this unit does. The shelves sit on cleats, but are not attached. You can add

79

CLOSET ORGANIZER EXPLODED VIEW

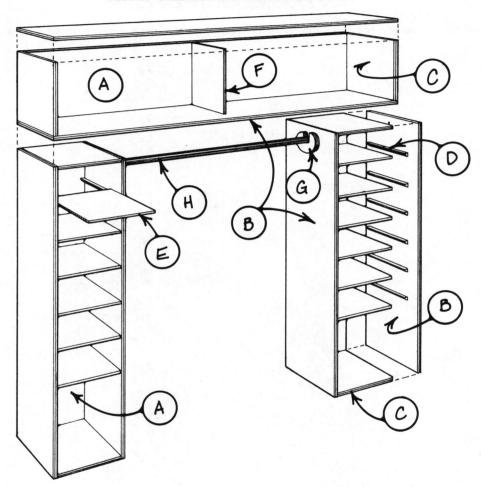

(A) BACKS • 3 PCS. ¾" × 14½" × 64½"

(B) SIDES • 6 PCS. ¾" × 16" × 66"

(C) ENDS • 6 PCS. ¾" × 14½" × 16"

(D) CLEATS • 24 PCS. ¾" × 12" QUARTER ROUND

(E) SHELVES • 12 PCS. ½" × 14½" × 15"

(F) DIVIDER • 1 PC. ½" × 12" × 14½"

(G) ROD SUPPORTS • 2 PCS. 1" × 6" DIA. PLYWOOD

(H) CLOTHES ROD • 1 PC. 1¼" DIA. CUT TO FIT

TOP, FRONT, AND SIDE VIEWS

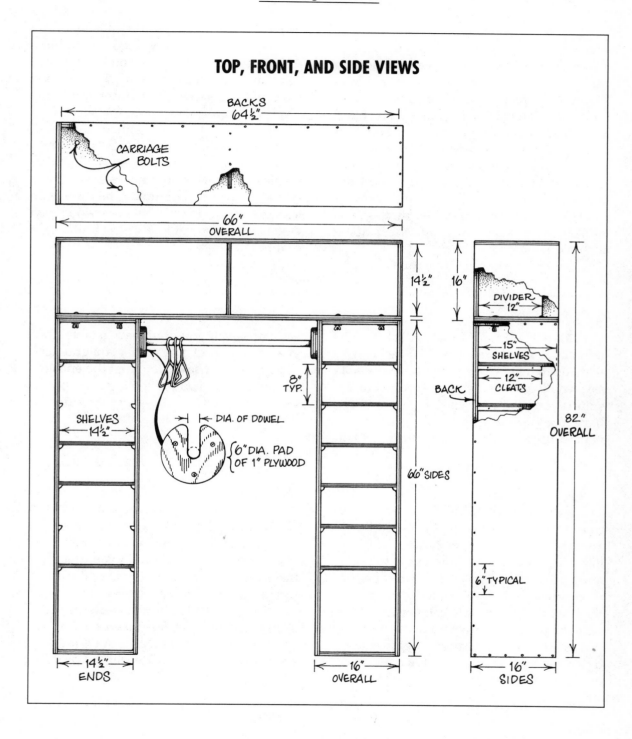

BACKS
64½"

CARRIAGE
BOLTS

66"
OVERALL

14½"

16"

DIVIDER
12"

8"
TYP.

15"
SHELVES

12"
CLEATS

BACK

SHELVES
14½"

DIA. OF DOWEL

6" DIA. PAD
OF 1" PLYWOOD

82"
OVERALL

66" SIDES

14½"
ENDS

16"
OVERALL

6" TYPICAL

6" TYPICAL

16"
SIDES

shelves or remove them as your storage needs change. The top box has a divider to stiffen it as it spans the two vertical boxes and also to create his and hers spaces.

The dimensions illustrated are for a unit that fits into our master bedroom closet. The 16-inch width of the vertical boxes should work for any large closet, but other dimensions will have to come from measuring the depth, height, and width of your closet. Our unit required three sheets of ¾-inch plywood and one sheet of ½-inch plywood.

You can make this unit from any ply-wood you like. Before you go out and buy A Grade hardwood plywood, however, keep in mind that most of the plywood faces will be against the closet walls. Besides, the unit is in a closet. We suggest an AB interior plywood, either softwood, birch, or maple. Use the A faces of the best panels for the areas that show. Birch or maple are a particularly nice surface if you intend to paint your unit. They are both less expensive than other hardwood ply-woods. You also could give the unit a light coat of oil.

1. CUT THE PARTS TO SIZE. All of the parts in our unit are either 14½ inches wide or 16 inches wide. If you have a table saw, you'll get the cleanest, quickest results if you plan your cutting so you only have to adjust your rip fence twice. You may want to start by rough-cutting with a circular saw. If you don't have a table saw, you can make all cuts with a straightedge-guided circular saw. Note that the ends in the illustration include the tops and bottoms of the vertical boxes and the sides of the top box.

2. INSTALL THE CLEATS. We used quarter round because it has a nice finished look. You could use ¾ × ¾-inch rips if you like. Cut the quarter round cleats to length. Lay two vertical shelf sides on the workbench with their inside faces up and their back edges butting each other. Make sure the top and bottom edges of the pieces are flush. Run a tape measure down the butting edges and make a mark on both pieces every 8 inches. Separate the pieces and use a square to extend the marks into pencil lines. Carefully align each cleat and predrill and countersink for two 1-inch drywall screws. Even though the screws are self-tapping, they'll split the cleats if you don't predrill.

Put yellow glue on the cleats and align them on the sides. Insert the screws. Clean up glue that squeezes out with a wet sponge as you go. Repeat the procedure for the remaining vertical sides.

3. **LAY OUT THE TOP BOX DIVIDER.** Measure to halfway along one edge of the inside of the top of the top box (33 inches in our case). Subtract ¼ inch and make a mark. Use a square to extend the line to a pencil mark, which you'll use to align the divider. Make a little X to denote which side of the line the divider will go on. Align the top piece on the bottom piece with all edges flush. Use the top piece to lay out the line on the inside of the bottom piece and make another little X.

4. **ASSEMBLE THE BOXES.** Dry assemble one of the boxes with clamps. Predrill and countersink for ½-inch #8 wood or drywall screws every 6 to 9 inches. Most of the screws won't show, but if you want to putty or plug those that will, drill counterbores. Clamp the sides to the back. Make sure all edges are aligned and then predrill holes through the sides and into the back. Put the ends in place and predrill through the back and sides and into the ends. Disassemble the box. Apply glue and then screw the box together. Repeat the process for the other two boxes.

Install the top box divider with screws. Slightly break all front edges with a block plane and sand smooth. Do the same for the shelves.

5. **APPLY FINISH.** Plug or putty the screws that will show, if you wish. Prime and paint the unit or oil it. Finish the shelves outside the boxes.

6. **ASSEMBLE THE UNIT.** You may want to do this right in the closet. Put the top box in position on the bottom boxes and align it carefully. Then drill four ⅜-inch-diameter holes as shown in the top view. Insert two 1 × ⁵⁄₁₆-inch carriage bolts and tighten them with washers and wing nuts.

If the floor of your closet is carpeted, the unit may wobble a bit. If it does, secure it by putting two 3-inch drywall screws through the back of the boxes and into wall studs.

7. **MAKE AND INSTALL THE CLOTHES POLE SUPPORTS.** Use a compass to draw 6-inch-diameter circles on a scrap of ¾- or 1-inch plywood. You could also use a contrasting piece of hardwood. Most wooden clothes poles are 1¼ inches in diameter. Use the pole itself to lay out the slots in the circles. Cut out the pads with a jigsaw. Predrill and countersink the pads for 1- or 1¼-inch wood or drywall screws.

Cut the clothes pole to fit and hold it up in the closet to see how high you want it. You might even put your longest piece of clothing on a hanger and put the han-ger on the pole. You may decide you want two poles, one on top of the other. When you are happy with the height, mark the location of one support on the side of the unit and level across to determine the location of the other support. Screw both supports into place. Install the pole and shelves.

ACCESSORY SHELVES

We're sure you'll find plenty of uses for this small, versatile shelving unit. It's ideal for organizing magazines, newspapers, mail, and file folders atop or beside a desk. You might place it at bedside where the top shelf could be a nightstand for a clock, radio, lamp, and/or phone. It might find its way into the bathroom or the shop and it works great in a kid's room to keep the endless piles of books and magazines sorted.

The unit is freestanding and the shelves slide into place a little short of the back so there is space for electrical wires.

ACCESSORY SHELVES EXPLODED VIEW

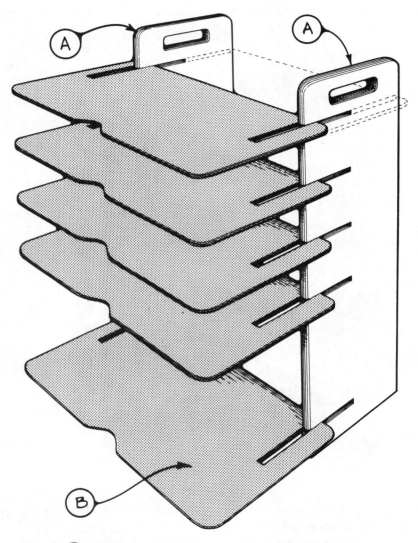

(A) SIDES · ¾" PLYWOOD · 2 PCS. 8" × 26"
(B) SHELVES · ⅜" MARINE PLYWOOD · 5 PCS. 9½" × 19"

TOP, FRONT, AND SIDE VIEWS

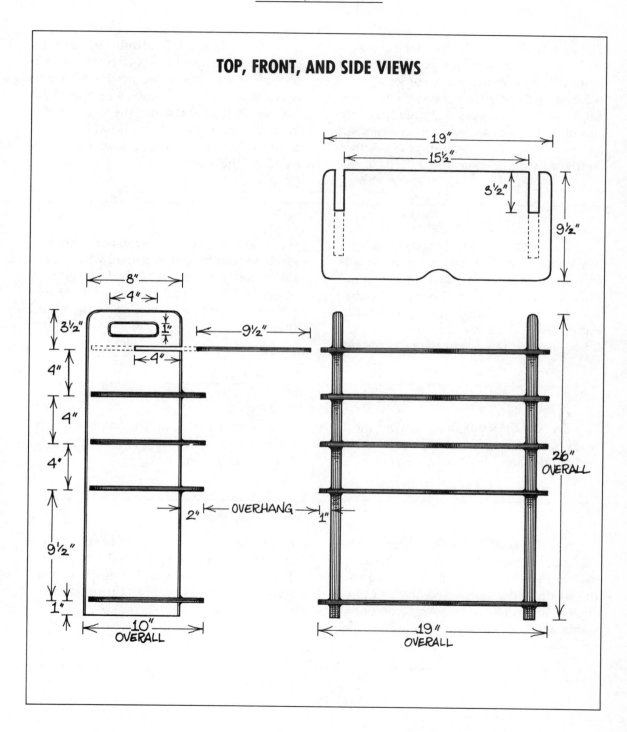

The handles and small size make it easy to move the unit for storage or to clean around it. The entire piece comes apart in seconds and packs flat for travel or storage. All in all, this is a very versatile little storage unit. Of course, you can customize it for specific uses by changing the width or depth or by adding shelves.

We made the sides from high density overlay (HDO) and the shelves from marine plywood. When the marine plywood is oiled, it contrasts nicely with the HDO surface. You could make the entire piece from marine plywood or, as another nice contrast, you could use oak or birch plywood for the sides.

1. **CUT THE SIDES** Cut the sides to the dimensions listed. With a compass or a 3-inch-diameter can lid, draw a 1½-inch radius on the top corners. We cut the radii by clamping the sides together and cutting both sides at the same time on a band saw. If you use a jigsaw to cut the radii, it's bet-ter to do it in two cuts because the blade tends to wander out of square when cutting through too thick a board. Bevel the edges slightly by making two or three passes with the block plane and then sand them.

2. **CUT THE HANDHOLDS.** Lay out the hand hold on one side. Drill a starter hole and cut the hand hold with a jigsaw. Smooth and square up the hand hold with a file or rasp, then use it as a pattern to lay out the other hand hold.

3. **CUT SLOTS IN THE SIDES.** Measure the thickness of your shelf plywood because it may not be exactly ⅜ inch thick. Adjust the width of the slots accordingly. If the shelves are too loose, the unit won't be stable when it is assembled. On the other hand, the shelves shouldn't fit so tightly that they have to be pounded into place. You can cut the slots with a jigsaw or with a router and pattern. See "Cutting Slots," page 14.

4. CUT THE SHELVES. Cut the shelves to size and then round the front corners with the same 1½-inch radius as the sides. You can round the back corners or leave them square. Also optional is the indent in the front of the shelves. The indent makes it a little easier to pull files or papers from the shelves. To cut the indent, use the same 1½-inch radius and cut 1¼ inches into the shelf.

5. APPLY FINISH. The HDO surfaces need no finish at all. We just applied some tung oil to the exposed plywood edges of the HDO and to the shelves. If you used hardwood plywood or marine plywood for the whole project, it will look great and be easy to keep clean if you oil or varnish the whole thing.

MUG AND SPICE RACK

This wall-mounted rack will save counter-space and keep your spices in one place where they can be easily seen and quickly selected. The rack is designed for two sizes of seasoning or spice containers—the larger containers in the bottom and the shorter ones on the top. There is also space to hang mugs, mixing spoons, or other kitchen tools from screw-in hooks along the bottom edge of the rack.

The back of the rack is made of ½-inch birch plywood with a pair of decorative swans cut out of the top edge. The rest of

the rack is constructed of 1-inch birch plywood. Use any hardwood plywood you like. The sliding doors are clear or smoky acrylic.

We left the plywood edges of our rack exposed, but if you prefer, you could easily cover the edges with wood veneer tape or even ½-inch-thick solid wood. You can make the cabinet and shelf narrower by the thickness of your facings, or use the dimensions given here and just notch the shelf deeper so the doors will clear after the facing is applied.

MUG AND SPICE RACK EXPLODED VIEW

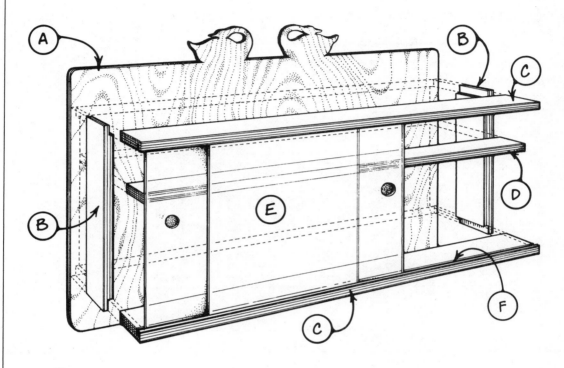

(A) **BACK** • 1 PC. ½" × 24" × 36" (PATTERN CUTOUT IN TOP 3")

(B) **SIDES** • 2 PCS. 1" × 3" × 14½" (DADOS AS SHOWN)

(C) **TOP & BOTTOM** • 2 PCS. 1" × 3" × 35" (GROOVE AS SHOWN)

(D) **SHELF** • 1 PC. 1" × 2⅜" × 34"

(E) **DOORS** • 2 PCS. PLASTIC ⅛" × 13" × 18"

(F) **GROOVE DIVIDER** • 2 PCS. HARDWOOD ⅛" × ¾" × 35"

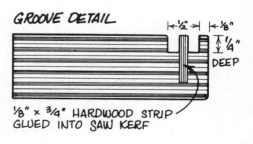

GROOVE DETAIL

|←½"→| |←⅛"

¼" DEEP

⅛" × ¾" HARDWOOD STRIP GLUED INTO SAW KERF

TOP, FRONT, AND SIDE VIEWS

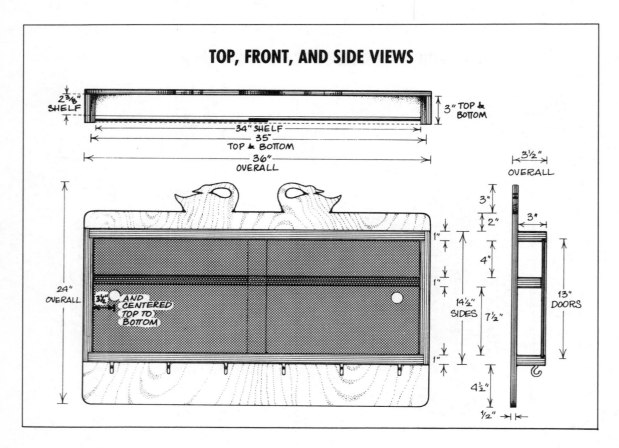

SWANS LAYOUT

EACH SQUARE = ½"

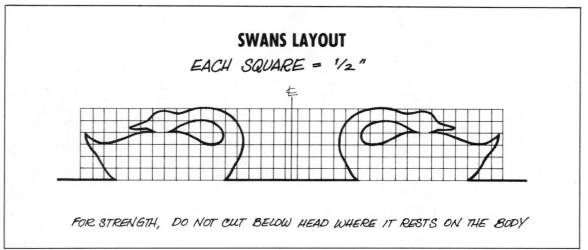

FOR STRENGTH, DO NOT CUT BELOW HEAD WHERE IT RESTS ON THE BODY

1. LAY OUT AND CUT THE BACK. Cut the back to the overall dimensions illustrated. These dimensions allow 3 inches of height for the swan cutouts, so make the back only 21 inches high if you want to skip them. A scaled pattern is provided for the swans. Cut the figures with a jigsaw on slow speed with a fine cutting blade. Drill a starter hole to get your jigsaw into the closed neck area. The corners of the back have a 2-inch radius. Clean up your cuts with a rasp and sandpaper.

---

2. CUT AND RABBET THE SIDES. Cut the sides to size on the table saw. The rabbets can be made on the table saw or radial arm saw. If you don't have a dado blade for your saw, lay out the rabbets and remove the material with several passes through the saw. Clean up the bottom of the cuts with a chisel and/or rabbet plane.

TIP ▶

You can make rabbets, such as the ones in the sides of the spice cabinet, with your table saw even if you don't have a dado cutter. Use the rip fence of your saw as a stop. To make the rabbet 1 inch wide, set the fence 1 inch from the outside of your saw blade as shown. Set the blade height to the depth of the rabbet, in this case ⅜ inch. With the workpiece supported against the saw's miter gauge, make a kerf along the edge of the workpiece. Make repeated, overlapping kerfs by moving further into the workpiece until the workpiece runs against the fence, completing the rabbet.

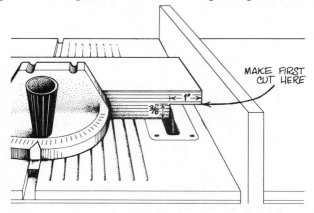

MAKE FIRST CUT HERE

3. **MAKE THE TOP AND BOTTOM.** Cut the top and bottom to size on the table saw. As shown in the groove detail, the doors slide in a groove in each piece. The doors are separated by a hardwood strip that is glued into a saw kerf in the groove.

Start by making a ¼ × ¼-inch groove in the top and bottom pieces. Make the groove ³⁄₁₆ inch from the front edge of each piece. You can make the groove with a dado cutter in the table saw or with a straightedge-guided router.

Set your table saw fence ⁹⁄₁₆ inch from the nearest side of the blade. Set the blade height to ¾ inch. Run the top and bottom pieces over the saw so that the blade makes a kerf in the middle of each groove.

Rip a ⅛-inch-wide strip off a 35-inch-long piece of clear hardwood. Do this by setting your fence so that most of the stock is between the fence and the blade and the ⅛-inch strip falls off the other side of the blade.

Test-fit the strips in the kerfs. They should be snug, but not so tight that you can't press them in with your hands. If they are too tight, thin them with a block plane. When they fit, put yellow glue in each groove and press the strips in place.

4. **MAKE THE SHELF.** Dry assemble the top, bottom, and sides with a couple of clamps. Check the length you need for a snug-fitting shelf and then cut the shelf to size.

5. **CUT THE DOORS.** Cut the two acrylic doors to size on the table saw. Cut a slight chamfer on all edges to make them softer to the touch and to make the doors slide easily in their slots.

6. **CUT FINGER HOLES IN THE DOORS.** The finger holes are centered vertically and located 3½ inches from the edge of each door. Place each door down on a piece of scrap wood and drill the holes slowly with a sharp 1¼-inch spade bit. Use a drill press if you have one. Keep the pressure light to avoid splitting the acrylic.

7. **ASSEMBLE THE RACK.** All assembly is done with 1¼-inch #10 Phillips-head wood screws. Use two screws at each end of the bottom, shelf, and top. Screws that go into the sides of the rack are predrilled, countersunk, and plugged.

First, assemble one side to the top, bottom, and shelf. Insert the doors and make sure the top, bottom, and shelf are square to both sides before attaching the other side. Finally, screw the back to the rack. Plug the screws as described in "Plugs," page 21.

---

8. **APPLY FINISH.** You can paint, oil, or varnish the rack. If you choose to stain the rack, realize that the plywood edges will come out darker than the face veneers.

---

9. **ADD OPTIONAL HOOKS.** We put six mug hooks on the bottom of our rack to make it even more useful. These are screw-in hooks that are available in brass or coated with plastic or rubber. You can buy them at a home-supply store, hardware store, or lumberyard.

---

10. **MOUNT THE RACK.** Mount the rack with four screws inside the cabinet. Drive two screws at the top and two at the bottom, into studs in the wall.

KITCHEN KNIFE RACK

K eep your knives handy and off the counter with this simple, wall-mounted knife rack made from two pieces of plywood scrap. We made ours from 1-inch-thick hardwood plywood. You could use ¾ inch or ½ inch, depending on what you have around and how thick you want the rack to look. You could also use softwood plywood.

The length of the rack and the width of the slots shown in the drawing are laid out to accommodate our complement of knives. You can change the length for more or fewer knives and customize the slots by measuring your knife blades where they meet the handles. Leave at least 1 inch between slots to make it easy to withdraw the knives.

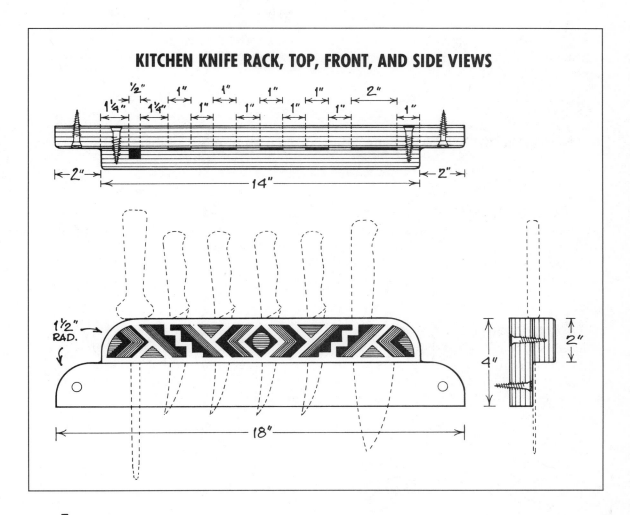

KITCHEN KNIFE RACK, TOP, FRONT, AND SIDE VIEWS

1. CUT THE PIECES. Cut the two pieces to overall dimensions on the table saw. Don't cut the curves yet.

2. CUT THE GROOVES. Set the saw blade to a height of ⅛ inch and cut the grooves in the small piece by making repeated passes over the blade. You could also use a dado blade. If you are cutting a slot for a sharpening steel, raise the blade to ½ inch to cut that groove.

3. ASSEMBLE THE PIECES. Predrill and countersink through the back for two screws. We used 1½-inch drywall screws. Use shorter screws if you are using thinner plywood. Screw the back to the front.

---

4. CUT THE CURVES. Draw the four 1½-inch radii on the ends. Cut them with a jigsaw.

---

5. MOUNT THE RACK. Since knife blades will protrude, pick a location where there is no danger of someone getting cut. Predrill and attach the rack to the wall with two roundhead wood screws. On our rack, the screws are 16 inches apart so we can screw into wall studs.

---

6. APPLY FINISH. The rack can be painted, stained, or oiled depending on your decor and the plywood you use. You should give it at least a light oiling to keep it from absorbing kitchen grime. Take the rack apart to make it easy to finish.

We decided to paint our rack with a southwestern motif that can be achieved freehand or by masking off areas with masking tape.

RECYCLING
BINS

Separating aluminum cans, glass, and newspapers is rapidly becoming a way of life. In fact, many states now require recycling and others will soon follow suit.

Yet the typical household still has no efficient means of separating and storing recyclables so they don't pile up and get in the way. We designed these bins to solve the problem.

The system consists of three bins, each sized to hold standard plastic garbage bags. The bins tilt out of a framework so they are easy to use and covered, without separate lids. The framework provides a shelf for stacking newspapers or for a can crusher.

We built our bins and framework from approximately one and a half sheets of ¾-

RECYCLING BINS FRAME EXPLODED VIEW

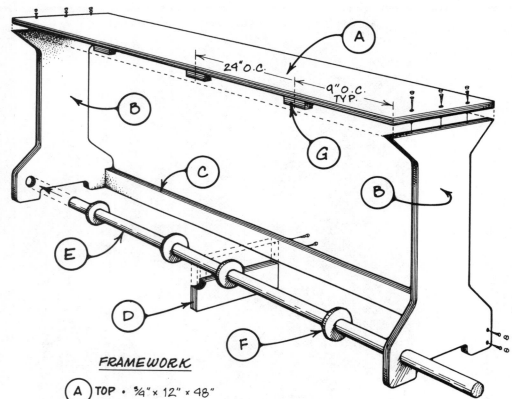

FRAMEWORK

A TOP • ¾" × 12" × 48"

B SIDES • ¾" × 12" × 23" (2 PCS.)

C REAR SUPPORT • ¾" × 2" × 46½"

D CENTER SUPPORT • ¾" × 2" × 9½"

E DOWEL • 1½" DIA. × 48"-49½" LONG

F SPACERS • ¼" × 3" DIA. PLYWOOD (4 PCS.)

G STOPS • ¾" × 1" × 3" PLYWOOD (3 PCS.)

RECYCLING BINS EXPLODED VIEW

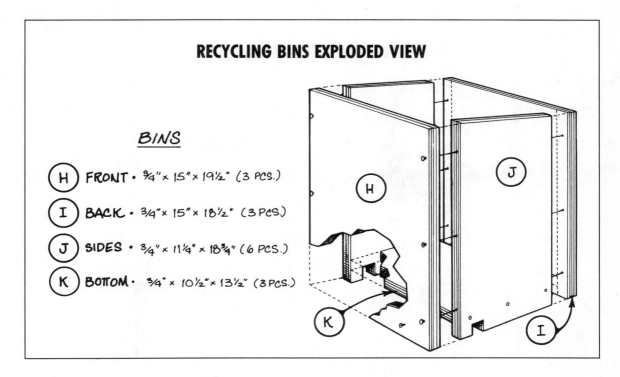

BINS

(H) FRONT • ¾" × 15" × 19½" (3 PCS.)

(I) BACK • ¾" × 15" × 18½" (3 PCS.)

(J) SIDES • ¾" × 11¼" × 18¾" (6 PCS.)

(K) BOTTOM • ¾" × 10½" × 13½" (3 PCS.)

inch high density overlay (HDO) plywood. HDO's impervious, easily cleaned surface is perfect for this project. It requires no more finish than some oil or paint on the exposed plywood edges. Unfortunately, HDO may be tough to get in many areas. The next best choice is BB Grade marine plywood that is primed and painted with exterior enamel. Either way, the bins are designed to stand up to outdoor use. If you keep them inside, you'll still need a finish that will stand up to frequent scrubbings with detergent.

1. CUT THE BIN SIDES, FRONTS, AND BACKS.

Begin by cutting all the parts for the bin, except the bottoms, to the dimensions listed. The ends have an angled cut at the top, from 19½ inches at the front to 18½ inches at the back. A quick way to make this cut on all six ends is to cut one with a straightedge-guided circular saw, sand the edge smooth, and then use it as a template to rout the rest with a flush trimming bit. If you do this, first cut the pieces to within ⅛ inch of the dimensions with the circular saw.

TOP, FRONT, AND SIDE VIEWS

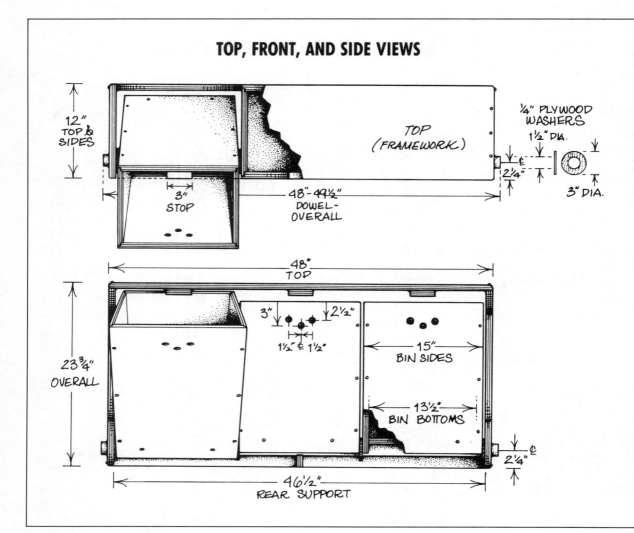

12"
TOP &
SIDES

3"
STOP

TOP
(FRAMEWORK)

48"-49½"
DOWEL-
OVERALL

¼" PLYWOOD
WASHERS
1½" DIA.

2¼"

3" DIA.

48"
TOP

23¾"
OVERALL

3"   2½"
1½"   1½"

15"
BIN SIDES

13½"
BIN BOTTOMS

2¼"

46½"
REAR SUPPORT

2. CUT THE DOWEL NOTCHES IN THE ENDS.
Each end piece has a notch near the back to allow the bins to pivot on the dowels. Cut the notches with a jigsaw.

3. ASSEMBLE THE BINS. Screw the bins together with 2-inch, galvanized, drywall-type screws. For HDO, you'll have to predrill. Slightly chamfer the edges of the bins with a block plane to prevent the face veneer or overlay from chipping.

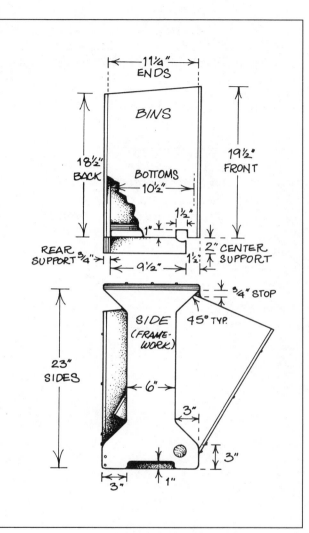

is flush with the tops of the notches. Screw the bottoms into place. To prevent moisture from getting into the joints when you wash the inside of the bin, you can run a bead of silicone caulk around the inside corners of the bin. Smooth the bead into a fillet with a gloved finger.

5. MAKE THE FINGERHOLDS. Lay out and drill three 1-inch-diameter holes in the front of each bin as shown in the front view.

6. CUT THE FRAMEWORK SIDES, TOP, REAR SUPPORT, STOPS, AND CENTER SUPPORT. Cut these pieces to the dimensions given in the materials list. These are the only critical cuts. Stack and clamp the two sides together. Then lay out the rest of the cuts as shown in *Top, Front, and Side Views.* Cut both pieces at once with a jigsaw. With the pieces still clamped together, drill the holes for the 1½-inch-diameter dowel. To prevent splintering, stop drilling when the tip of the bit protrudes through the back piece and then move the bit around to the other side to complete the hole.

Trace the curve of the dowel on the center supports. Cut along the line with a jigsaw.

7. MAKE THE WOODEN SPACERS. The ¼-inch plywood spacers prevent the bins from rubbing against each other. We made

4. CUT AND INSTALL THE BOTTOMS OF THE BINS. Measure the bottoms of the bins and cut them on the table saw to fit. Drill one ½-inch-diameter drainage hole in each corner of each bottom piece. Tap each bottom piece into place so that the underside

ours on the drill press using a 3-inch-diameter hole saw for the outside diameter and a 1½-inch-diameter hole saw for the dowel hole. In fact, the spacers don't have to be round on the outside. If you don't have a drill press, you could simply drill 1½-inch holes in 3-inch-square pads of plywood.

8. ASSEMBLE THE FRAMEWORK. Slip the spacers onto the dowel and then put the dowel through the hole in each side piece. The dowels should be snug, but you shouldn't have to force them into place.

If the holes are too tight, sand the inside with a piece of sandpaper wrapped around a smaller diameter dowel. With 2-inch, galvanized, drywall-type screws, fasten the rear support to the sides and then screw the top in place. Screw the center support to the rear support. Fasten the dowel to the center support with one screw. Fasten the stops to the top with 1-inch, galvanized, drywall-type screws. Put the bins in place from the front with the spacers separating them.

CHAPTER FOUR
INDOOR
TABLES

TRESTLE TABLE

The beauty of a traditional trestle table came from its simple, useful design. It answered the need for a large, heavy table that could easily be taken apart for moving or storage. It didn't try to disguise or adorn its solid plank construction or hide the wedges that held it together. The design stemmed from need and from the tools and materials on hand.

What kind of trestle table would our forefathers have designed if their material was high-quality hardwood plywood instead of planks and their tools were a table saw and a router instead of a hand saw and a plane? We asked ourselves these questions when we designed the table you see here.

The result is a table that, at 150 pounds, is heavy and structurally similar to a traditional trestle table. And, like a traditional table, it disassembles easily. Just remove four wingnuts, tap out two wedges, lift off the top, and remove the stretcher.

Rather than try to disguise its plywood construction by applying solid edges, this table celebrates the attractive, voidless

TRESTLE TABLE EXPLODED VIEW

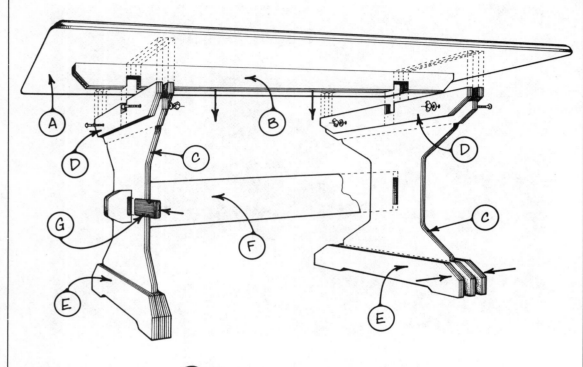

A TABLE TOP • 1 PC. 1" × 48" × 96"

B BEAM • 2 PCS. 1" × 4" × 72" (LAMINATED TOGETHER)

C POSTS • 2 PCS. 1" × 28" × 42"

D ARMS • 4 PCS. 1" × 4" × 42"

E FEET • 4 PCS. 1" × 5" × 42" (LAMINATED TO POSTS)

F STRETCHER • 1 PC. 1" × 8" × 62"

G HARDWOOD WEDGES • 2 PCS. ¾" × 3" × 5"

edges of high-quality hardwood plywood. Instead of the hourglass-shaped legs of a traditional table, our table is boldly angular simply because that's the design plywood dictates. The table top is 4 × 8 feet, taking full advantage of the size of a plywood panel. As a final expression of what can be done with modern tools and materials, we routed a detail along the edge of the table top.

---

1. SELECT THE SIDES. Pick the most attractive side of your best plywood panel for the top. Often both sides are quite attractive and it's just a matter of personal preference. The table will be most attractive if you cut both posts and all the arms and feet from one panel as shown in the *Cutting Diagram.* When you assemble the table, make sure all the surfaces that face in a given direction are from the same side of the same piece of plywood. Mark the pieces so they don't get reversed during construction.

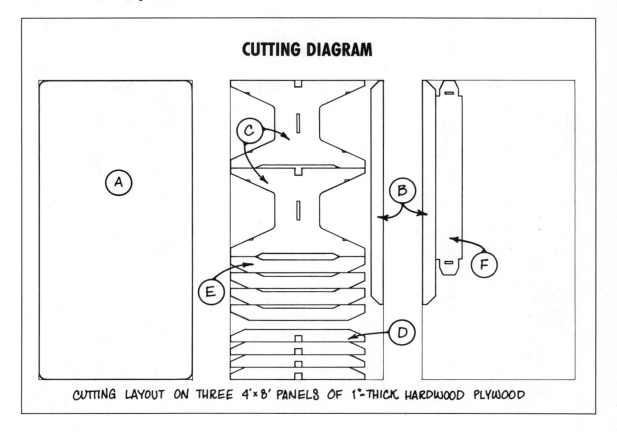

CUTTING DIAGRAM

CUTTING LAYOUT ON THREE 4'×8' PANELS OF 1"-THICK HARDWOOD PLYWOOD

2. **ROUND THE EDGES OF THE TOP.** The top requires only a rounding cut on each corner. Cut the corner to the radius shown with a jigsaw. Keep the cut as accurate as possible so the router detail will come out exact and smooth. Clean up the cut with a rasp, file, and sandpaper to remove small bumps. Run your hand around the curve and along the panel edges. Often you can feel small defects much easier than you can see them. You can finish the edges by sanding a slight round or you can cut a small bevel with a block plane.

We used a beading bit to rout a single

TOP, FRONT, AND SIDE VIEWS

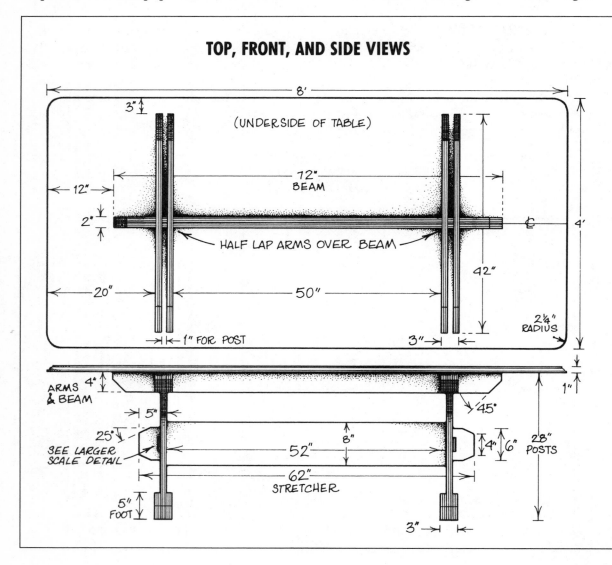

bead around the edge of the table. You might choose a ½- or ¾-inch round-over bit, a round-over bit with a bead on one or both edges or, for a more ornate look, try a roman ogee. The bead and the ogee are illustrated in *Tabletop Edge Options.* If you are undecided on the edge detail, hold off

until you are finished assembling the table. Seeing the size and proportions of the actual table will help you decide. Before routing the edges, check them for voids. If the roller-bearing guide dips into a void, it will cause a divot in your edge. If you find a void, fill it with wood filler.

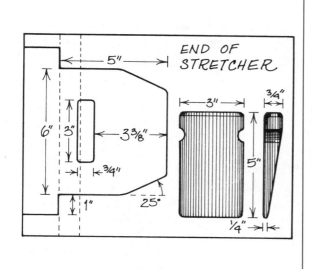

END OF STRETCHER

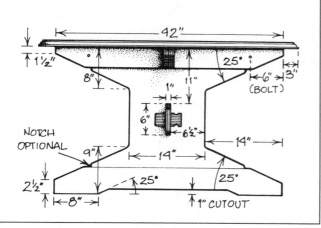

NOTCH OPTIONAL

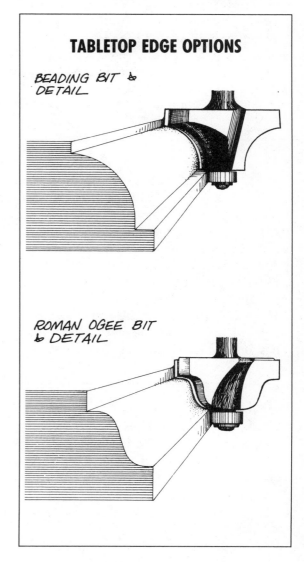

TABLETOP EDGE OPTIONS

BEADING BIT & DETAIL

ROMAN OGEE BIT & DETAIL

3. CUT THE POSTS, ARMS, AND FEET. Lay out one post and cut it with a jigsaw. Trace around it to lay out the other post. Cut out the post and then cut the 1-inch indentations that form the feet on the underside of each post. Cut about ⅛ inch to the waste side of the layout line and leave the cuts rough for now. Use the bottom of the posts as templates to lay out the feet. Later, after you've glued the feet to the posts, you will cut along the layout line that marks the bottom indentation. This will remove glue that squeezes out and ensure matching indentations.

Cut out one foot and one arm. Clean the cuts as necessary with a rasp or file and sandpaper. Rough-cut the other arms and feet and leave them half an inch or so larger on all sides than the final dimensions. Then use the first foot and arm as templates to rout the remaining arms and feet with a pattern bit or flush-trimming bit. For more information about pattern routing, see "Cutting Slots with a Router," page 14.

If you don't have a router, use the first arm and foot as templates to lay out the others and then cut them with a jigsaw.

---

4. MAKE THE BEAM. The beam consists of two thicknesses of plywood. You'll notice on the *Cutting Diagram* that each beam uses one factory edge. Instead of trying to get a perfect cut while wrestling a full panel through the table saw, start by ripping both pieces an ⅛ inch wider than the final dimension. Glue up the two pieces with yellow glue. After the glue has cured, scrape off any glue drips on the best edge. Then make a finish cut with a fine-cut carbide blade in the table saw. This cut removes glue that has squeezed out along the other edge. Make a steady, nonstop cut and clean up the saw marks with a couple of passes with a plane.

Cut the angle on each end of the beam. Note that this is a 45-degree angle while all other angles on the stretcher, arms, and feet are 25 degrees. Clean up the saw marks with a block plane or belt sander.

---

5. MAKE THE STRETCHER. The stretcher is one thickness of plywood. Again, because you are cutting it out of a nearly full sheet, you might find it easier to make a rough cut first before your final-width rips.

Lay out the ends of the tenons and cut them with a jigsaw.

---

6. MAKE STRETCHER SLOTS IN THE POSTS.
Lay out the slots and cut them with a jigsaw. Alternately, you can use a router as described in "Cutting Slots with a Router," page 14. After the slots are cut, use a scrap of the appropriate thickness to ensure a proper slip fit. With a file or fine rasp, cut a slight bevel on all edges of the slot. This will prevent the face veneer from chipping when you insert and withdraw the stretcher tenon. Don't cut the wedge slots now. Wait until the table is assembled so that you can locate them exactly.

7. ATTACH THE BEAM. Lay the tabletop upside down on a flat workbench. Center the beam in position on the tabletop and draw the outline of the beam with light pencil marks. Predrill for 3-inch #8 Phillips-head wood screws with a 1¼-inch counterbore. Use the seam between the layers of plywood as a guide to center the holes. Drill them on 12-inch centers. Apply glue to the edge of the beam and screw it to the bottom of the tabletop.

8. NOTCH THE BEAM. Cut the half-lap notch for the arms and the post in each end of the beam. Measure the actual combined thicknesses of the two arms and the post. Many plywood panels are ⅟₃₂ inch or even ⅟₁₆ inch smaller than normal size, so mark carefully using a ballpoint pen and a small square. Make the two side cuts with a backsaw. Make a number of kerf cuts to facilitate the removal of the notch. Then use a chisel and a mallet to make the notch.

9. NOTCH AND ATTACH THE ARMS. Cut a half-lap notch in the arms that fits snugly over the half-lap notch in the beam. Position each arm on the beam. Make sure the arm is parallel to the short edge of the table and get ready to glue it in place. Before you glue, however, place a 1-inch-thick spacer between each set of arms. Wax the spacers to prevent them from getting glued in place. After the glue dries, remove the spacers.

10. **NOTCH THE POSTS.** Make the half-lap notch in each post. Insert the posts between the arms. Make sure the notches let the posts butt flat against the bottom of the table.

11. **INSTALL THE CARRIAGE BOLTS.** Four 4 × ⅜-inch-diameter carriage bolts attach the posts to the arms. Bronze or brass bolts look better than chrome-plated bolts and they develop a nice patina. Use wide washers so you don't crush the wood. You can also use wing nuts so the table can be assembled without a wrench. Center the bolt hole in the width of the arm so you have room to manipulate the wing nut on the back side. Where the posts will be covered by the arms, mark one post left and one right so the bolt holes will always align.

Drill ½-inch-diameter holes so you won't have to pound the bolts in and out. When the table is assembled, the weight of the top will keep it stable, so the wing nuts don't have to be very tight.

12. **POSITION AND CUT THE WEDGE SLOTS.** The slots in the stretcher tenons extend ⅛ inch into the posts before the wedges are inserted. This ensures that the back side of the slot will not sit proud of the post and prevents the wedge from bearing against the post. To exactly position these slots, assemble the table on a flat surface. Insert the stretcher tenons in the post slots and then put the top in place. Bolt the top on.

With the posts tight against the tenon shoulders, scribe a line on each tenon where it meets the outside of each post. Disassemble the table. Make another line ⅛ inch closer to the shoulder than the first line. From this line, lay out the slot as shown in End of Stretcher detail.

You can cut the wedge slots with a jigsaw or a router and slot jig. See "Cutting Slots," page 14. A square slot with a square shoulder will work fine, but if you want to get fancy, cut the outboard shoulder of the wedge slots at the same angle as the wedges. If you do this, each wedge will fit from only one side, but the fit will be perfect.

13. **MAKE THE WEDGES.** Rip the wedges to width on the table saw and do the rough shaping with the band saw or jigsaw. Use a block plane to fine-tune the slope of the wedge and then bevel the top to prevent the wedge from splintering or splitting with use. Use a round rasp to form the finger-hold notches on both sides of the big end. You can sand the wedges if you like, but we liked the hand-worked look of the planed surfaces.

Assemble the table and test fit the wedges. They should tap into place with a light mallet. Adjust as necessary.

Soak the wedges overnight in a penetrating oil such as boiled linseed or Watco Danish. You can form a small soaking trough out of aluminum foil for each wedge to make it easier to pour the oil back into the can. After they soak overnight, wipe the wedges off and wet sand them with #400 grit sandpaper. Wipe and polish the wedges with a cloth until they are dry. More oil will bleed out of the wood, so set the wedges aside overnight and polish them one more time before using them. The oil soak waterproofs the wedges, makes them attractive, and helps them stand up better to repeated use.

14. **ASSEMBLE THE FEET.** With the wedges in place, remove the posts and stretcher from the table and set the assembly upright on a flat workbench. Place a piece of waxed paper under each post. Carefully align and glue all four feet to the posts using a clamp about every 9 inches.

When the glue sets, disassemble the table and make the final indentation cut on the underside of the posts and feet. You will be cutting through 3 inches of plywood, so use a long sharp blade in your jigsaw or get a helper to support the end and make the cut with a band saw. Clean the 25-degree surfaces on the feet with a block plane and slightly bevel all edges to match.

15. **BEVEL THE EDGES.** With the table disassembled, use a block plane to make a small bevel on the edges of all pieces except the tabletop. Bevel the edges of slots and notches with a file or small rasp.

16. **APPLY FINISH.** Do any final sanding and remove any pencil or pen marks. Take the table apart and bevel, rasp, and sand as required.

To finish our table, we started by saturating all the parts with Varathane #66 Clear Oil Finish. We let the oil dry for three days and then applied three coats of Varathane Liquid Plastic Exterior #93 Clear Satin to the top only. This gave added protection to the top, which will receive the brunt of abuse, and provided a nice contrast with the duller finish of the base.

A good alternative finish would be spar varnish with sunscreen. This finish will in time attain a mellow golden hue.

DROPLEAF
TABLE

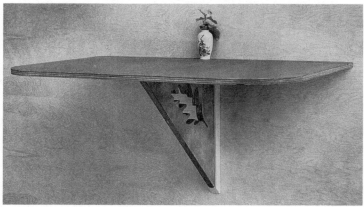

This dropleaf table is an idea borrowed from our boatbuilding days—they are standard equipment in sailboat cabins where space is at a premium. Now that we are landlocked, we find there are plenty of uses for this handy space-saver, so we adapted the design for use ashore. Perhaps you will use yours as an occasional desk or

117

DROPLEAF TABLE EXPLODED VIEW

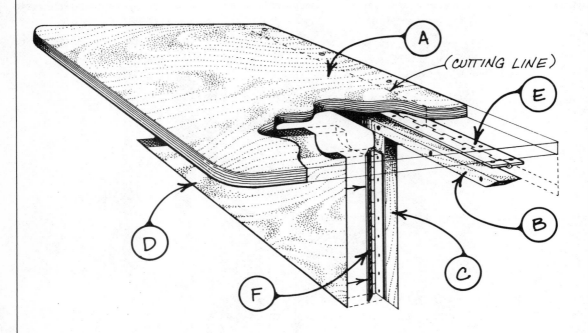

(CUTTING LINE)

A) TABLE • ¾" × 25" × 39" PLYWOOD

B) TABLE CLEAT • 1⅜" × 1⅜" × 32" SOLID WOOD

C) KNEE CLEAT • 1⅜" × 1⅜" × 18½" SOLID WOOD

D) KNEE • ¾" × 18" × 18" PLYWOOD

E) TABLE HINGE • ¾" × 36" LONG

F) KNEE HINGE • ¾" × 15" LONG

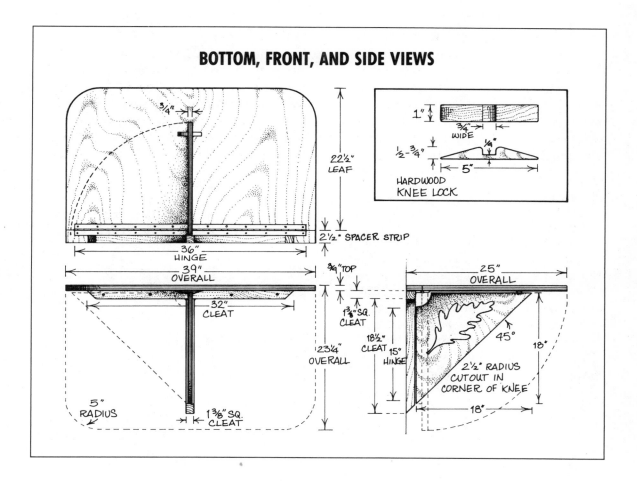

BOTTOM, FRONT, AND SIDE VIEWS

in a cozy eating nook for two. It's ideal for under a window and it's attractive with the dropleaf up or down. When down, the table protrudes less than 4 inches from the wall.

The top of a table should be about 30 inches from the floor. So we made our table top 25 inches wide to keep it well off the floor when it is folded down. We made our table of ¾-inch birch plywood and left the plywood edges exposed. You can use any hardwood plywood you like and even ap-

ply veneer tape to the edges if you don't like the exposed plies. Traditionally, drop-leafs are oval, but we made ours square and then rounded the corners.

The support knee of our table is embellished with a cutout in the shape of an oak leaf. We've provided a pattern for the leaf, but we encourage you to get creative and come up with your own cutout. Just be sure not to make the cutout so big that you weaken the knee. Of course, you can skip the cutout altogether.

1. MAKE THE TOP AND LOCATE THE HINGE.
Choose the best side of the plywood for the tabletop. Begin by cutting the drop leaf and the 2½-inch spacer strip from one piece of plywood. Cut the overall shape on the table saw or with a straightedge-guided circular saw and then cut the radii with a jigsaw. Make a line on the dropleaf where you will cut off the spacer, but don't cut it yet. First position the piano hinge over the line and drill the hinge screw holes. Remove the hinge and then cut through the center of the line. This method has two advantages: it ensures a consistent kerf-sized space between the spacer strip and the dropleaf, and it keeps the grain pattern aligned on the tabletop.

2. MAKE THE KNEE.
Cut the triangular knee as shown. Then cut out the 2-inch radius round on the top inside corner. See *Maple Leaf Cutout* if you wish to add the leaf design. Drill a starter hole and then cut out the leaf design as closely as you can with a jigsaw. Clean up the design with a rasp and #60 grit sandpaper wrapped around a pencil or narrow file.

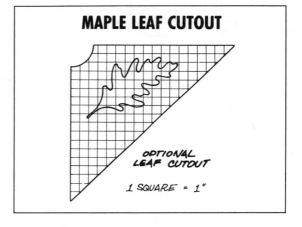

MAPLE LEAF CUTOUT

OPTIONAL LEAF CUTOUT

1 SQUARE = 1"

3. MAKE THE CLEATS.
The cleats are 1⅜ × 1⅜-inch fir. We ripped ours from a clear 2 × 4. The cleats can be stained or painted to match the table, or they can be left natural. If you've chosen a hardwood plywood for the table, you may want to make the cleats of matching solid stock.

· We made our horizontal cleat 32 inches long because we wanted it hidden well under the table and we intended to mount it on a wooden wall with a continuous attachment for screws. If you will be mounting your table on a wall with studs on 16-inch centers, make the horizontal cleat 35 inches long. This way you'll be able to center the vertical cleat on a stud and attach the horizontal cleat to a stud on both sides.

Cut a 45-degree angle at the bottom of the vertical cleat and at both ends of the horizontal cleat. Plane and sand off any saw marks and break the edges slightly with a block plane.

4. **APPLY FINISH.** We stained and oiled our table. You could paint yours. Whatever you do, it's easier to apply a finish before the table is mounted on the wall.

---

5. **MOUNT THE TABLE.** How you attach the table to the wall will depend on the way your house is constructed. It's particularly important that the horizontal cleat be firmly attached because it takes most of the stress. For most situations, we recommend predrilling and countersinking for 3-inch #12 flathead wood screws.

Measure 29¼ inches up from the floor and use a 4-foot level to draw a horizontal line. Mount the horizontal cleat. Now mount the knee cleat. Use a framing square to keep it square to the horizontal cleat.

Attach the hinge to the knee and then to the knee cleat. Note that the top of the knee must be ¼ inch below the top of the horizontal cleat to allow the knee to clear the tabletop hinge. The ¼ inch is taken up by the knee lock so that the table will be level when open.

Attach the hinge to the tabletop and the spacer strip. Predrill and counterbore for 1½-inch #10 flathead wood screws and attach the spacer strip to the horizontal cleat. Fill all counterbores with plugs or putty.

---

6. **MAKE AND ATTACH THE KNEE LOCK.** The knee lock can be made from any 1-inch-thick piece of hardwood. None of its dimensions are critical except that the notch must be ¾ inch wide and deep enough to keep the knee ¼ inch from the tabletop. Lay out the shape on the edge of a piece of stock that is at least 3 × 5 inches so you can clamp it to your bench with a little more than 1 inch of the width overhanging. Cut out the tapers and the notch with a jigsaw and then clean them with a rasp while the piece is still clamped to the bench. Now make the 5-inch cut to separate the knee lock from the piece of stock. Sand the lock smooth and give it a few coats of penetrating oil. Even if you paint the rest of the table, we don't recommend painting the knee lock. The paint will quickly wear away with use.

Swing the knee out and slip the knee lock into position. Check that the knee is exactly square to the horizontal cleat. Check that the knee lock is square to the knee. Mark the location of the knee lock. Swing the knee off center so it is out of the way, but still holds up the tabletop. Put yellow glue on the knee lock and clamp it into position. If you don't have a clamp that will reach, leave the lock and knee in position and predrill and counterbore for a ¾-inch #6 flathead wood screw on each side of the notch. Then glue and screw the knee lock into position. The screws won't be visible when the table is open or closed.

BED AND BREAKFAST TRAY

This tray is ideal for breakfast in bed and it's just right for reading, writing, or eating when sitting on the floor. It makes a good homework desk for kids who enjoy working on the floor, and it can be lifted and carried by one handle.

The top of our tray is a nice old piece of spruce left over from another project. We made the legs for our tray from Appleply, a high-quality multi-ply with a maple face veneer that is made by States Industries. A European multi-ply, called baltic birch, is commonly available in lumberyards.

Perhaps you have squirreled away a piece of wood that would be perfect for this tray. Any wide piece of good solid stock

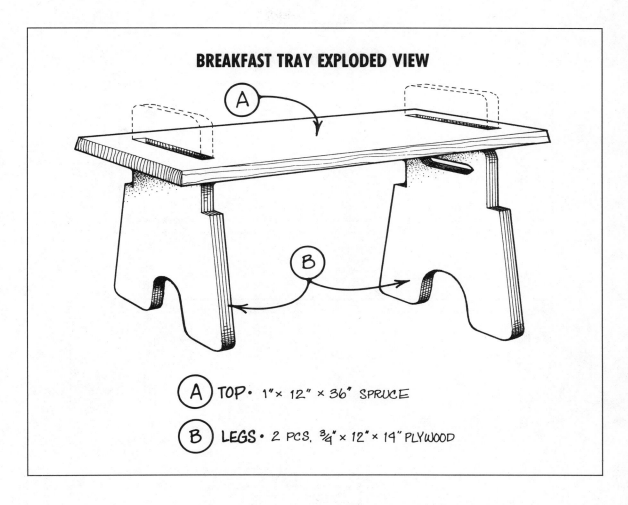

BREAKFAST TRAY EXPLODED VIEW

(A) TOP • 1" × 12" × 36" SPRUCE

(B) LEGS • 2 PCS. ¾" × 12" × 14" PLYWOOD

will do as long as it is at least ¾ inch thick. There is no glue or fasteners in this project. The legs are held in place by friction and the tray can be disassembled for storage. A top made of 1-inch stock will provide an even better grip on the legs. Of course, you could use multi-ply for the top too, if you want a slicker looking tray.

1. PREPARE AND CUT THE PARTS. If the top is solid wood, plane it flat on both sides. Whether solid wood or plywood, cut the top to size on the table saw, with the blade set for an 8-degree bevel.

TOP, FRONT, AND SIDE VIEWS

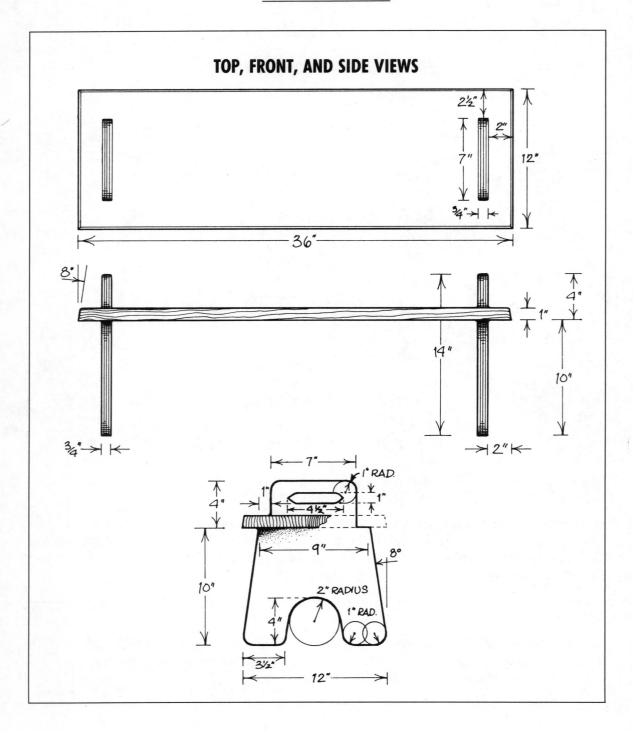

2. LAY OUT AND CUT THE LEGS. Lay out one leg as shown in *Top, Front, and Side Views.* Cut it with a jigsaw. The crucial dimensions are the part of the leg that must fit through the slot in the top. Drill a starter hole for the jigsaw to cut the carrying slot. Use the first leg as a template to lay out the second leg. Cut the second leg.

TIP ▶

> If you find your tray is getting used on the floor more than on the bed, you can tack foam rubber strips to the bottom of each leg to prevent the tray from slipping on hardwood or tile floors.

3. CUT THE SLOTS IN THE TOP. Carefully lay out the slots on a scrap of the plywood left over from the legs as described in "Cutting Slots with a Jigsaw," page 16.

4. APPLY FINISH. We finished our tray with three coats of spar varnish. An oil finish would be nice, too. We don't recommend paint if you intend to disassemble the tray because paint will rub off the legs.

Surprise someone with breakfast in bed!

CHAPTER FIVE

PLYWOOD
AND EPOXY
PROJECTS

In this chapter you will find six projects, five of which are designed to withstand constant exposure to the weather. These five projects rely on epoxy to make them weatherproof.

If you have never worked with epoxy, you shouldn't be deterred from tackling these projects. Some of the techniques will be new, none will be difficult. More often than not, epoxy simplifies rather than complicates the woodworking skills and equipment you need to complete a project. This is because epoxy can be used as a surface coating, as a glue, or even structurally to replace cleats or complex joinery. In fact, the sixth project in this section, the fireplace bench, is an indoor project that uses epoxy only to simplify joinery.

We first began using epoxy with plywood more than 15 years ago when we were making our livings building boats. In fact, boatbuilding is by far the most common use of epoxy with plywood. Wood has traditionally been used to build boats because it is strong and buoyant. Unfortunately, when wood is exposed to water it rots, swells, warps, and won't hold paint. Coating wood with epoxy solves these problems by encapsulating the wood in plastic so that no significant amount of moisture can get to the wood. No moisture means no rot and no movement. Since plywood is designed to counteract movement anyway, combining it with epoxy gives you an extremely stable building material.

Boatbuilders also like epoxy because it is an extremely strong glue that, when thickened with fillers, will fill and seal gaps up to ¼ inch. Another plus is that, unlike other glues, epoxy requires little or no clamping pressure.

When we moved away from the ocean and boatbuilding, we began to experiment with other applications for epoxy. After all, we reasoned, if epoxy will stand up to salt water, it should be great for anything left out in the weather. We found epoxy to be such a strong and versatile material that we often use it for indoor projects as well. You'll find epoxy offered as an alternative construction technique in several projects. For example, the camp box project offers the option of using epoxy fillets instead of the more typical wooden cleats to make the box easy to clean and to save space. But the other five projects in this section stand apart because epoxy is essential to their design. They are the only projects in this book that can't be built without epoxy.

Epoxy, the System

Epoxy has two parts: resin and a hardener. When you mix these two ingredients together, a chemical reaction causes the mixture to cure into a hard plastic. In some applications, one of several types of filler is added to the mixture to make it hold a shape until it hardens.

Over the years, we have tried various brands of epoxy. Our favorite is West System epoxy made by Gougeon Brothers. That's the brand we used for the projects in this book. As a result, much of the information in this chapter is based on Gougeon Brothers literature as well as our own experience with West System epoxy.

The key to the successful use of epoxy is to mix proper proportions of resin and hardener. One of the things we like best about West System epoxy is the company's calibrated mini pumps that screw directly onto the resin and hardener cans. The pumps are calibrated so that one stroke on the resin pump and one stroke on the hardener pump will give you the correct mix of resin and hardener.

All of the projects in this book use West System 205 hardener. This hardener has a pot life of about 15 minutes. This means that you have that long to work with it before it begins to harden. This epoxy mixture cures into a strong, rigid plastic that creates a virtually waterproof bond with wood. All hardeners have a wet lay-up time of about twice as long as the pot life. This means that if you have 15 minutes to apply the epoxy, you have about 30 minutes to get everything assembled and all the clamps or weights adjusted.

For the projects in this book, we use West System 105 Resin. This is a clear, light amber, low-viscosity epoxy resin. When spread with a roller, it flows out and self-levels. It can be cured in a wide temperature range and can be sanded and shaped after it has cured. The resin cures to a clear finish so you can achieve a natural finish by coating it with varnish. It has no solvent odors or vapors.

Gougeon makes 11 fillers that are designed to give the epoxy mixture various characteristics while it is being worked and when it is cured. We use 6 of them for projects in this book. When we use epoxy to glue butt or scarf joints, we add 403 Microfibers, which gives the mixture excellent gap-filling characteristics. This addition also prevents the epoxy from soaking into the end grain, which could leave too little epoxy on the surface for a good bond.

Any time we use epoxy as a glue on large areas, such as when laminating, we use a filler that consists of approximately equal parts of 407 Low-Density Filler and 406 Colloidal Silica. The low-density filler is less goopy than the microfibers and creates a mix that spreads more evenly with a roller or squeegee. The silica makes the mixture smoother and less drippy. It also makes the surface more resistant to abrasions, a quality that is especially important for the rowing dory and camper cap projects. The more low-density filler you add, the more easily the epoxy will sand; the more silica, the stronger the bond.

For making fillets in furniture projects such as the fireplace bench, we use 405 Filleting Blend, which will take a natural or stained finish and is relatively easy to sand. For fillets that must be super strong, such as those in the rowing dory and hot tub projects, we use a 50/50 mix of the filleting blend with 404 High-Density Filler. The high-density filler is designed for maximum strength. We design our projects so that the joints will flex slightly (for example, when you fill the hot tub) and we find that 404 alone is so hard and inflexible that the epoxy may tear the plywood when the joint tries to flex. So, we add a pinch of silica to the mixture when we are making large fillets. It makes the mixture slide smoothly off the filleting paddle.

In one project, the rowing dory, we use 423 Graphite Powder. This black filler produces a low-friction coating that has increased scuff resistance and durability. We add it to the mixture that is used to coat the bottom of the dory.

Unlike the ratio of resin to hardener, knowing the amount of filler to add is not an exact science. For the projects in this book, we will refer to specific fillers that are to be combined with the resin and hardener to create mixtures of three basic consistencies: catsup, mayonnaise, and peanut butter, as shown in *Epoxy Consistencies*. These descriptions are only a guide. It won't alter the effectiveness of the epoxy if your mixture is a little thicker or thinner than the one we describe. In fact, as you

EPOXY CONSISTENCIES

CATSUP CONSISTENCY
FOR LAMINATING

SLIGHTLY THICKENED MIX THAT
SAGS DOWN VERTICAL SURFACES

MAYONNAISE CONSISTENCY
FOR GENERAL BONDING

MODERATELY THICKENED MIX
CLINGS TO VERTICAL SURFACES,
PEAKS FALL OVER

PEANUT BUTTER CONSISTENCY
FOR FILLETING

MAXIMUM THICKNESS MIX
CLINGS TO VERTICAL SURFACES
& FORMS STIFF PEAKS.

become familiar with epoxy and fillers, you may develop your own favorite epoxy/filler blend by combining two or more fillers in various ratios that work best for you.

Measuring and Mixing

As mentioned, the West System mini pump makes measuring easy. You use one stroke of resin to one stroke of hardener. The best mixing container is a clean, flexible plastic pot, such as a margarine container, because when epoxy hardens in the container you can flex the pot and pop it out.

After you dispense the proper proportions of resin and hardener into a mixing pot, thoroughly stir the two ingredients together with a disposable wooden stick. Thoroughly scrape the sides and bottom of the pot. If the project requires that a filler be added to the epoxy, continue to stir while you add filler, until you achieve the consistency you want. Continue stirring until all the ingredients are well blended.

Controlling Cure Time

Several factors control the pot life and cure time of epoxy. When you mix the resin and hardener together, you create an exothermic, or heat-producing, reaction. The more heat generated, the shorter the pot life and the faster the cure. Heat generated by this reaction can be dissipated if you pour the mixture into a container with a large surface area, such as a roller pan. This will extend the pot life.

You can use a hot air gun, hair dryer, or heat lamp to add heat to the surface and speed the cure time, but it's unlikely you'll have to do this when you build the projects in this book.

Estimating How Much Epoxy You Will Need

When you use epoxy as a surface coating, you will need to apply at least two, and usually three coats. Wood absorbs a lot of epoxy, so the first saturation coat usually requires about 25 percent more epoxy than subsequent coats. A quart of 105 or 106 resin and the .44 pint of hardener that goes with it will cover 90 to 105 square feet on the first coat and 120 to 135 square feet on subsequent coats.

Cleanup

Resin, hardener, and uncured epoxy can be cleaned from surfaces with Gougeon Brother's 850 Cleaning Solution. Before you apply the cleaner, scrape off any excess epoxy with a sharpened mixing stick or putty knife. Then dampen a clean rag or paper towel with the cleaning solution and wipe off the remaining epoxy.

If you get resin, hardener, or uncured epoxy on your skin, wash it off with a waterless skin cleaner. Do not use solvent directly on your skin. We avoid getting epoxy on our skin by wearing disposable surgical gloves for small projects or heavier, dishwashing gloves for larger projects.

Application Techniques and Procedures

Whether you are using epoxy as a glue, a surface coating, or to reinforce joints with fillets, it's important that all surfaces are clean and free of paint, varnish, grease, oil, or wax.

Epoxy as a Glue

If you are used to working with traditional woodworking glues, you know that they need well-matched surfaces and clamping pressure to work. Traditional glues can't fill gaps because they can't form a bond unless wood fiber is pressed against wood fiber. But epoxy can fill gaps because when it is mixed with fillers it forms a mass that is stronger than the wood itself. This means that joints do not have to fit tightly. In fact, we often purposely leave joints loose so that epoxy can flow in and seal the wood inside the joint. An example of this is the bottom of the hexagon hot tub.

Because of epoxy's ability to fill gaps, you don't need any more clamping pressure than it takes to hold the parts together until the epoxy cures. Often, a few weights will take the place of long and/or specialized clamps. You never have enough clamps is a woodworker's cliche that doesn't apply when you use epoxy.

Whether you are using epoxy to attach a small piece to your project or to glue up layers of plywood, the basic procedure, as shown in *Using Epoxy as a Glue*, is the same.

Any time you use epoxy, the surfaces must be clean and sanded. Apply the epoxy to the joint in two steps. First, apply the resin/hardener mixture that doesn't have an added filler to the surfaces that are to be bonded. Use a disposable brush or firm urethane roller. Keep recoating the surfaces until the wood stops soaking up

the epoxy. If a surface has been precoated with epoxy, you don't need to add more. Just wipe the area with a damp, clean paper towel and lightly sand it before proceeding to the second step.

For the second step, you will need to slightly thicken the epoxy with filler. In general, the bigger the gap you want to fill, the thicker you should make the epoxy. Use *Epoxy Consistencies* as a guide to determine how thick the epoxy should be for different applications. There are two reasons to add filler. First, it gives the epoxy some body and increases its gap-filling ability. Second, it prevents the epoxy from soaking into the wood, which could result in a joint that is partially bare of epoxy.

Once you have the correct consistency, immediately apply the thickened epoxy over the surface. Do not wait for the initial coating to dry. Apply an even coat of the epoxy/filler mixture to one of the surfaces that is to be joined. Use enough epoxy so that a small amount squeezes out when the surfaces are joined together with a force equivalent to a firm hand grip.

Any method of clamping is fine as long as the parts that are to be joined are held so that they can't move while the epoxy cures. Staples are often used as a clamping tool. Steel staples, however, must be removed after the epoxy cures. If you want to leave the staples, use ones made of a noncorroding alloy such as bronze or stainless steel. Other methods of clamping include spring, C, and adjustable bar clamps; heavy rubber bands cut from inner tubes; nylon-reinforced packaging tape; and heavy weights. When you apply the clamp, it's wise to use duct tape, polyethyl-

USING EPOXY AS A GLUE

PRECOAT WITH UNTHICKENED EPOXY TO PREVENT A RESIN-STARVED JOINT.

APPLY ENOUGH THICKENED EPOXY SO THAT IT SQUEEZES OUT OF THE JOINT WHEN CLAMPED

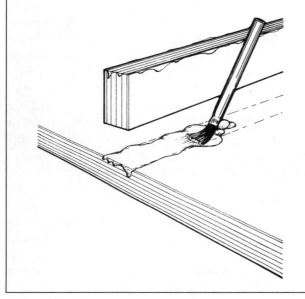
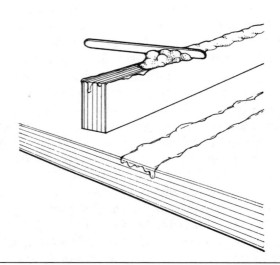

ene sheeting, waxed paper, or a Gougeon Brothers product called Peel Ply between the wood and the clamps so that they don't inadvertently become bonded together. Remove any excess adhesive that squeezes out of the joint before the epoxy cures. It is far more difficult to sand away excess epoxy after it has cured.

Epoxy as a Coating

Epoxy makes wood virtually waterproof, but sunlight is its Achilles' heel. The ultraviolet rays of direct sunlight can cause the resin to break down. As a result, outdoor projects need a final coating of paint or ultraviolet-resistant varnish. Because no moisture can get under the paint or varnish, you won't have problems with the final finish cracking, peeling, or lifting off.

As mentioned, wood surfaces should be coated with at least two coats of epoxy. We usually use three coats. Epoxy works well as a coating for hardwood plywood and any kind of solid wood. But we find it doesn't work well when it is applied di-

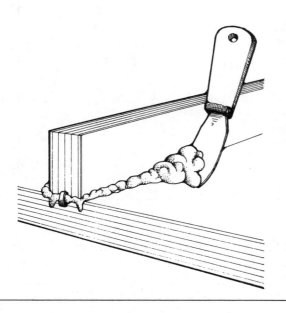

AVOID UNNECESSARY & VERY DIFFICULT
SANDING BY REMOVING EXCESS EPOXY.

rectly to softwood plywood. Before you coat softwood plywood, you should sheathe the surface with a fiberglass mesh, but we don't coat softwood plywood in any projects in this book. Before you apply the epoxy, do any final shaping of your project and sand it with #50 or #80 grit sandpaper to provide an adequate mechanical bonding surface for the epoxy. Holes or gouges can be filled after the first coat of epoxy.

When epoxy is used as a coating on the projects in this book, it does not require the addition of fillers. Epoxy's viscosity

plays an important role in how well it will penetrate the wood fiber. If you are working in a cool shop, warm the resin and hardener to approximately 70°F to reduce viscosity. Often, you can warm the epoxy enough by placing the resin and the hardener in separate containers near a light-bulb. Sometimes we trap the heat by putting a box over the resin, hardener, and light bulb. The fast hardener we use for all the projects in this book lets you sand and recoat about every 12 hours.

When you work with the fast hardener, mix only as much epoxy as you can use in 10 or 15 minutes. Begin with small quantities. As you become familiar with the epoxy and how to apply it, you can increase the size of the batch you mix.

If you move plywood from a warm room to a cool one, or vice versa, make sure the wood's temperature has stabilized before you coat it. As wood warms up, air is released from its grain, which is a phenomenon called outgassing. If you apply the first coat while the wood is outgassing, tiny bubbles will appear in the epoxy.

Disposable, firm, urethane-foam roller covers are the most practical tool for coating wood with epoxy. Cut the rollers into small pieces, if necessary, to reach tight areas. Roll on the epoxy with long, easy motions to achieve a uniform coat. The surface will be stippled when the epoxy is applied with a roller. Reduce stippling and remove any air bubbles by lightly smoothing the uncured epoxy with a foam brush or a roller cover that has been cut in half, then into thirds, and then placed in a slotted stick as shown in *Making a Brush*.

After the coat of epoxy has cured, you

MAKING A BRUSH

CUT A FOAM ROLLER COVER IN HALF, THEN IN THIRDS FOR AN INEXPENSIVE FOAM BRUSH GOOD FOR REMOVING STIPPLED SURFACE

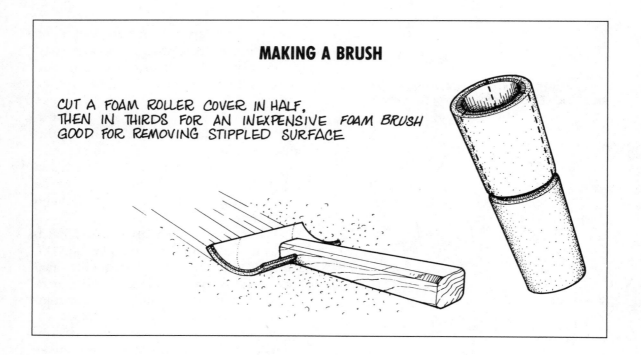

can smooth it with a sharp hand cabinet scraper. Remove any air bubbles that may have formed on the surface as well as dust or even insects that may have alighted and gotten stuck.

The amount of epoxy that you will need to coat a bare wooden surface is affected by things such as the wood specie and grain. If some areas, particularly the end grain, look dry a few minutes after you coat them, recoat the surfaces. Watch the surface area for the next 15 minutes and roll more epoxy on any areas that look dry.

You can fill major voids, gouges, or fastener holes any time after the first coat is applied. You don't have to wait for the first coat to cure. To make a filler that will sand and plane easily, add a low-density filler to the resin/hardener mixture until you get a peanut butterlike consistency. Trowel the mixture onto the surface with a plastic squeegee as shown in *Filling Voids*. Remove any excess before the epoxy cures.

After the first coat has cured, the surface is usually somewhat fuzzy and rough because the wood grain has expanded slightly after absorbing the epoxy. Lightly sand the surface with #80 grit sandpaper before you apply subsequent coats.

Sometimes a water-soluble, waxy substance called blush will appear as the epoxy cures. Blush is a byproduct of the curing process that will clog sandpaper and contaminate subsequent coats if it is not cleaned from the surface. The best way to remove blush is to scrub the cured surface with clean water and a 3M Scotch Brite pad. Wipe the surface dry and clean it with paper towels.

To save time and sanding, you can recoat the surface before the epoxy cures. As soon as the first coat has become tacky and will support the weight of another coat without running or sagging, the next coat may be rolled on. After a coat has cured, however, you'll have to wash the surface with water and a 3M Scotch Brite pad and lightly sand it to create a good mechanical bonding surface before you apply another coat. As a general rule of thumb, if the epoxy has cured enough to allow you to sand the surface without clogging the sandpaper, you should sand the surface before you recoat it. After you sand, dust the surface clean of any sanding residue before you proceed with additional coats. If you have never worked with epoxy be-

fore, you might find it worth the extra work to play it safe and wait until the epoxy cures before you recoat the surface.

Bonding with Fillets

When two pieces meet at a right angle in conventional woodworking, a cleat is often used to strengthen the joint. The cleat adds mass to the joint and increases the area to be glued and/or fastened. Because filler-thickened epoxy has mass and strength, you can replace cleats with a cove-shaped fillet of epoxy.

A fillet offers several advantages over a cleat. First, if you are already using epoxy for a project, it is easier and quicker to apply fillets than to fit, cut, and fasten cleats. Fillets can conform to any shape, but it's not easy to use cleats on curved surfaces. The cove shape eliminates sharp corners

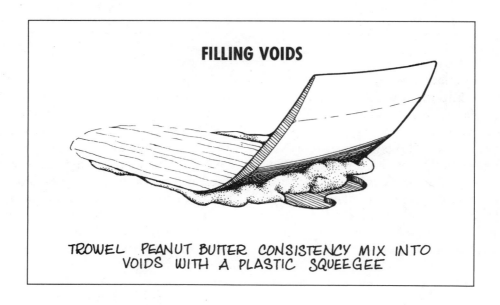

FILLING VOIDS

TROWEL PEANUT BUTTER CONSISTENCY MIX INTO VOIDS WITH A PLASTIC SQUEEGEE

MAKING FILLETS

APPLY A LIBERAL AMOUNT OF FILLETING MIX & CLAMP, NAIL, OR STAPLE INTO PLACE. MIX SHOULD SQUEEZE OUT EVENLY ALONG JOINT.

APPLY ENOUGH ADDITIONAL MIX TO MAKE AN EVEN FILLET OF DESIRED RADIUS.

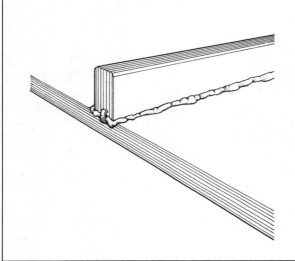
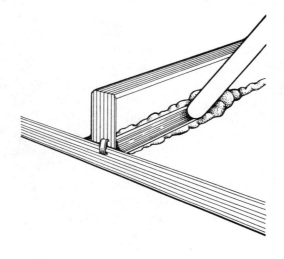

and creates joints that are easier to clean. And most importantly for outdoor projects, the fillet makes the joint waterproof.

Make your filleting mix as described in the above section, "Epoxy, the System." To save mixing and preparation time, it's best to precut and fit as many parts as practical. That way you can make as many fillets as possible in one session. Precoat the prepared bonding surfaces with the resin/hardener mixture.

Next, mix filler into the epoxy mixture. Good, smooth fillets depend on a filleting mixture of the correct thickness. With a

little experience, you'll learn which mixture works best for your conditions and materials. Generally, a smooth-textured filler with a peanut butterlike consistency is best.

Apply a liberal amount of the filleting mixture to the mating edge of the joint. Position the part and use staples, small nails, or clamps to hold the pieces in place. Some of the epoxy mixture should squeeze out of the joint. The rest will fill any gaps or imperfections in the materials that are being bonded together, as shown in *Making Fillets.*

Apply more filleting mixture along the

CAREFULLY CLEAN OFF EXCESS EPOXY
WITH A PUTTY KNIFE BEFORE IT CURES.

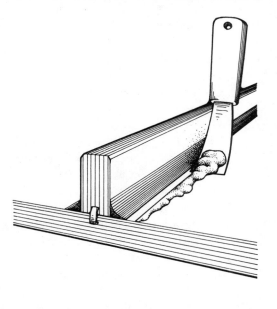

joint line with the mixing stick. Use enough mixture to create a fillet of the desired size. Shape the fillet by scraping the excess epoxy along the joint with a radiused tool or gloved finger so that you leave a smooth cove shape. The tool will leave a narrow, strip on each side of the cove. Carefully clean the area on each side of the fillet with a sharpened scraping stick or putty knife.

When the fillet is fully cured, sand it smooth with #80 grit sandpaper. Wipe the surface clean of any dust and apply a coat of resin/hardener over the entire fillet area

to seal the surface. After a final sanding, the fillet can be painted or varnished along with the rest of the project.

Reinforcing Epoxy with Fiberglass Mesh Tape

When you use epoxy to join plywood parts, you can make the joints stronger by adding fiberglass mesh tape. When soaked in epoxy, the fiberglass becomes transparent and barely detectable on the finished surface. So, you can use it even if you want a natural wood finish.

Sometimes, entire plywood surfaces are covered with epoxy-impregnated fiberglass mesh, but that's not necessary for any of the projects in this book. However, three projects—the rowing dory, camper cap, and hexagon hot tub—do employ 2-, 4-, and/or 6-inch-wide fiberglass mesh tape. You can buy the mesh tape in rolls for this purpose. We recommend that you use the rolls that are bound on the edges. If you cut strips from sheets of fiberglass, the loose edges will make it harder to do a neat job. Fiberglass tape is available from Gougeon Brothers. (See "Sources," page 295.)

Applying Fiberglass Strips

For joints that won't be abused, for example those in the hexagon hot tub, plenty of reinforcement will be provided by one layer of fiberglass. But for joints that will be subjected to rugged conditions, such as the chines of the dory, which are sure to get knocked around, we use as many as four layers of fiberglass. Regardless of the number of layers, the procedure is the same.

Cut the strips you'll need to the required length. Then saturate the joint with epoxy. (Whether the epoxy is thickened or not depends on the application.) Put on your protective gloves and saturate the first fiberglass strip on a piece of cardboard. Use a plastic squeegee to work the epoxy into the fiberglass. The fiberglass is white when it's dry. You'll know it's saturated when it becomes clear. Lift the saturated strip off the cardboard and stretch it slightly as you apply it to the joint. Squeegee out any air bubbles and apply more epoxy if necessary. You can add additional layers of fiberglass without waiting for the epoxy to cure. To trim the fiberglass in place, let the epoxy cure for a few hours until it has set enough to keep from moving under the pressure of a knife, but is still rubbery and pliable enough to cut easily.

Safety

Epoxy is safe to use if you follow the proper precautions, which you'll find on epoxy product containers and literature. Here's some points to keep in mind.

- Avoid all direct skin contact with resin, hardeners, and mixed epoxy. Wear plastic or rubber gloves whenever you handle epoxy. Barrier skin creams provide additional protection if you have sensitive skin, allergies, or a lot of messy work to do.
- Never use solvents to remove epoxy from your skin. Waterless skin cleaners work well in most cases. Always wash thoroughly with waterless cleaners and rinse thoroughly with water immediately after skin contact with resin, hardener, or solvent.
- Protect your eyes from contact with resins, hardeners, mixed epoxy, and solvents by wearing safety glasses or goggles. If contact should occur, immediately flush your eyes with liberal quantities of water at a low pressure for 15 minutes. If discomfort is present, see a doctor immediately.
- Use epoxy only in well-ventilated areas.
- Wear a dust mask if you sand epoxy. Take extra care if the epoxy has cured less than a week.
- Be clean, neat, and organized when you use epoxy. This is largely a matter of common sense. Not only will it make your work safer, it will produce better results.

MAHOGANY PICNIC TABLE

During the spring and summer months at our Montana cabin, we spend most of our time outdoors. When the bugs aren't too bad, we enjoy eating outside. After a few frustrating seasons trying to resurrect and maintain a picnic table that was built of solid cedar planks, we decided to apply some boatbuilding techniques to the problem and build a table suited for the great outdoors. The result is an attractive table that will last for years with minimal main-

tenance. The epoxy finish is virtually waterproof, which prevents rot, warpage, and splitting.

One of the boatbuilding techniques we used was to prefinish as much of the table as possible with epoxy. The epoxy not only glues the pieces together, it seals all the components and keeps moisture out. We applied a final finish of varnish.

This basic table design can be applied to a larger version by using the same wood-

MAHOGANY PICNIC TABLE EXPLODED VIEW

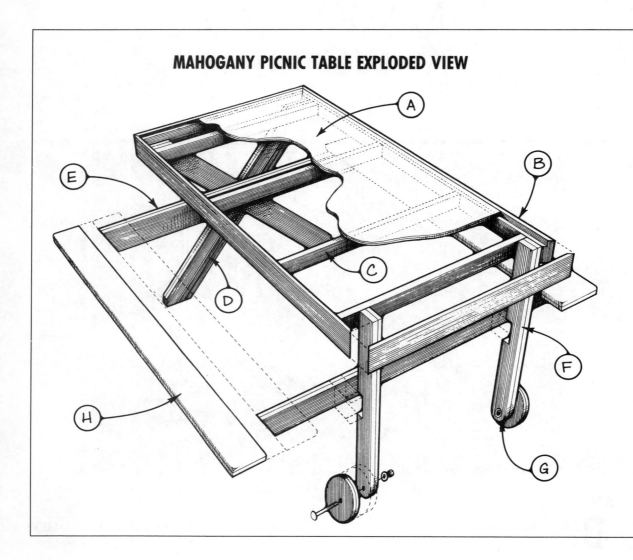

epoxy plywood techniques. With the framing and molding attached, ½-inch-thick plywood is strong and stiff enough for the table shown. For a larger, say 4 × 8-foot tabletop, ¾- or even 1-inch-thick plywood would be a better choice.

For the top, try to choose an attractive piece of plywood that has good grain and a minimum number of defects. Since we used plywood with a luan-mahogany face veneer for the top, we chose solid mahogany for the molding, legs, and seats. The face veneer could just as well be oak, alder, or any attractive veneer. Make the mold-

(A)	PLYWOOD TABLETOP	• 1 PC. ½" × 40" × 72" MAHOGANY PLYWOOD
(B)	TABLETOP MOLDING	• 2 PCS. ¾" × 3" × 40¾" (OR TO FIT) 2 PCS. ¾" × 3" × 72¾" (OR TO FIT) MAHOGANY, MITERED AT EACH END ⁹⁄₁₆" RABBET ON TOP SIDES
(C)	TABLETOP BLOCKING	• 4 PCS. FIR 2×4 RIPPED TO 2⅜" CUT TO 39¼" (OR TO FIT)
(D)	LAMINATED DIAGONAL LEGS	• 4 PCS. ¾" × 4" × 51¾" MAHOGANY LAMINATED INTO TWO PIECES
(E)	LAMINATED SEAT SUPPORTS	• 4 PCS. ¾" × 4" × 64¾" MAHOGANY LAMINATED INTO TWO PIECES 65° ANGLE CUT ON EACH END
(F)	LAMINATED VERTICAL LEGS	• 4 PCS. ¾" × 4" × 28" MAHOGANY LAMINATED INTO TWO PIECES TOPS CUT SQUARE, BOTTOMS ROUND
(G)	LAMINATED WHEELS	• 8" DIAMETER & 1½" WIDE BUILT FROM MAHOGANY SCRAPS
(H)	LAMINATED SEATS	• 4 PCS. ¾" × 8" × 72¾" MAHOGANY LAMINATED INTO TWO PIECES ⅜" ROUND OVER ON TOPS

ESTIMATED EPOXY RESIN NEEDED

2 gallons

ings and legs to match. The bracing under the table won't be seen, so it doesn't have to match the visible parts of the table. You might save money by substituting clear fir or another solid wood. We laminated many of the pieces for the table because we had the stock on hand and because an epoxy laminated piece resists warping and splitting better than single pieces of the same dimension, which was another fact that we borrowed from our boatbuilding days. Of course, you may use single pieces of 2 × 4 where we glue up two 1 × 4s if 2 × 4 stock is what you have on hand.

Before beginning this project, be sure to read the introduction to this chapter, which begins on page 127.

1. CUT AND PREFINISH THE TABLETOP.

Mark and cut the tabletop to the size listed. Coat the top and edges with epoxy as described in "Epoxy as a Coating," page 132. When the epoxy has cured, flip the tabletop over and coat the bottom. The top will be given two more coats of epoxy after the molding has been installed.

2. RIP AND RABBET THE EDGE MOLDINGS.

Rip the four pieces of stock to a width of 3 inches and then cut them to lengths about ½ inch longer than specified on the drawing. This will give you a little margin later when you cut miters for the corners. Rabbet the pieces to receive the tabletop. The rabbet is ⅜ inch wide and ⁹⁄₁₆ inch deep, which is ¹⁄₁₆ inch deeper than the thickness of the tabletop. This ¹⁄₁₆ inch allows you to trim the molding flush after it has been attached and the epoxy has set.

3. CUT AND ATTACH THE EDGE MOLDINGS.
You should now have four sections of
edge molding. Each should be slightly
longer than the length it must cover. Start
by making careful 45-degree miter cuts on
one end of each piece. Next fit the molding to the table. It's easier to fit the long
sides first. Start by clamping one long
piece in position on the tabletop, after you
have carefully aligned the end with the
miter cut. Then, predrill and counterbore
for a couple of 1½-inch #10 Phillips-head
wood screws. Use the screws to temporarily attach the molding. Now mark the
position of the miter on the other end of

the molding. Repeat this sequence for the
other three pieces of molding. When all
the molding pieces are fitted, take them off
and apply epoxy to all surfaces as described in "Epoxy as a Glue," page 131.
Reattach the pieces to the table. Drive the
screws into the existing holes to automatically align the pieces. Space more screws
about 9 inches apart. Plug the screws with
matching wood plugs. If you don't have a
supply of matching plugs, make your own
from scraps of the molding you are using.
(See "Plugs," page 21.) Shave the plugs
flush.

4. TRIM THE MOLDINGS FLUSH. Once all
four pieces of molding are glued in place
and the epoxy has cured, lay the tabletop
on a flat surface. Carefully trim the hardened epoxy drips and the extra ¹⁄₁₆ inch of
excess wood from the top edge of the

molding. Use a sharp, finely adjusted
block plane for the initial trimming. Then
finish with a freshly sharpened cabinet
scraper to bring the surfaces flush without
gouging the face veneer of the tabletop.

5. ROUND THE MOLDING EDGES. On our
table, we rounded over the top and bottom edges of the molding slightly with a
block plane followed by sandpaper. If we
were to do it over, we would simply chamfer the top and bottom edges with a hand
plane or a router with a chamfer bit. In our
opinion, the chamfer would give the piece

a much classier, hand-built look. You
might prefer to rout an ogee or cove detail.
(See *Tabletop Edge Options,* page 111.) The
round or chamfered edge will make the
table more comfortable and safer around
kids. It also will hold a finish much better
than a sharp edge.

6. **FINISH THE TOP.** Apply two more coats of epoxy to the top and molding. You don't need to add additional coats to the bottom. Take special care to fill any voids and cracks, however small, between the molding and the tabletop. Brush or roll epoxy into the crack until it is filled. Scrape between coats if dust and bugs are a problem. Otherwise, a final scraping can wait until just before you varnish the assembled table.

---

7. **CUT AND INSTALL THE UNDERSIDE BLOCKING.** The blocking not only stiffens the plywood top, it also provides a place for the legs to be attached. Use a sheet or blanket to keep from scratching the tabletop while you work. Lay the top upside down on a perfectly flat surface. Cut and fit each block individually to ensure a proper fit. Space the blocking as shown in *Front View.* Leave 4 inches for the vertical legs and 1½ inches for the diagonal legs. If you make an 8-foot table, use six pieces of blocking instead of the four pieces shown here. Glue each piece of blocking to the table bottom with epoxy. Use large C-clamps with protective pads so that you don't mark the table. You'll need to clamp just the ends of the blocking because epoxy requires only enough clamping pressure to ensure contact. In fact, you could put weights on the blocking and skip the clamps.

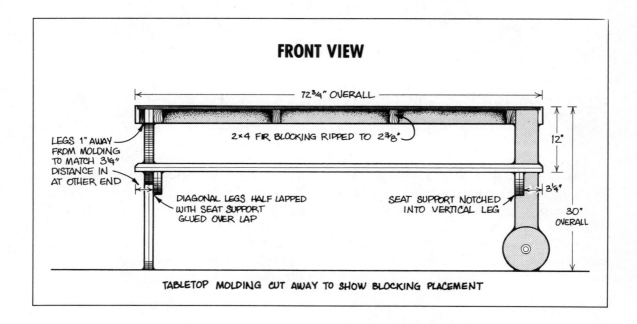

FRONT VIEW

72¾" OVERALL

2×4 FIR BLOCKING RIPPED TO 2⅜"

12"

LEGS 1" AWAY FROM MOLDING TO MATCH 3¼" DISTANCE IN AT OTHER END

DIAGONAL LEGS HALF LAPPED WITH SEAT SUPPORT GLUED OVER LAP

SEAT SUPPORT NOTCHED INTO VERTICAL LEG

3¼"

30" OVERALL

TABLETOP MOLDING CUT AWAY TO SHOW BLOCKING PLACEMENT

SIDE VIEW

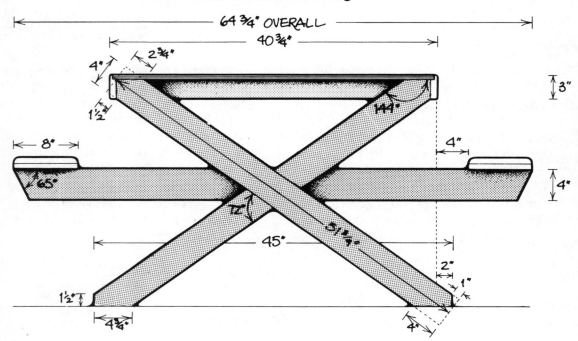

END WITH DIAGONAL LEGS

64¾" OVERALL

40¾"

4"

2¾"

3"

1½"

144°

8"

4"

65°

4"

71°

45°

51¾"

2"

1"

1½"

4¾"

4"

TABLETOP MOLDINGS CUT AWAY TO SHOW PLACEMENT OF LEGS

8. CUT AND GLUE UP THE DIAGONAL LEGS.
The legs on one side of the table are joined with diagonal half-lap joints. The other side of the table has straight legs with wheels. This system makes the table easy to move around, but stable in place.

As mentioned, each of the legs con-sists of two laminations of ¾-inch stock. To make the diagonal legs, cut the four pieces to the lengths and angles shown on the cutting list and in *Side View*. Then glue them together with epoxy and clamps. Be careful and use only moderate clamping pressure.

 END WITH VERTICAL LEGS (TYPICAL)

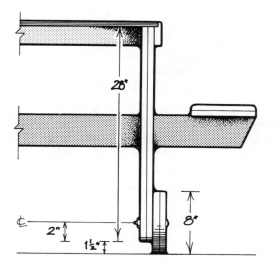

proper fit all around and to obtain the exact angle for the half-lap cuts. Mark the half-lap joint on the two pieces that are to be cut. Unclamp the legs. Then make the necessary cuts exactly halfway through each piece. Cut the sides of the joint square with a portable circular saw or table saw and then make kerf cuts every ¼ inch or so to the proper depth. Use the epoxy glue line at the middle of the laminated leg as a depth-of-cut guide. When you get to it, you know you're halfway through the leg. Use a ¾-inch-wide chisel to take out the balance of the wood by using the kerf cuts as a guide. Don't try for a tight fit. There should be slight clearance on all sides so that the epoxy can seal the grain of the wood and prevent rot pockets from developing.

10. GLUE THE DIAGONAL LEGS TOGETHER.

Run a trial fit. Make adjustments if necessary, then apply epoxy and clamp the legs together with moderate pressure. Wipe off the excess epoxy that squeezes out of the joint during assembly. It's much easier to remove it now than after it has hardened and must be chiseled and sanded away. Wipe the joint carefully with a heavy paper towel or a clean, dry rag so that you leave a perfect, small, round fillet. Work carefully. If you incorrectly clamp the legs together when you glue with epoxy, the error is there to stay, even after the clamps are removed. The legs should stand square and plumb when they are glued into position under the tabletop.

9. HALF-LAP THE DIAGONAL LEGS. Half-

lapping produces a very strong joint and allows the legs to cross in the same plane. This creates a much cleaner look than the staggered legs on most picnic tables. After you laminate the legs, temporarily clamp them in place under the table to ensure a

TIP ▶ If you don't have large enough clamps, you can glue and screw the seat support to the diagonal legs. Counterbore and screw the legs together with two or three 1-inch screws that are arranged in an attractive pattern. Seal the holes with matching wood plugs.

11. **MAKE THE VERTICAL LEGS.** Glue up both vertical legs and cut them to length. Mark out and cut notches in the vertical legs to receive the seat supports. Note that unlike the diagonal legs, the vertical legs are installed with the wide sides against the long sides of the table. Make sure the legs stand square to the underside of the table by checking with a framing square and tape measure. With a jigsaw or band saw, round the bottoms of the vertical legs to a 1¾-inch radius. Measure and drill the holes for wheel bolts. First, drill a 5/16-inch-diameter hole and then seal the hole by thoroughly swabbing it with epoxy. Let the epoxy cure, then swab it again. After the second coat has cured, redrill the hole to ¼-inch-diameter. This will seal the wood grain inside the hole and prevent it from rotting. It also will protect the wood from the corrosive salts that leach from metal when it is exposed to moisture. Glue the legs to the tabletop.

12. **MAKE THE WHEELS.** The wheels are 8 inches in diameter and are cut from two pieces of ¾-inch solid mahogany or a wood that matches the table. Each wheel is made of two pieces that have been glued together. The grain should be staggered at a 90-degree angle for strength and durability. The wheels could also be made of laminated plywood scraps from the tabletop, but solid timber that matches looks better. Laminating two pieces of ¾- inch stock makes a 1½-inch-thick wheel, which normally is wide enough for use on grass, gravel, and packed dirt. If you are going to use the table on a beach or in deep sand, make a wider wheel by using additional laminations. They should work better in that situation. Rubber or carpet strips tacked around the perimeters of the wheels will allow the wheels to roll smoothly, quietly, and nondestructively on hard surfaces.

13. **DRILL THE WHEELS.** Drill the holes for the wheels the same way you drilled the holes for the legs. Coat the entire wheel with three coats of epoxy.

14. **INSTALL THE WHEELS.** We used bronze carriage bolts because bronze looks good and acquires a rich, antique patina with age and exposure. Stainless steel also works well, even though it doesn't match mahogany as well as bronze. Avoid cheap, plated bolts that will soon rust. Use a small Teflon or plastic washer to provide clearance between the wheel and leg and to ensure easy rolling. Tighten the bolt moderately, then back off half a turn for clearance. To prevent the nuts from working off the bolt while you roll the table, place a dab of silicone seal on the bolt end and let it set overnight before you move the table.

15. **MAKE AND INSTALL THE SEAT SUPPORTS.** Cut the four pieces of ¾-inch stock to length. Laminate them into two supports and prefinish them before you attach them to the table. One seat support rests in notches that are cut into the vertical legs. Glue and screw the other seat support across the diagonal legs. The tricky part is to achieve a perfect alignment and an even distance down from the tabletop on both sides and at all four corners. Mark the distances with a framing square then clamp the supports in place. Sight across to ensure alignment. When the supports are in place and properly aligned, carefully predrill the screw holes in the diagonal legs so that you'll be able to screw them into place when the epoxy is applied.

16. **CUT AND INSTALL THE SEATS.** Laminate the seats and cut them to length. For comfort and safety, cut a small bullnose (full round) or bevel on the top edges. Center them on the seat supports, mark the support location, apply epoxy to the marked areas, and clamp the seats to the supports.

17. **PREPARE FOR FINISH.** Before you finish the table, wash the components with a 3M Scotch Brite pad and sand the components with #80 or #100 grit sandpaper.

18. **APPLY FINISH.** Paint is the most durable finish for an epoxy-sealed table because the pigment blocks out the Sun's radiation, which eventually will break down the epoxy resin. This is the Achilles' heel of epoxy when it is used as a sealant. Epoxy must be protected from long-term exposure to sunlight. But it's a shame to cover all that beautiful wood and careful workmanship, so you'll probably opt to put a clear finish over the epoxy. If you want a clear finish, we recommend that you use a spar varnish with sunscreen. Intended for outdoor use, spar varnish dries softer than other clear finishes. It's also inexpensive and easy to apply. If you use spar varnish, you'll have to lightly sand and recoat the table about every other year, or perhaps more often if the table is exposed to a lot of direct sunlight. Apply the varnish at full strength from a freshly opened can. Use thinner only if the varnish will not spread evenly. Add thinner sparingly and experiment constantly. For ease of application, use a 6-inch-wide foam roller. Brush out any bubbles and drips with a small, disposable foam brush or a better quality China bristle brush. If you pay attention to the recoat times on the varnish can label, you may be able to apply a number of coats during the suggested recoat times without having to sand between coats. Apply at least three coats of varnish, let them dry a couple of days, and serve breakfast at sunrise on the patio.

CAMP
BOX

Rugged and waterproof. We kept those two words in mind when we designed this camp box. Half-inch plywood and a sturdy piano hinge took care of rugged. Marine plywood and epoxy-filled joinery made the box waterproof. The lip around the top and the piano hinge cleat are solid wood. The rest of the box is made from one sheet of plywood.

We find that the box is particularly handy as a galley box for storing cooking gear by the fire. It's right where we need it and it doubles as a fireside bench. It could be just as handy for such items as sleeping bags, tents, pillows, and blankets.

You could build this box without epoxy by using ¾ × ¾-inch cleats instead of the fillets. Just predrill the cleats for 1-

CAMP BOX EXPLODED VIEW

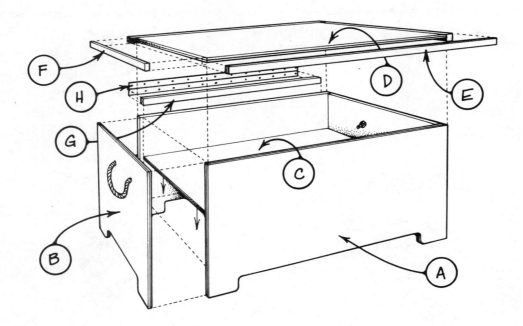

(A) PLYWOOD FRONT & BACK • 2 PCS. ½" × 16" × 36"

(B) PLYWOOD SIDES • 2 PCS. ½" × 16" × 23"

(C) PLYWOOD BOTTOM • 1 PC. ½" × 23" × 35"

(D) PLYWOOD TOP • 1 PC. ½" × 24⅛" × 36⅛" (CUT TO FIT)

(E) FRONT & BACK MOLDING • 2 PCS. ¾" × 1" × 37⅝" (CUT TO FIT)

(F) SIDE MOLDING • 2 PCS. ¾" × 1" × 24⅛" (CUT TO FIT)

(G) CLEAT • 1 PC. ¾" × 1" × 36"

(H) HINGE • ¾" × 36" LONG

ESTIMATED EPOXY RESIN NEEDED

1 quart

inch wood screws and coat the two adjacent edges with glue. Then screw the cleats together in the corners and under the bottom. The epoxy fillets, however, offer at least three advantages. First, they don't waste space inside the box. Cleats get in the way of being able to pack right into the corners. Second, the rounded fillets make it easier to clean the inside of the box. Finally, the epoxy makes the joints waterproof. If you decide to use epoxy, before you begin be sure to read the introduction to this chapter, starting on page 127.

1. CUT THE PLYWOOD BOX PARTS. Cut the front, back, sides, and bottom to the dimensions in the materials list. You can cut the top to approximate size while you are slicing up the sheet, but don't make the final cuts. You can cut the top to a perfect fit after the box is assembled.

2. CUT THE FEET. With a jigsaw, make the cutouts that form the feet in the front, back, and sides of the box. Sand out any saw marks.

3. ASSEMBLE THE BOX. To help position the bottom, make four 3-inch-thick spacers from scrap material. Put the spacers on a flat work surface and place the bottom on the spacers. Clamp the front, back, and sides to the bottom. If you don't have long clamps, predrill and countersink the front, back, and sides. Attach them to the bottom with 1-inch drywall screws. Fill the countersinks with wood putty and sand them before you paint. Use a framing square to make sure the box is square. If the box is not square, use a long clamp to hold it square while you make the fillets.

TIP ▶ If your clamps aren't long enough to assemble this box, use spanish windlasses. Tie a length of rope around the box. Insert a stick between the rope and the box and rotate the stick until the rope is taut and the joints are tight. Tie the stick to the rope to keep it from unwinding.

TOP, BACK, AND SIDE VIEWS

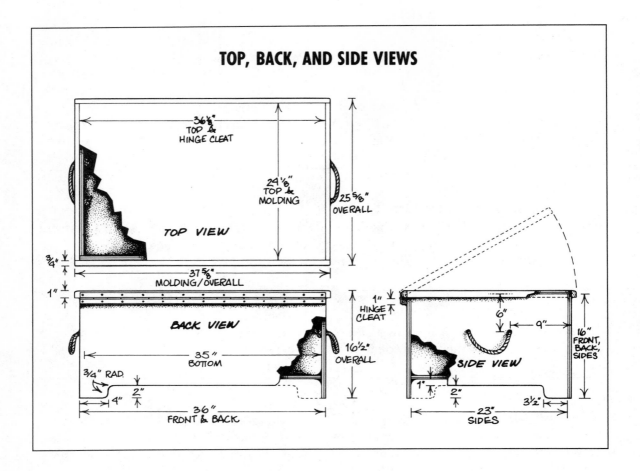

4. MAKE THE FILLETS. Fillets are used on the inside of the box and under the bottom wherever two pieces of plywood meet (see "Bonding with Fillets," page 135). Rather than trying to make complete fillets with the heavy clamps in place, use a rubber-gloved index finger to dash in short, shallow mini-fillets around the inside seams of the box. Check to make sure the box is square again before the epoxy cures. After the mini-fillets have cured, remove the clamps. Now you can easily move the box around as you run the completed fillets right over the shorter fillets. Flip the box over and run the fillets under the bottom. While you are at it, seal the bottoms of the legs with epoxy to prevent them from soaking up moisture when you set the box on the ground.

5. **DRILL HOLES FOR THE ROPE HANDLES AND PREPARE THE BOX FOR FINISHING.** Drill ½-inch-diameter holes in the sides for the rope handles. Slightly round all the edges and corners of the box with sandpaper or a block plane. Scuff up the fillets with #80 grit sandpaper so they will hold paint.

6. **CUT THE TOP TO FIT.** Measure the exact width and length of the box and cut the top ⅛ inch larger in both dimensions. This will allow 1/16 inch of clearance between the lip of the top and the sides of the box all the way around.

7. **ATTACH THE SOLID WOOD MOLDINGS.** Put the top upside down on waxed paper that has been laid on your flat work surface. Cut the side moldings about ½ inch longer than the width of the lid. Apply epoxy to the moldings and clamp them in place with a ¼-inch or so overhang on each end. If you don't have long clamps, secure the molding with 4d finish nails. Predrill the nail holes to prevent the molding from splitting.

After the epoxy has cured, use a backsaw to cut the side moldings flush with the corners of the top. Attach the front and back moldings in the same manner. Run them a little long and then cut them flush to the sides of the side moldings after the epoxy has cured. Test fit the top. You may have to sand or plane the inside edges of the lip a bit for a smooth fit. If you like, round-over the molding with a block plane or router. Sand the box and slightly round the edges so that they will hold paint.

8. **INSTALL THE HINGE.** Mark the location of the hinge and then use epoxy to glue the solid wood spacer cleat to the back of the box. The spacer provides a flush surface for both sides of the hinge. After the epoxy has cured, attach the hinge. Make sure that the lid opens and closes properly and has the right amount of clearance. You may have to plane a bit off the bottom inside edge of the rear molding so that it will clear the back of the box. Install a hasp or locking mechanism at this time, if required. Finally, remove the hinge and other hardware before you finish the box.

9. **APPLY FINISH.** Two coats of exterior paint are the best finish for this box. It's easy to apply, durable, and weather-resistant. If the paint gets dirty or beat up, you can always add another coat. You could also varnish the box, but varnish won't last as long or protect as well as paint.

HEXAGON HOT TUB

If you are about to flip past this project because you figure a hot tub *must* be too tough to build, don't do it! Even if you have only the most rudimentary carpentry skills, you can be soaking in your new hot tub a couple of weekends from now.

It is natural to assume that a hot tub would be tricky to construct. After all, almost since man began working in wood he has struggled with the problem of how to make a wooden structure that will hold water and not leak or rot. Traditional solutions have involved cutting and joining to very close tolerances.

The six-sided tub you see here takes a completely different approach. While it still is important to cut the pieces to the proper sizes, this tub uses epoxy and 6-inch-wide fiberglass tape to achieve strength and water-tightness, instead of tight, complex joinery. In fact, the bottom is deliberately cut for a loose fit to allow the epoxy to do its job.

This tub certainly doesn't sacrifice beauty for simplicity. It's built of ⅜-inch hardwood plywood. We used luan mahogany, a readily available, reasonably priced plywood. Mahogany is naturally a rot-resistant wood, but since the entire tub is coated with epoxy, you can use any hard-

HEXAGON HOT TUB EXPLODED VIEW

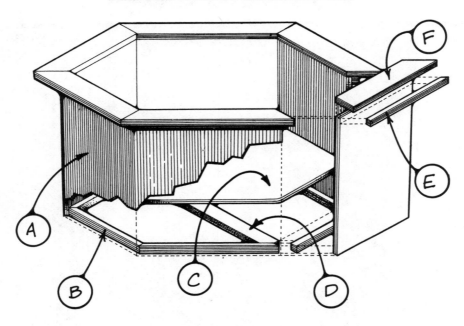

A **TUB SIDES** • 6 PCS. 3/8" x 24" x 24" PLYWOOD

B **BOTTOM CLEATS** • 15' OF 2" x 2" SOLID WOOD CUT TO LENGTH

C **TUB BOTTOM** • 3/8" PLYWOOD CUT TO HEXAGON PATTERN

D **BOTTOM SUPPORT** • 2" x 6" SOLID WOOD CUT TO LENGTH

E **TOP MOLDING CLEATS** • 15' OF 1" x 1" (NET) SOLID WOOD CUT TO LENGTH

F **TOP MOLDING** • 15' OF 3/4" x 2 1/2" (NET) SOLID WOOD CUT TO LENGTH

ESTIMATED EPOXY RESIN NEEDED

3 gallons

wood plywood and matching or contrasting solid hardwood that you like. The coating of epoxy and sunscreen varnish shows off the natural beauty of the wood. If you'd like to paint your tub, we recommend birch or maple plywood, whichever you can get cheaper. Both veneers make excellent bases for paint. Make the perimeter cap molding out of the hardwood of your choice.

The tub may be heated with an external, commercial hot tub system that comes complete with jets and a hot water heater. In the summer months, it can be filled with a hose and used as a wading pool for the kids.

The tub shown is 45 inches at its widest dimension across the bottom. That's perfect for two people, or three if they are good friends. You can build the tub larger if you like, but use thicker plywood if you do. Use ⅝-inch plywood for anything more than 45 inches and ¾-inch plywood for 60 inches or more. If you change the size of the tub, we recommend that you make your own scale drawing to calculate measurements.

Before you start building this tub, be sure to read the introduction to this chapter, starting on page 127.

1. LAY OUT AND CUT THE SIDES. To simplify every subsequent step, when you build the tub it's important to make all six sides exactly the same size. Otherwise, you'll find yourself trimming the bottom and painstakingly fitting each cleat and piece of molding. Make your layout with a fine-tipped ballpoint pen.

Decide which sides of your plywood panels will be the exterior of the tub. You'll want the best faces out, unless you'll be painting the tub. Keep this in mind when you cut the bevels on the vertical edges of each side.

The adjoining edges of each side are cut at a 30-degree angle. Because of the epoxy and fiberglass joints, the tub will be structurally sound and watertight even if the edges are not cut perfectly. The tub will look better and be easier to finish, however, if you make the cuts carefully. So, make test cuts until you get your saw set exactly to the right bevel. If you have a table saw, leave the blade at 90 degrees and cut all six sides 1 inch wider than the dimension you need. Then cut the pieces to size by setting the blade for a 30-degree cut. Once you've cut the bevels, cut the sides to length.

2. PREFINISH THE SIDES. Coat both sides and all the edges of each side piece with three coats of epoxy as described in "Epoxy as a Coating," page 132.

TIP ▶ If you don't have a table saw, you can bevel the sides of the tub with a straightedge-guided circular saw. Set your saw blade for 30 degrees. Make a sample cut to check the angle. Align the blade of your saw with the cut line and mark where the shoe of the saw will run along the straightedge. Clamp the straightedge to the plywood and check to make sure it is square. Make the cut.

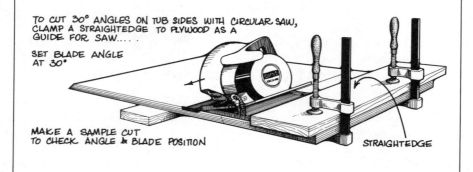

TO CUT 30° ANGLES ON TUB SIDES WITH CIRCULAR SAW, CLAMP A STRAIGHTEDGE TO PLYWOOD AS A GUIDE FOR SAW.....

SET BLADE ANGLE AT 30°

MAKE A SAMPLE CUT TO CHECK ANGLE & BLADE POSITION

STRAIGHTEDGE

3. ASSEMBLE THE SIDES. Assembly will be easier with the help of two support jigs, as shown in *Jigs for Assembling Tub*. Make the jig on plywood and set the plywood on the benchtop.

As illustrated, put waxed paper under each joint so that the glue doesn't attach the tub to the jig. As described in "Epoxy as a Glue," page 131, saturate both beveled edges of one side piece with epoxy and place it in the bottom of the jig. Next, saturate the beveled edges that will join with the piece in the bottom of the jig and place two more sides as shown. Then thicken the epoxy to the consistency of mayonnaise with about equal parts of low-density filler and silica. Lay a small bead of the new mixture on the seams.

Lay a single strip of epoxy-saturated 6-inch-wide fiberglass tape over each seam as described in "Reinforcing Epoxy with Fiberglass Mesh Tape," page 137. Let the joints cure until they are hard. Then, carefully remove the tub section from the jig.

Assemble the remaining three sides in the same way. When the second half of the tub has cured, put both halves of the tub in the jig with one of the unglued joints positioned at the bottom. After this joint has been taped, epoxied, and cured, turn the tub and make the final joint in the bottom of the jig. Let the final joint cure.

JIGS FOR ASSEMBLING TUB

BUILD FOUR 30° ANGLED *SUPPORT JIGS* & FASTEN SECURELY TO A FLAT SURFACE

SET HALF THE TUB SIDES INTO PLACE & FILLET EACH CORNER (2).........LET EPOXY HARDEN, SAND FILLET SMOOTH & APPLY 6" FIBERGLASS TAPE OVER FILLETS..... LET EPOXY HARDEN COMPLETELY BEFORE REMOVING FROM JIG

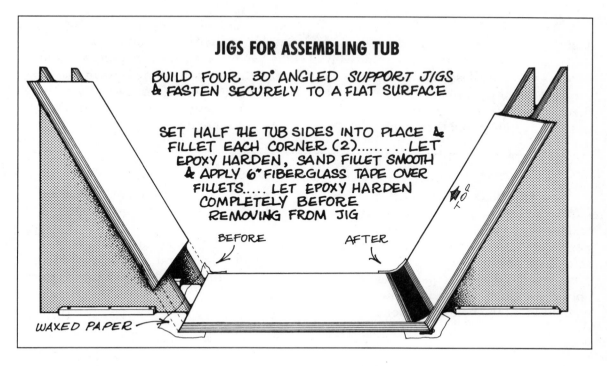

BEFORE

AFTER

TOP

WAXED PAPER

GLUING UP THE SIDES

STACK HALVES TOGETHER IN JIG TO FILLET & TAPE REMAINING TWO SEAMS INSIDE, ONE AT A TIME

SAND, FILL & TAPE OUTSIDE OF SEAMS, TWO AT A TIME

ROTATE IN JIG (ONLY AFTER EPOXY HAS CURED) TO EXPOSE THE NEXT TWO SEAMS & REPEAT THE SAME STEPS UNTIL ALL SIX SEAMS ARE COMPLETED INSIDE & OUTSIDE

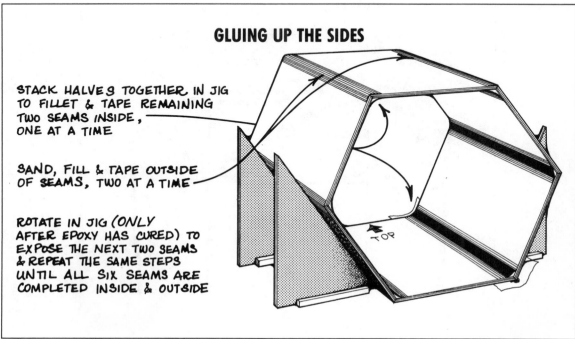

TOP

4. TAPE THE OUTSIDE SEAMS. Start by slightly rounding the outside corners of the plywood with a block plane. This will let you wrap fiberglass tape around the corner without it wrinkling or lifting. If there are any gaps in the outside seams, use a putty knife to fill them with thick-ened epoxy. Leave the tub in the jig and apply 6-inch fiberglass tape and epoxy to the two outside seams that are facing up. After the epoxy has cured, rotate the tub. Tape and epoxy the remaining seams two at a time. Always let the joints cure before you move the tub.

---

5. CUT AND INSTALL THE BOTTOM SUPPORT CLEATS. Cut the six bottom cleats to overall lengths of 24 inches with opposing 30-degree angles at each end. Put the tub upside down on a flat surface. Glue the cleats around the inside perimeter with epoxy. Use clamps to position the cleats ¼ inch proud of the bottom of the plywood. This keeps the bottom of the tub off the ground and protects it from damage and rot.

When the epoxy has cured, flip the tub right side up and, if necessary, use a chisel and/or block plane to level the tops of the cleats.

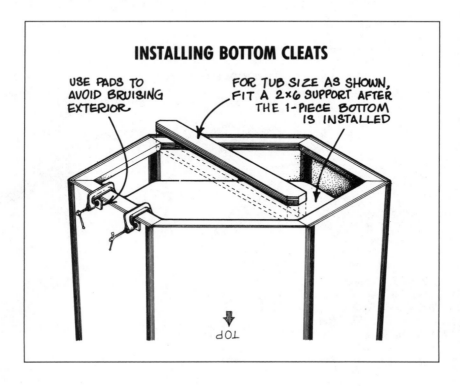

INSTALLING BOTTOM CLEATS

USE PADS TO AVOID BRUISING EXTERIOR

FOR TUB SIZE AS SHOWN, FIT A 2×6 SUPPORT AFTER THE 1-PIECE BOTTOM IS INSTALLED

TOP

6. CUT AND INSTALL THE BOTTOM. *Laying Out the Bottom* provides a method for cutting the hexagon bottom. As mentioned, the bottom should not fit tightly to the tub walls. Rather, there should be a ⅟₁₆- to ⅛-inch gap all around to allow the epoxy to seep in, seal the edges of the bottom, and bond the bottom to the tub walls. A bottom that has to be forced into place not only forfeits this seal, but may crack the side joints. Measure the inside bottom edges of the tub before you cut the bottom piece, so you can adjust for any variation from the listed dimensions.

If you make a tub larger than the one shown, one sheet of plywood won't be wide enough for the bottom. You'll have to butt-join two pieces as shown in *Joining Bottom of a Larger Tub.* Use a plywood block and an additional support cleat. First countersink, screw, and epoxy the plywood butt block to the support cleat. Then

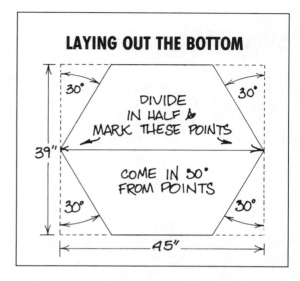

LAYING OUT THE BOTTOM

30°   30°

DIVIDE IN HALF & MARK THESE POINTS

39"

COME IN 30° FROM POINTS

30°   30°

45"

epoxy and screw this assembly to the bottom sections to form the butt joint. Wet the screw holes with a few drops of epoxy before you insert the screws. To prevent rust, use stainless steel screws in the bottom of the tub. Or, after the epoxy has

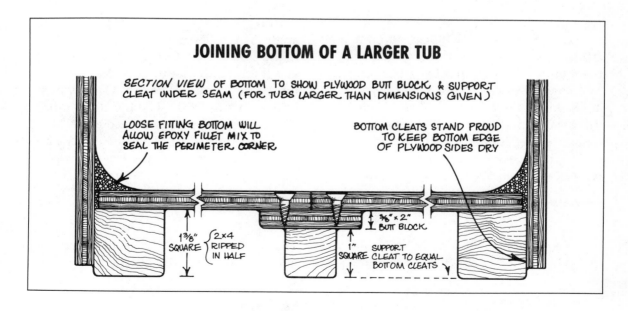

JOINING BOTTOM OF A LARGER TUB

SECTION VIEW OF BOTTOM TO SHOW PLYWOOD BUTT BLOCK & SUPPORT CLEAT UNDER SEAM (FOR TUBS LARGER THAN DIMENSIONS GIVEN)

LOOSE FITTING BOTTOM WILL ALLOW EPOXY FILLET MIX TO SEAL THE PERIMETER CORNER

BOTTOM CLEATS STAND PROUD TO KEEP BOTTOM EDGE OF PLYWOOD SIDES DRY

1⅜" SQUARE { 2×4 RIPPED IN HALF

⅜" × 2" BUTT BLOCK

1" SQUARE SUPPORT CLEAT TO EQUAL BOTTOM CLEATS

cured, remove the screws and fill the holes with a few drops of epoxy.

When the bottom is ready to install, put epoxy on the tops of the perimeter cleats and around the perimeter of the underside of the bottom. Put the bottom in place and weigh it down with a few bricks or other heavy objects until the epoxy has cured.

Flip the tub over again and cut the 2 × 6 bottom support to fit and then use epoxy to attach it to the bottom of the tub. Hold the bottom support in place with a few screws that you have predrilled through the bottom of the tub. When the epoxy has cured, remove the screws and fill the holes with a few drops of epoxy.

---

7. MAKE THE BOTTOM FILLET. Fill the gap between the bottom and sides with un-thickened epoxy (see "Bonding with Fillets," page 135). Then thicken the epoxy to the consistency of peanut butter by using approximately equal parts of the filleting blend and high-density filler. With a putty knife and tongue depressor, apply the thickened epoxy in a fillet around the pe-rimeter of the tub. Make the fillet with a radius of approximately 1 inch. Clean off the excess epoxy with the putty knife and allow the fillet to cure.

A generous fillet provides all the strength you need for a tub of the size shown. If you are building a bigger tub, you may want to reinforce the joint by putting fiberglass tape under the fillet.

---

8. CUT AND INSTALL THE CAP MOLDING CLEATS. These cleats will show, so make them out of the same hardwood as the cap moldings. Start by cutting a 30-degree angle on both ends of each cleat. Clamp that cleat in place. Cut a 30-degree angle on one end of another cleat. Hold the second cleat in position with the uncut end under the installed cleat and scribe the angle. This will compensate for variations in the side angles. Cut to the scribe line and then clamp that piece in place. Repeat this process around the tub. When you are satisfied with the fit of all the cleats, un-clamp them. Apply epoxy and then clamp them together again. After the epoxy has cured, plane the top of the cleats flush to the top of the tub, if necessary.

---

9. CUT AND INSTALL THE TOP MOLDINGS. Individually fit the moldings in the same way you fit the cleats. Glue the miters to-gether and the molding to the tub.

INSTALLING TOP CLEATS AND MOLDING

EPOXY GLUE CLEAT FOR MOLDING
TO TOP PERIMETER OF TUB

WHEN HARD, PLANE SURFACE
SMOOTH

FIT CAP MOLDING
LEAVING A SMALL
OVERHANG INSIDE TO
SEAL PLYWOOD EDGE

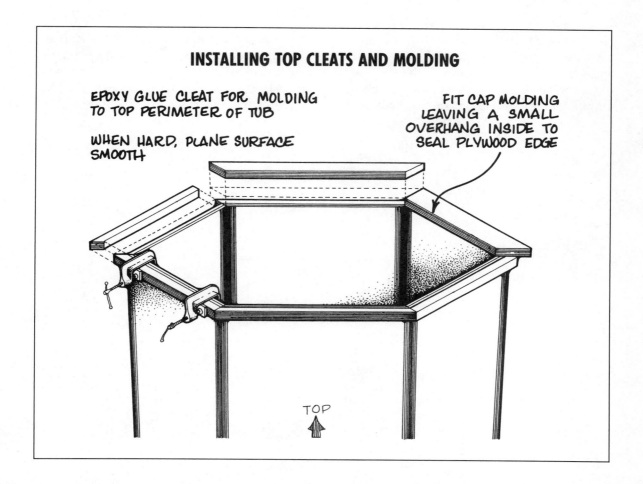

TOP

10. SHAPE AND FINISH THE CAP MOLDINGS. When the epoxy has cured, remove the clamps. If the top is uneven, carefully plane or sand it flat. Rout a small round over on the top edges or just plane and/or sand it to a pleasing shape.

11. INSTALL THE PLUMBING. Every plumbing system is a little different, so it's best to buy your system and plumb the tub accordingly. Check under hot tubs in the phone book. When you make holes in the tub for the plumbing, seal the plywood edges inside the hole with epoxy.

12. **APPLY FINISH.** Seal the moldings and cleats with three coats of epoxy before you apply varnish or paint. If the tub is exposed to sunlight, and you won't be painting it, coat the outside of the tub with an exterior varnish that has a sunscreen. No finish, except epoxy, should be applied on the inside of the tub. Now settle in for a good long soak. You've earned it!

ROWING DORY

This 15-foot dory is light enough to carry on a car roof rack, yet strong enough to handle rough water. Epoxy and plywood create the great strength-to-weight ratio. The epoxy also eliminates the need for tight joinery. Gaps of about ⅜ inch are left between the joined parts of the hull to let plenty of epoxy seep in and seal the plywood edges. This makes extremely strong joints. It also makes the boat waterproof and easy to build.

And while you've got plenty of work ahead to make the dory, no special tools or skills are required. Just be sure to read the introduction to this chapter, page 127, before you begin. We hope this little boat will be as much fun to build as it will be to use.

We designed the boat to accept a commercially available sliding seat. Excluding the seat, the boat weighs only about 60 pounds—perfect for fast rowing in calm water. The drop-in sliding seat can be removed easily, so one strong person can hoist the boat onto the roof of a car. The boat has sealed compartments fore and aft that ensure that it will float if it capsizes.

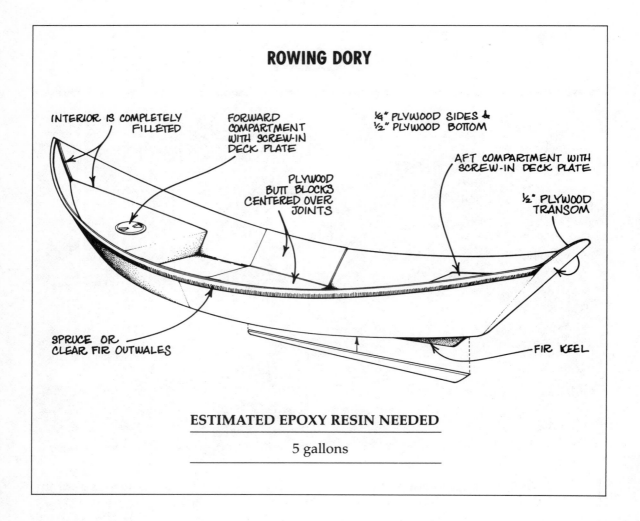

ROWING DORY

INTERIOR IS COMPLETELY FILLETED

FORWARD COMPARTMENT WITH SCREW-IN DECK PLATE

¼" PLYWOOD SIDES & ½" PLYWOOD BOTTOM

AFT COMPARTMENT WITH SCREW-IN DECK PLATE

PLYWOOD BUTT BLOCKS CENTERED OVER JOINTS

½" PLYWOOD TRANSOM

SPRUCE OR CLEAR FIR OUTWALES

FIR KEEL

ESTIMATED EPOXY RESIN NEEDED

5 gallons

The compartments can be fitted with watertight, screw-in hatches so they can be used for storage. These hatches are available from Beckson Marine. (See "Sources," page 295.)

If you are more interested in rough-water boating than fast, calm-water rowing, we suggest that you use a fixed seat instead of the sliding seat. For rough water, you'll want to use small sandbags or other ballasts in the bottom of the boat or in the compartments. Extra weight will carry the hull through small wind chops that otherwise would stall progress.

We built our boat from luan mahogany plywood. We used 6-millimeter sheets for the sides and compartments and 9-millimeter panels for the bottom.

1. ASSEMBLE THE BUILDING-BASE LADDER.

Nearly half the work for this project is to assemble the mold around which you will build the boat. This mold has two parts—the building-base ladder and the frames.

The building-base ladder is actually a base that supports and aligns the frames while you fit, attach, and joint the sides, bottom, and transom. The overall length and width of the ladder are not crucial. One that is about 16 feet long and 16 inches wide will work well. The rungs of the ladder are spaced at 18-inch intervals. These rungs are called *frame stations*, be-

cause the frames are attached to them. It's important to select straight 2 × 4s for the ladder and to mark the frame stations accurately across the top. Mark the frame stations on the ladder sides before you assemble the ladder by clamping both side pieces together and using a square across both pieces. Place a rung at each frame station and secure it with two 2½-inch #12 screws at each end. Check that the ladder is square. Place the ladder across two level sawhorses to achieve a comfortable working height.

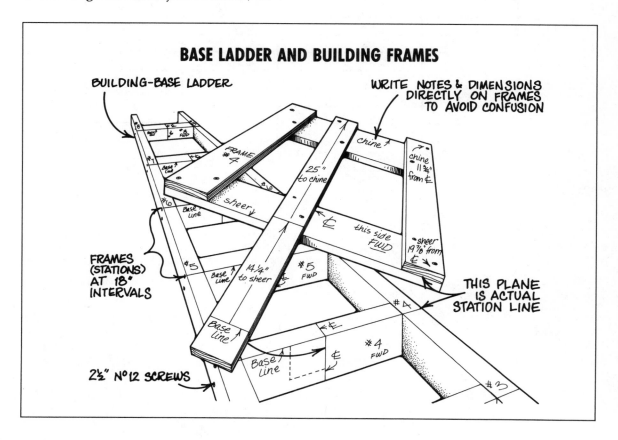

BASE LADDER AND BUILDING FRAMES

TABLES OF OFFSETS AND LINES DRAWING

TABLE OF OFFSETS

DISTANCES FROM CENTERLINE		STA. Nº	HEIGHTS ABOVE BASELINE	
AT SHEER	AT CHINE		AT CHINE	AT SHEER
—	—	S	—	1 3/4"
6 5/8"	—	0	19 3/4"	5 3/4"
12 1/4"	4 1/4"	1	23 1/4"	9 1/4"
16 1/2"	8 3/8"	2	24 1/4"	11 3/4"
19"	11 1/8"	3	24 3/4"	13 1/2"
19 7/8"*	11 3/4"*	4	25"*	14 1/4"
19 1/4"	10 7/8"	5	25 1/4"	14 1/8"
17 1/4"	8 1/2"	6	25"	13 3/8"
13 7/8"	5"	7	24 5/8"	11 3/4"
9 7/8"	7/8"	8	23 3/4"	9"
5 3/8"	—	T	—	5 1/8"

* INCLUDES 1/4" DEDUCTION FOR BUTT BLOCKS (1/4" THICK PLYWOOD)

NOTES:

- ■ DIMENSIONS GIVEN IN TABLE OF OFFSETS ARE TO THE *INSIDE* OF THE DORY HULL.

- ■ THE *BASE LINE* REFERRED TO IS THE WORKING TOP OF THE BUILDING-BASE LADDER.

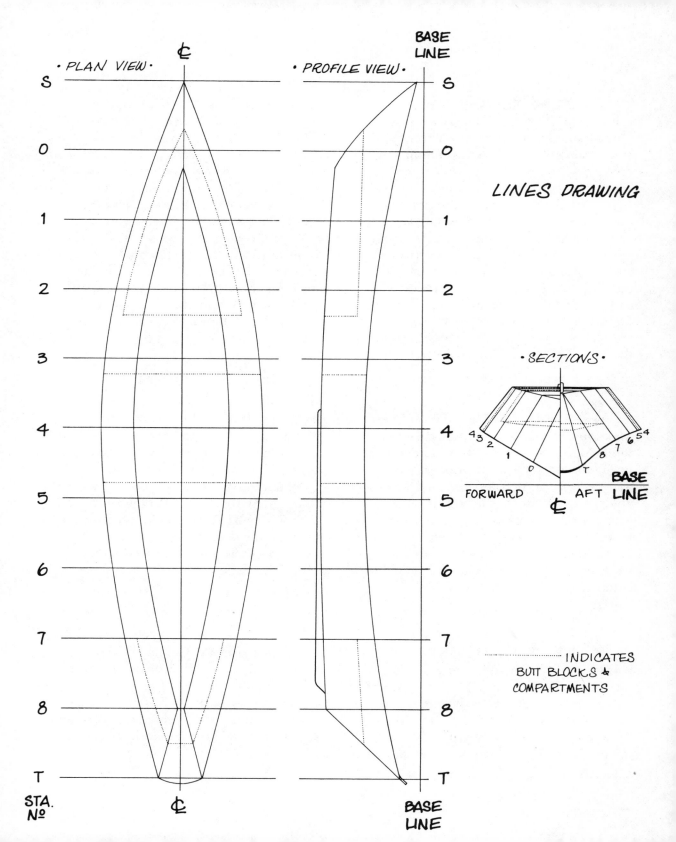

· PLAN VIEW ·

· PROFILE VIEW ·

BASE LINE

· LINES DRAWING ·

Ȼ

Ȼ

BASE LINE

· SECTIONS ·

4 3 2 1 0 T 8 7 6 5 4

FORWARD   AFT

Ȼ

BASE LINE

·········· INDICATES
BUTT BLOCKS &
COMPARTMENTS

STA.
Nº

S
0
1
2
3
4
5
6
7
8
T

BASE LINE

2. ASSEMBLE THE FRAMES. Two curves run the length of the boat on each side. One set of curves, called the chines, runs along the joints between the bottom and each side. Another curve is called the sheer. This runs along the tops of the sides. The sheer curves are compound— they curve out as well as down from each end of the boat. The frames are sized and positioned along the ladder to define these curves and to provide places where you can temporarily attach screws as you cut and assemble the parts of the boat.

Lay out each full-scale frame on a piece of plywood. Use the dimensions in the Table of Offsets. Use 1 × 4 stock to build the frames right on the plywood. You can use the same piece of plywood for all the frames as long as you don't get your lines mixed up. *Base Ladder and Building Frames* shows how these dimensions are used to build the frame for station #4, as an example. Notice in *Base Ladder and Building Frames* that the longest vertical piece is not centered on the frame. Instead it is offset to one side so that one edge defines the centerline. Assemble the frame with 1¼-inch #8 drywall screws and mark them for reference as shown. Include centerlines, sheer, chines, and distances to base line.

3. ATTACH THE FRAMES TO THE LADDER. Make sure the ladder is level. Strike a centerline down the length of the ladder. First install the largest frames, which are in the middle of the boat. Then alternate sides and work out toward the ends. Clamp each frame into position, eyeball the centerline from both ends, and then check it with a level to ensure that it's perfectly vertical before you screw the frame to the ladder. Note on the Table of Offsets that the midship frame is inset ¼ inch from the curves on the chines and sheer. This is to allow for butt blocks on each side. These blocks will reinforce plywood joints.

Watch the frame as you work. If a frame is the wrong size or in the wrong position, it will become obvious when you align it on the ladder. Also be sure your frames are placed on the correct side of each ladder station.

4. BEVEL THE OUTSIDE EDGES OF THE FRAMES. Later, when you bend the sides of the boat along the sides of the frames, the curves will be more fair if the edges of the frame are beveled to follow the curves. These bevels need not be exact. To find the bevels, use a wooden batten as shown in *Beveling the Frames*. Get two helpers and have one hold each end of the batten in place along the top of the frames as you mark the angles of the bevels. Then make the approximate bevels with a block plane. See "Making and Using a Flexible Layout Batten," page 19.

BEVELING THE FRAMES

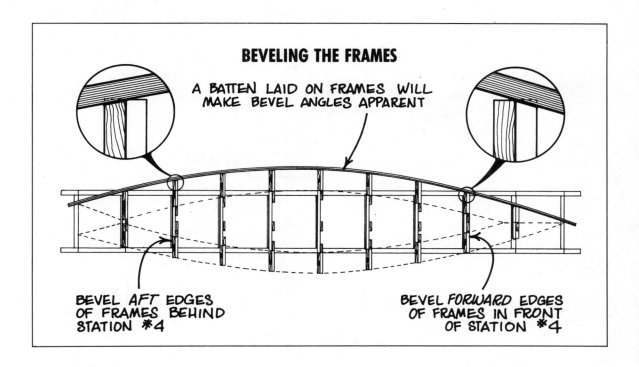

A BATTEN LAID ON FRAMES WILL MAKE BEVEL ANGLES APPARENT

BEVEL AFT EDGES OF FRAMES BEHIND STATION #4

BEVEL FORWARD EDGES OF FRAMES IN FRONT OF STATION #4

CUTTING DIAGRAM

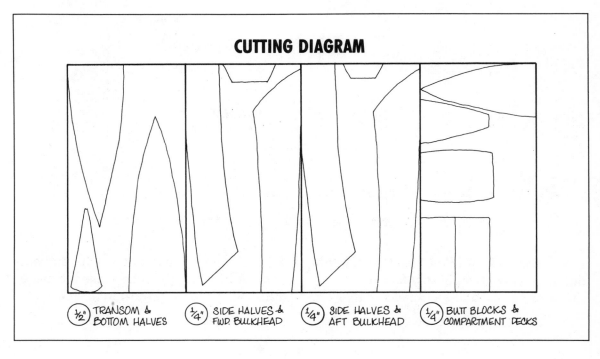

½" TRANSOM & BOTTOM HALVES

¼" SIDE HALVES & FWD. BULKHEAD

¼" SIDE HALVES & AFT BULKHEAD

¼" BUTT BLOCKS & COMPARTMENT DECKS

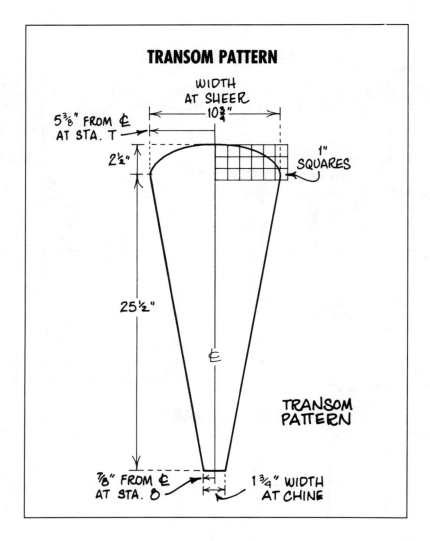

TRANSOM PATTERN

WIDTH
AT SHEER
10¾"

5⅜" FROM ℄
AT STA. T

2½"

1"
SQUARES

25½"

℄

TRANSOM
PATTERN

⅞" FROM ℄
AT STA. 0

1¾" WIDTH
AT CHINE

5. **CUT THE TRANSOM.** Cut the transom according to the *Transom Pattern*.

6. **ROUGH-CUT THE BOTTOM AND SIDES.** In this step, you'll temporarily fasten full sheets of plywood to the frames so that you can roughly lay out the sides and bottom of the boat. The rough cuts are made because it is too awkward to position full sheets for accurate marking. It's possible to accomplish this step alone with the help of temporary screws and clamps, but it's a lot easier if you have a helper to hold things in place while you screw or clamp.

The bottom and both sides are made from two sheets of plywood each. You only need to mark one side. After you cut it you can use it as a pattern for the other side. It doesn't matter whether you mark the bottom or the sides first. Position a full sheet so that one of its short edges overlaps the bow frame station by about 3 inches. This means that Station O will be about 21 inches from the end of the plywood as shown in *Rough-Cutting the Bow.* Shoot a few drywall screws through the side and into the frames when you have the sheet in place. Now hold another sheet against the frame, this time leaving just enough plywood to meet the frame at the transom. Let the second piece overlap the first sheet at midship and insert a few more temporary positioning screws. Mark the stern and bow for rough cuts and run your pencil down the end of the second sheet where it overlaps the first sheet. Remove the plywood and use a jigsaw to rough-cut the chines, stern, bow, and sheer. Make your rough cuts about ½ inch outside your final marks.

The curve of the sheer will be defined roughly by the framing stations that are set every 18 inches. The exact shape of the curve will be refined near the end of the building process when you attach the boat gunnels. The gunnels will give you a smooth continuous curve at the sheer, so

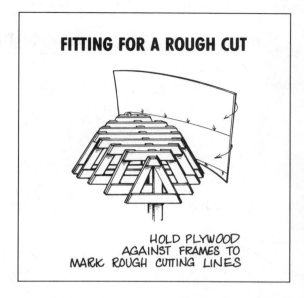

FITTING FOR A ROUGH CUT

HOLD PLYWOOD
AGAINST FRAMES TO
MARK ROUGH CUTTING LINES

that all you have to do is plane the plywood sides flush to the top of the gunnels. The exact curve of the bow is not crucial, in fact it doesn't have to be curved at all. It's basic shape will fall into place when you assemble the boat around the frames after the final cuts. All you'll need to do is fine-tune it with a block plane to a pleasing fair shape.

Rough-cut all four side pieces. Cut the aft pieces 1 inch longer than the scribe line. You'll need the overlap to make a scarf joint.

The bottom is easier to mark for a rough cut because the plywood will lay flat on the frames. But it's still a good idea to insert a few screws to help you realign the bottom during later construction steps. Overlap and cut the two sheets as you did for the side and again add 1 inch for the scarf joint.

ROUGH-CUTTING THE BOW

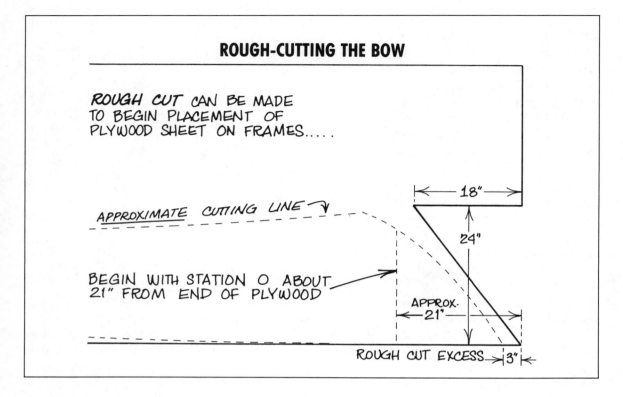

ROUGH CUT CAN BE MADE
TO BEGIN PLACEMENT OF
PLYWOOD SHEET ON FRAMES......

APPROXIMATE CUTTING LINE

BEGIN WITH STATION O ABOUT
21" FROM END OF PLYWOOD

18"

24"

APPROX.
21"

ROUGH CUT EXCESS 3"

7. **FINISH CUT THE SIDES AND BOTTOM.** Put the two parts of one side on the frame again and screw them in place through the same holes. Check that your scarf-cut marks are correct. Mark for final cuts. Put the bottom pieces in place and mark them for the final cuts so that you have a gap of about ⅜ inch at the chines. The gap is to let epoxy flow in and make the chines waterproof and strong. Use the two sides as patterns to trace the pieces for the other side. Finish cut these pieces.

8. **CUT THE SCARF JOINTS.** When scarf joining, two edges are cut back at the same angle so that they can overlap. This increases the gluing area and the strength of the joint. Making scarf joints in plywood is really easier than it looks, espe-cially the short scarf needed here. Still, if you have never done it before, you might want to try one on scrap material first. Start by making a diagonal line on the side of each end that is to be scarfed. As *Making a Scarf Joint* shows, the line runs from the 1-inch overlap line to the end of the piece on the opposite side. Do the same for the other piece that is to be joined and then clamp them together on your workbench. Shave down both pieces with a block plane as shown in *Making a Scarf Joint*. Sand or lightly rasp the scarfs to prepare them for gluing. Use the glue lines inside the plywood as a guide when you cut flat scarfs. If the glue lines are straight across, the scarf will be straight across.

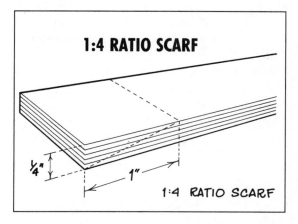

1:4 RATIO SCARF

¼"   1"

1:4 RATIO SCARF

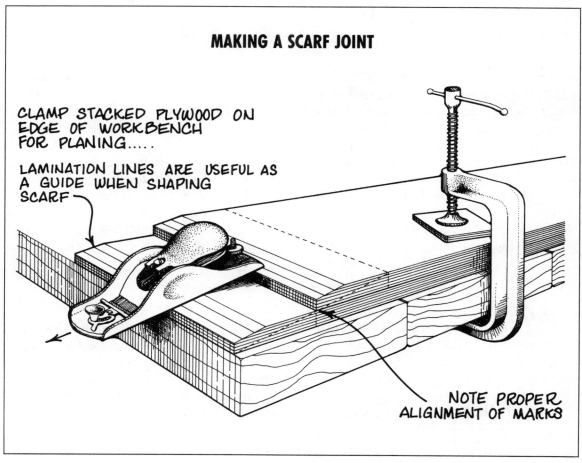

MAKING A SCARF JOINT

CLAMP STACKED PLYWOOD ON EDGE OF WORKBENCH FOR PLANING.....

LAMINATION LINES ARE USEFUL AS A GUIDE WHEN SHAPING SCARF

NOTE PROPER ALIGNMENT OF MARKS

9. GLUE THE SCARF JOINTS. Lay some waxed paper on your work surface. Saturate both surfaces that are to be joined with epoxy. Then thicken the epoxy slightly with equal parts of microfibers and silica and apply it to both surfaces. Assemble the joint on the flat surface and put waxed paper over it. Lay a 2 × 4 over the waxed paper to distribute even pressure. Clamp the joint together. If you don't have deep clamps, you can put small finish nails right through the 2 × 4. Let the epoxy cure at least overnight. Then remove the clamps and/or nails and sand the scarf lightly.

10. COAT THE PARTS WITH EPOXY. To totally seal the plywood, it's necessary to apply epoxy before you assembly the dory. Apply three coats as described in "Epoxy as a Coating," page 132.

11. GLUE THE BUTT BLOCKS OVER THE JOINTS. The scarf joints are reinforced with large, interior butt blocks. Make the blocks for the sides the same thickness as the sides and the block for the bottom the same thickness as the bottom. The blocks are 28 inches long and run the full width of the joints they cover. Rough scribe the sheer curve of the sides for the side butt blocks and cut the blocks to that curve. Later, the blocks will be planed flush to the gunnels and the sides. To attach the butt blocks, lay the sides and the bottom on a flat wooden surface, center the blocks over the joints, and mark their locations. Apply epoxy to both surfaces. Put the blocks in place and place weights on the blocks. Since epoxy is slippery, it may help to use small nails at the corners to hold the blocks in the proper position. When the epoxy has cured, finish and seal the edges of the blocks with small fillets as described "Bonding with Fillets," page 135.

12. REASSEMBLE THE BOAT ON THE FRAME. Use the existing screw holes to realign the sides and bottom on the frames. Hold the transom in place by taping it with duct tape to the sides as shown in *Taping Outside Joints.* Don't make a tight fit between the sides and bottom at the chines. If these pieces fit tightly together in spots, use a circular saw to cut at least a ⅜-inch gap between the two pieces. This gap will allow the epoxy to seal the end grain of the plywood in the chines. It also will allow the chine-fillet mixture of epoxy to squeeze into place more easily.

GLUING A SCARF

LAY PLYWOOD *FLAT* ON WORKBENCH..... GLUE & CLAMP OR
NAIL WITH A 2×4 TO SPREAD FORCE EVENLY ON SCARF

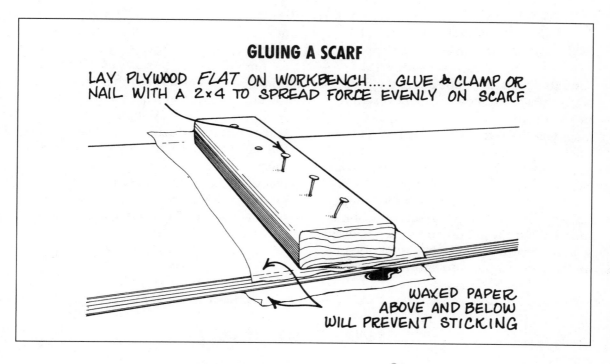

WAXED PAPER
ABOVE AND BELOW
WILL PREVENT STICKING

INTERIOR BUTT BLOCKS

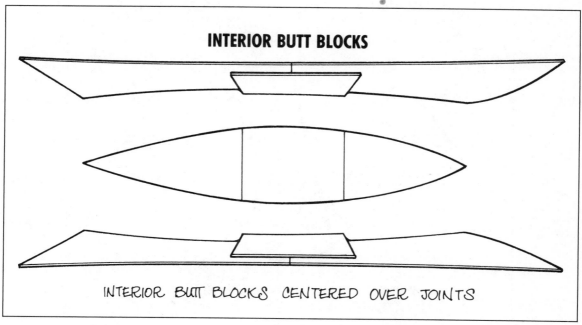

INTERIOR BUTT BLOCKS CENTERED OVER JOINTS

13. **TAPE THE TRANSOM, CHINES, AND BOW.** Position the transom, then apply 4- to 6-inch long tack strips of epoxy-saturated fiberglass tape along the transom, chines, and bow to hold everything in alignment. After the tack strips of fiberglass tape have hardened, remove the duct tape and apply one layer of epoxy-saturated 4-inch-wide fiberglass tape over the tack strips on the transom. See "Reinforcing Epoxy with Fiberglass Mesh Tape," page 137. Put one layer of saturated 4-inch tape around the chines and bow. Then put a layer of saturated 3-inch tape on top of all the 4-inch tape. Add another layer of 4-inch and another layer of 3-inch saturated tape to the chines. You can add more layers for a really rough-service boat, but we think four layers at the chines and two at the bow and transom are plenty for most conditions, especially since all the joints will be reinforced with fillets inside. Cut the tape in 3-foot-long strips. As you use them, saturate them on a piece of cardboard and work the epoxy into the fiberglass tape with a roller and squeegee. Butt the ends of the strips and stagger the joints with each layer. You don't need to let the epoxy cure between layers.

TAPING OUTSIDE JOINTS

TAPE ALL JOINTS FIRST WITH 4" FIBERGLASS TAPE, THEN BEGIN SECOND LAYER WITH 3" FIBERGLASS TAPE ALTERNATING WIDTHS UP TO FOUR LAYERS

THE TRANSOM CAN BE HELD IN PLACE WITH DUCT TAPE UNTIL PARTIAL TAPING HAS HARDENED

14. **FAIR THE JOINTS.** After the epoxy has cured, carefully shave any loose fiberglass fibers or epoxy lumps with a sharp block plane. Add equal parts of low-density filler and silica to the epoxy until the mixture reaches a peanut butterlike consistency. Use a 3-inch-wide putty knife to fill any dents with the mixture. You can also use it to build up a pleasing round where the chine joints may have flattened across the gap. It's better to fair, or smooth things out, by adding the fairing mixture, than to try to sand things flat. Sanding creates dust and removes epoxy, which weakens the joints. After the fairing mixture has cured, you can fine-tune the shape with a block plane and then a long sanding block. Remove all the screws. Dab a little unthickened epoxy into the holes and then fill them with thickened epoxy.

15. **FILLET THE HULL.** Flip the boat over onto the sawhorses. Carefully support the hull so you maintain the proper shape when you fillet. To help support the hull, remove the #4 frame from the building base and insert it into the upright hull at the correct position.

Make the fillets as described in "Bonding with Fillets," page 135. Use a filler comprised of equal parts of filleting blend and high-density filler. Add silica until the mixture is stiff, but slides smoothly off the filleting paddle. You may find it easier to build up neat, consistent fillets in two or three layers by letting the epoxy cure between layers. This is especially true of the large chine fillets. If you do the fillets in two or three layers, you can ease the chore of sanding by using only the fillet blend for the last layer.

To make the fillets, make a paddle from ⅛- or ¼-inch plywood. Cut a 1-inch radius on one end and 1½-inch radius on the other. This way, by turning the paddle

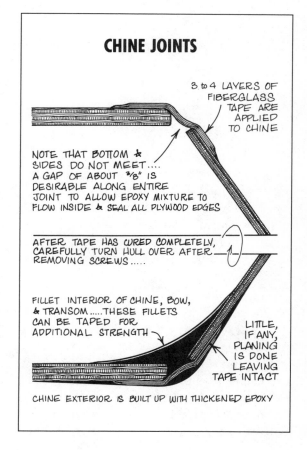

CHINE JOINTS

3 to 4 LAYERS OF FIBERGLASS TAPE ARE APPLIED TO CHINE

NOTE THAT BOTTOM & SIDES DO NOT MEET.... A GAP OF ABOUT ⅜" IS DESIRABLE ALONG ENTIRE JOINT TO ALLOW EPOXY MIXTURE TO FLOW INSIDE & SEAL ALL PLYWOOD EDGES

AFTER TAPE HAS CURED COMPLETELY, CAREFULLY TURN HULL OVER AFTER REMOVING SCREWS.....

FILLET INTERIOR OF CHINE, BOW, & TRANSOM.....THESE FILLETS CAN BE TAPED FOR ADDITIONAL STRENGTH

LITTLE, IF ANY, PLANING IS DONE LEAVING TAPE INTACT

CHINE EXTERIOR IS BUILT UP WITH THICKENED EPOXY

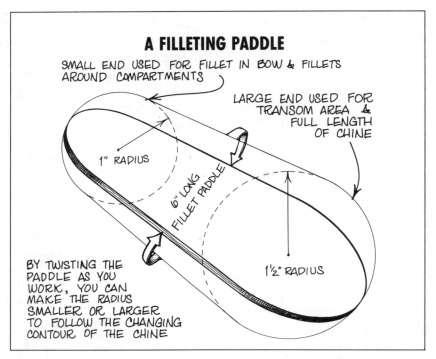

A FILLETING PADDLE

SMALL END USED FOR FILLET IN BOW & FILLETS AROUND COMPARTMENTS

LARGE END USED FOR TRANSOM AREA & FULL LENGTH OF CHINE

1" RADIUS

6" LONG FILLET PADDLE

1½" RADIUS

BY TWISTING THE PADDLE AS YOU WORK, YOU CAN MAKE THE RADIUS SMALLER OR LARGER TO FOLLOW THE CHANGING CONTOUR OF THE CHINE

you can change the radius of the fillet. This paddle, along with a gloved finger, makes all the fillet sizes you will need. A large radius is required on the chine joints because of their wider, open angles. A smaller radius is necessary on acute angles in the hull, such as the bow, where the two sides come together. After final sanding, seal all fillets with a coat of unthickened epoxy. If your boat will see rough service, you can make the fillets even stronger by covering them with a layer of 4-inch-wide fiberglass tape that has been saturated with epoxy. Don't sand the tape.

---

16. INSTALL THE KEEL. Because this is a multi-purpose boat, we made the keel longer and deeper than what is usual for a dory. This keel provides excellent directional stability and makes the bottom stronger and stiffer. It also protects the bottom of the boat. Taper the keel either by cutting 2 or 3 degrees off each side on the table saw or by shaping it with a hand plane. The exact shape is not critical.

Flip the boat upside down on the sawhorses, center the keel, and mark one edge down the length. Saturate both of the surfaces that will be glued with epoxy.

Then thicken the epoxy with microfibers and apply the mixture to both surfaces. Put the keel in place. Have someone hold the keel in position while you duck under the sawhorses and drive temporary screws through the bottom and into the keel. After the epoxy has cured, remove the screws and fill the holes with thickened epoxy. If the keel gets damaged or worn down, you can plane it off and attach a new one. Our boat has had three keels.

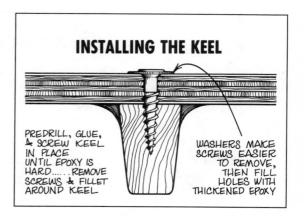

INSTALLING THE KEEL

PREDRILL, GLUE, & SCREW KEEL IN PLACE UNTIL EPOXY IS HARD......REMOVE SCREWS & FILLET AROUND KEEL

WASHERS MAKE SCREWS EASIER TO REMOVE, THEN FILL HOLES WITH THICKENED EPOXY

17. CUT AND INSTALL THE COMPARTMENTS. The hull has two sealed flotation and storage compartments—one forward and one aft. The compartments have flush-fitting Beckson screw-in ports, which seal them from leaks even when they are fully immersed. Of course, if you are willing to sacrifice the storage space, you can skip the ports. Either way, the water-tight compartments ensure that the boat won't sink if it is swamped. Filleted securely to the hull, the compartments also strengthen the bow and stern and eliminate the need for internal ribs or frames. You can make the compartments from the same thickness of plywood that was used for the sides. If adults will frequently sit on them, however, it's better to make them the same thickness as the bottom.

Each compartment has a vertical bulkhead and a deck. Cut these parts with a jigsaw according to the dimension in *Compartment Layouts.* Test fit the parts in the boat. The decks should fit with a slight slope for drainage. A slight error is bound to have crept into the building process, so the bulkheads and decks probably will be slightly large or slightly loose. If they are a bit loose, that's no problem because the fillets you will use to attach them can fill gaps up to ¼ inch. If the bulkheads are too tight, scribe them to fit as shown in *Scribing the Bulkheads.* Set a bulkhead into the boat as far as it will go. Set your compass a hair wider than the gap between the bottom of the boat and the bottom of the bulkhead. Then scribe the bulkhead. Be careful to keep the two points of the compass vertical throughout the scribe. The decks can be scribed in the same way, but we find that we can usually just trim the decks with a block plane until they fit.

After you fit the bulkheads and decks, apply epoxy to a ¾ × ¾-inch wood cleat and attach the cleat to the inside top edge

COMPARTMENT LAYOUTS

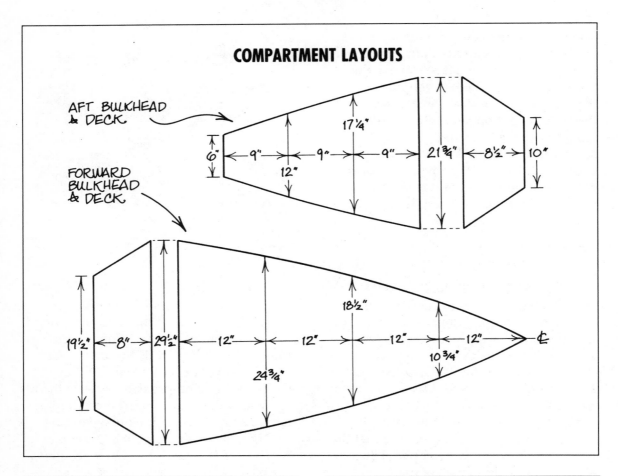

AFT BULKHEAD & DECK

6" 9" 9" 9" 17¼" 12" 21¾" 8½" 10"

FORWARD BULKHEAD & DECK

19½" 8" 29½" 12" 12" 18½" 12" 12" 24¾" 10¾" ₵

SCRIBING THE BULKHEADS

KEEP COMPASS VERTICAL AT ALL TIMES WHEN FITTING BULKHEADS DOWN INTO HULL

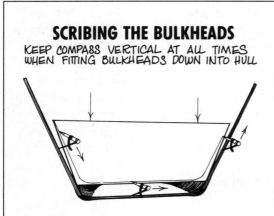

FILLETING THE COMPARTMENTS

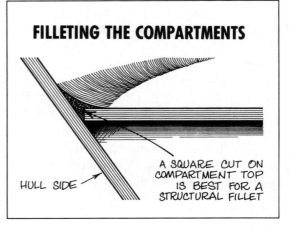

HULL SIDE

A SQUARE CUT ON COMPARTMENT TOP IS BEST FOR A STRUCTURAL FILLET of each bulkhead. This is the joint that would be under your knees if you sat on the compartment.

As *Filleting the Compartments* shows, there is no need for cleats on the sides of the boats. And when you cut the compartment tops, there is no need to make angle cuts that conform to the angled sides of the hull. It's better to leave a gap for the epoxy to flow into when you fillet the top in place. Apply epoxy to the cleats and use small nails or screws to hold the top in place until the epoxy cures. Then remove the fasteners and fill the holes with thickened epoxy. After the top is secured, round the front edge slightly with sandpaper and apply a layer of fiberglass tape and epoxy across the edge to reinforce the compartment and seal the joint. Finally, fillet the top to the hull. Install the ports by using the template and instructions provided by the manufacturer.

18. **INSTALL THE GUNNELS.** Flip the boat upside down again for this operation so that any epoxy-glue drips will be along the top of the sheer where they can be planed off easily. The gunnels are simply ⅝ × 1½-inch strips of spruce that have been cut to length. But they are an important structural part of the hull. We made them of spruce because it is light. Fir would be a little heavier and a little more abrasion resistant.

To attach the gunnels, brush or roll a coat of epoxy on both of the surfaces that will be glued. Then put a thin coat of slightly thickened epoxy on both surfaces as described in "Epoxy as a Glue," page 131. Attach the gunnels to the sides with small clamps set very 4 to 6 inches. Use pads of scrap plywood to protect the wood under the clamps. Check that the gunnels are flush to the sheer. Remember, you only need enough clamping pressure to hold the gunnels in place. Clamping them too tightly will squeeze out too much epoxy and make a weak bond.

After the epoxy has cured, remove the clamps and flip the boat right side up. Use a block plane or a belt sander to fair the top edges and ends of the gunnels. Sand a small round on the edge of the gunnel, or cut a small bevel with a block plane and then sand it.

INSTALLING THE GUNNELS

PADS PREVENT BRUISES WHEN CLAMPING GUNNEL

19. COAT THE BOTTOM WITH EPOXY AND GRAPHITE. Graphite powder, one of the West System fillers (see "Sources," page 295), is a fine black powder that, when mixed with epoxy, forms a scuff-resistant, low-friction surface that is ideal for the bottom of small boats. The black graphite also is a very effective sun barrier, which is important for boats that will be stored upside down.

Mix the graphite into the epoxy according to the directions on the container. Mix well until all the graphite is soaked with epoxy. Work out of direct sunlight when you apply the mixture to the boat because the black graphite could absorb enough heat to set the epoxy before you are done working.

Apply masking tape along the sides at the chines, in case any of the mixture drips off the edge while you are applying it. Make sure you remove the tape before the epoxy starts to cure. Pour the mixture of epoxy and graphite onto the bottom and spread it out with a squeegee and then a foam roller. The mixture is self-leveling. Small imperfections will smooth themselves if they are given adequate time before the epoxy starts to cure.

After the epoxy has cured, you may wish to use a sharp scraper to remove any small dust craters or kamikaze bugs from the surface. After you use the boat for a few seasons, you may wish to patch any dings and scratches on the bottom of the boat with thickened epoxy and then recoat it with graphite. The bottom of the boat may also be waxed to further reduce friction, but the wax will need to be removed before you recoat the bottom.

20. APPLY FINAL FINISH. The bottom of the boat gets no further finish. Rough up the rest of the boat with #100 grit sandpaper to provide a proper tooth for varnish or paint. If the epoxy clogs the sandpaper, it probably needs more time to cure. If you build in areas with air pollution, the surface may become cloudy and waxy. While this is not a problem between coats of epoxy, it can degrade the bond between the epoxy and varnish or paint. Wash the entire boat with soap and water just before you finish it. If that doesn't remove any contamination, wash the surface with paint thinner. Spar varnish with sunscreen is the easiest natural finish for epoxy-sealed wood. Apply three or four coats as per the instructions on the can. By carefully using the recommended recoat times, multiple coats may be applied without having to sand between coats. Varnish may be brushed or rolled on with a foam roller. Boats that are exposed to sunlight most of the time may have to be lightly sanded and revarnished every year, but if you keep the boat out of sunlight as much as possible, you may get by for years without refinishing.

Several coats of marine enamel paint will last for years without any maintenance at all.

21. INSTALL THE THWART AND OARLOCKS.

The fixed thwart is the rower's seat. If you intend to use a sliding rowing seat, you can make the thwart removable or you can skip it altogether. Oarlocks are not used with the sliding seat. Make the seat of ½-inch plywood. It should be 10 inches wide and scribed to fit between the sides of the boat. As shown in *Installing the Thwart*, use epoxy to glue the cleats to the sides. Center the cleats between the bow and the stern and locate them 5 to 7 inches below the sheer, depending on the rower's height. If you don't have deep-throated clamps, you can cut a batten that is slightly longer than the distance between the cleats and use it to wedge both cleats in place until the epoxy cures. Plane the

tops off the cleats, as shown in *Installing the Thwart*, to make a level surface onto which you will attach the thwart. Fasten the thwart in place with 1¼-inch #10 stainless steel or silicone bronze screws.

If you are using a sliding seat, you won't need oarlocks. If you do install oarlocks, depending on the oarlocks you purchase you'll probably have to mount them on blocks that have been glued with epoxy to the inside of the gunnels. For most people, oarlocks should be 10 or 11 inches away from the thwart. If you wish to customize the boat to one rower, temporarily clamp the oarlock blocks in place and try the boat out. Adjust the position for the most efficient stroke.

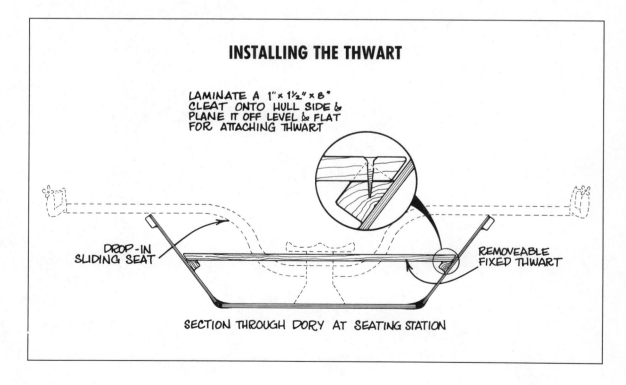

INSTALLING THE THWART

LAMINATE A 1" × 1½" × 8"
CLEAT ONTO HULL SIDE &
PLANE IT OFF LEVEL & FLAT
FOR ATTACHING THWART

DROP-IN
SLIDING SEAT

REMOVEABLE
FIXED THWART

SECTION THROUGH DORY AT SEATING STATION

22. **INSTALL THE SLIDING SEAT.** This slim dory will provide efficient rowing even with a fixed thwart and gunnel-mounted oarlocks. But you can't beat a sliding seat and quality oars for speed and enjoyment. Sliding seats let you use your entire body, including the large leg muscles, for a smooth, nontraumatic aerobic workout.

Drop-in sliding seat units that come complete with attached outriggers and oarlocks have the added advantage of being easy to remove from the boat before you transport it. Install the seat according to the manufacturer's instructions. Oars are available in a wide variety of styles, sizes, and quality. Fine lightweight spruce or basswood oars are a pleasure to use and look at, and will make the dory come alive in the water. See "Sources," page 295, for where to buy sliding seats, oarlocks, and oars.

CAMPER
CAP

Looking at the photograph, you already realize that this is not a typical homemade camper cap. Most homemade versions are built under the assumption that the use of plywood forces the design to have boxy right angles. Since pickup trucks, especially late models, aren't built with right angles, the caps end up looking like awkward afterthoughts. The problem isn't just aesthetic; the box is not an aerodynamic shape. Buffeted by the wind, a boxy cap reduces gas mileage and degrades handling.

From building plywood boats, we knew that plywood doesn't have to mean a box. We knew that by combining plywood with epoxy, we could design a cap that would blend with the lines of the truck and slip through the air as efficiently as a boat slips through water. The result is, in fact, a capsized version of a plywood and epoxy boat—watertight, weatherproof, and easy to build.

That's right, easy to build. We don't mean to imply that you'll snap this cap together this weekend or next because there

CAMPER CAP EXPLODED VIEW

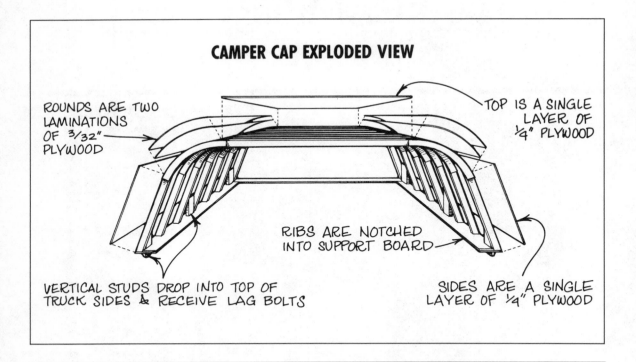

ROUNDS ARE TWO LAMINATIONS OF 3/32" PLYWOOD

TOP IS A SINGLE LAYER OF 1/4" PLYWOOD

RIBS ARE NOTCHED INTO SUPPORT BOARD

VERTICAL STUDS DROP INTO TOP OF TRUCK SIDES & RECEIVE LAG BOLTS

SIDES ARE A SINGLE LAYER OF 1/4" PLYWOOD

MEASURING YOUR TRUCK

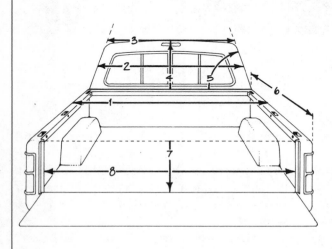

1• MAXIMUM WIDTH OF CAP/TRUCK BED

2• WIDTH OF CAP/CAB HALFWAY UP

3• WIDTH OF CAP/CAB AT MAXIMUM HEIGHTH

4• MAXIMUM HEIGHTH OF CAP/CAB

5• ANGLE OF SIDES ON CAP/CAB

6• MAXIMUM LENGTH OF CAP/TRUCK BED

7• ADDITIONAL LENGTH FOR BACK PANEL

8• WIDTH OF BACK PANEL AT TAILGATE

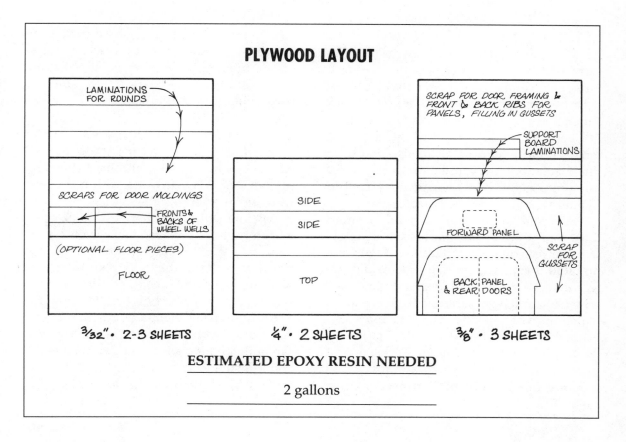

PLYWOOD LAYOUT

LAMINATIONS FOR ROUNDS

SCRAPS FOR DOOR MOLDINGS

FRONTS & BACKS OF WHEEL WELLS

(OPTIONAL FLOOR PIECES)

FLOOR

3/32" • 2-3 SHEETS

SIDE

SIDE

TOP

1/4" • 2 SHEETS

SCRAP FOR DOOR FRAMING & FRONT & BACK RIBS FOR PANELS, FILLING IN GUSSETS

SUPPORT BOARD LAMINATIONS

FORWARD PANEL

SCRAP FOR GUSSETS

BACK PANEL & REAR DOORS

3/8" • 3 SHEETS

ESTIMATED EPOXY RESIN NEEDED

2 gallons

is plenty of labor involved. We do mean, though, that no step is beyond the ability of a handy person with basic skills and tools. Do take the time to read carefully through the project before you begin so you'll understand all the steps and how they relate to each other. This will help you to avoid mistakes because sometimes the logic behind early steps isn't evident until you read later steps. It is equally important that you read the introduction to this chapter, page 127, as well as the literature that is supplied by the manufacturers of the epoxy and hardware that you use. If you have never worked with epoxy, practice a

little. Spread some out to see how it soaks into the plywood. Mix some up with various ratios of silica and filler and make a few fillets. When you do start using epoxy on the cap, do small, easy areas first. It doesn't take long to get a feel for how this material works.

Unlike other projects in this book, we can't supply you with exact dimensions of all the parts. That's because the cap has to be made to fit your particular truck. Instead, we provide a precise method for custom-fitting the cap. The key to this method is that much of the building is done right on the truck.

There's plenty to do, but we think you'll be quite pleased with the results. We certainly are. As of this writing, we have used our camper for nearly four years in weather ranging from 100-degree desert sun to 40-degree-below Montana winters. It's been left outside most of the time and traveled more than 90,000 miles. Thanks to the insulation and ventilation, it stays cool in summer and heats surprisingly well in winter with just the truck heater.

Pleased as we are with our camper cap, four years of use has shown us a few things we would do differently if we were to build it again. Essentially, we would upgrade some of the hardware and windows. For light and ventilation, we put a small hatch in the top of the cap. This hatch, designed for recreational vehicles, is flimsy. We'd replace it with a large Beckson boat hatch that would serve as a sunroof and provide much more light and ventilation (see "Sources," page 295). We'd further increase ventilation by using Beckson black-plastic opening boat ports in the sides instead of fixed plexiglass. We'd still use fixed windows in the back doors because open rear windows could suck dust and dangerous fumes into the truck. Finally, we'd shop around a bit more for the best door hardware, hinges, and hasp. We'd replace RV-quality hardware with boat hardware where ever possible.

Before you start, here's a quick summary of what's involved. After you design your cap, you'll build support boards that sit on the sides of the truck bed. Next, you will build the ribs, sheathe them, and assemble the sides. Then you'll build the doors and install them along with the windows and top hatch. If you want, you also can build and install carrying racks. Finally, you'll insulate, weatherstrip, and then install a fabric liner on the inside.

1. MEASURE THE TRUCK AND DESIGN THE CAP.

Because we wanted a cap that would be aerodynamic and complement the shape of our truck, we decided to match the rear profile of the cab. This meant that the cap would have to have sloping sides that meet at the top with a round. By keeping the cap the same height as the cab, we are able to carry a 20-foot boat that extends over the truck cab.

We have a full-size pickup with an 8-foot bed. We didn't want the cap to be longer than the bed because we wanted to leave the tailgate in place to protect the back of the camper. We also like tailgate picnics. This made it easy to design a cap that uses full 8-foot sheets of plywood. Obviously, the plans can be adapted to smaller trucks simply by cutting the plywood to shorter lengths. But we don't recommend trying to adapt these plans to make a taller, wider, or longer cap. Larger caps would create wind-load and joinery considerations that these plans are not designed to handle.

The eight measurements you'll need to adapt these plans to your own truck are shown in *Measuring Your Truck*. Armed with these dimensions, a scale ruler, and a triangle, make the side and rear view scale drawings for the cap. Triangular in section, scale rulers have two or more scales on each edge. As you read across any of the scales, one increment equals 1 inch. The 3/32 scale is the most useful for this project.

While we don't recommend that you change the basic size or shape of this design, we do encourage you to customize the size and location of the doors, windows, hatches, and hardware. For example, if you will use your cap only for camping, you might only want one small rear door. Since we often haul full sheets of plywood, we made large double doors. When you customize your cap design, it might help to photograph the side and rear views of your truck. Photocopy the photos and use them to sketch ideas.

2. PROTECT THE TRUCK. Since much of the building work is done right on the truck, it's a good idea to cover the sides of the truck and the bed with plastic to keep from marring the paint with hand tools or splattering it with epoxy. Take note, though, that epoxy will sometimes bond even through plastic, so wipe up drips immediately.

3. BUILD THE SUPPORT BOARDS. The base of the cap consists of three support boards that lay on top of the sides and rear of the truck bed as shown in *Building the Support Boards*. Each support board is built from two layers of 3/8-inch mahogany plywood. Later, you will be notching the support boards to accept the ribs. By using two layers of 3/8-inch plywood instead of one layer of 3/4-inch, it will be easier to cut the notches exactly halfway through. Also, you'll be able to use the rest of the sheet to build the front or back panel of the cap. The support boards are 6 inches wide in order to provide adequate support and a small shelf around the interior of the truck. Make the two side supports 1 1/4 inches shorter than your truck bed. This is to allow 1/2 inch for the front panel and 3/4 inch for the rear panel and door hardware. Cut the rear support board to fit between the other two.

As shown in *Building the Support Boards*, clamp the two diagonal braces to the support boards to keep them in alignment. Cut two butt blocks of 3/8-inch plywood to fit under the front corners of the support boards as shown in the detail drawing on *Building the Support Boards*. The exact dimensions of the blocks will be

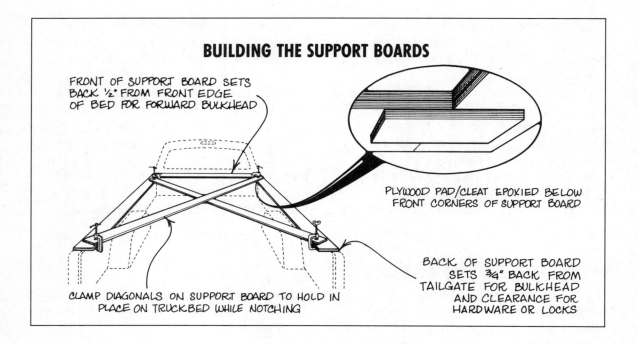

BUILDING THE SUPPORT BOARDS

FRONT OF SUPPORT BOARD SETS BACK ½" FROM FRONT EDGE OF BED FOR FORWARD BULKHEAD

PLYWOOD PAD/CLEAT EPOXIED BELOW FRONT CORNERS OF SUPPORT BOARD

CLAMP DIAGONALS ON SUPPORT BOARD TO HOLD IN PLACE ON TRUCKBED WHILE NOTCHING

BACK OF SUPPORT BOARD SETS ¾" BACK FROM TAILGATE FOR BULKHEAD AND CLEARANCE FOR HARDWARE OR LOCKS

determined by the lip on your truck bed; ours are about 3 × 6 inches. Check that the support boards are perfectly aligned. Put thickened epoxy on the bottom of the blocks, but don't spread it on a perimeter of about ½ inch around the blocks. This is to prevent the epoxy from squeezing out onto the truck when the pieces are clamped. Then clamp the blocks in place. Wipe up any glue that squeezes out.

4. CUT AND INSTALL THE STUDS AND MAKE BOLT HOLES. Most pickup-truck beds have four rectangular stud holes—one in each corner of the top of the sides. These holes usually are sized to accept 6 to 8 inches of 2 × 4. As shown in *Installing the Studs*, there's also a round hole on the inside of the sides so that you can lag-bolt the studs in place.

If your truck doesn't have holes along the sides for studs, eliminate the vertical studs and drill holes for ⅜-inch carriage bolts every 12 inches through the support boards and the top edge of the truck-bed sides. The length of the bolts will be determined by your truck. It's important to use lock washers under the nuts. Without them, road vibration could loosen the bolts.

If your truck does have square stud

holes, mark and cut the holes for the vertical alignment studs that extend through the support boards and into the holes. Drill pilot holes in the plywood and make the cuts with a jigsaw. We used mahogany for the studs, but any strong wood will do. Clear fir or spruce also are good choices. Cut the studs so that they are about 12 inches in length and use a block plane to taper one end of each stud to help them find the holes easier when you put the cap on the truck.

With the support boards in position, put the vertical studs through the notches and into the holes in the truck-bed sides. Predrill the studs for lag bolts, which fit the round holes that are perpendicular to the square stud holes. Use large washers under the lag-screw heads. (Lock washers aren't necessary for screws that are put into wood.) Attach the studs to the support boards with tongue-depressor-size

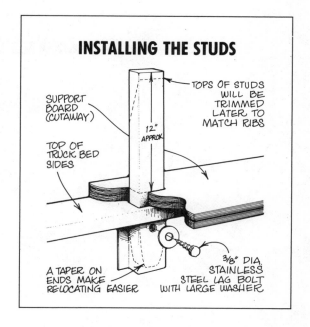

INSTALLING THE STUDS

SUPPORT BOARD (CUTAWAY)

TOP OF TRUCK BED SIDES

12" APPROX

TOPS OF STUDS WILL BE TRIMMED LATER TO MATCH RIBS

A TAPER ON ENDS MAKE RELOCATING EASIER

3/8" DIA. STAINLESS STEEL LAG BOLT WITH LARGE WASHER

epoxy fillets as described in "Bonding with Fillets," page 135. Leave everything in place until the fillets have cured.

---

5. BUILD THE RIBS. The exact shape and size of your ribs will be derived from the scale drawing you did earlier. We used a 12-inch radius for the round where the sides meet the top. This is about the tightest radius that easily can be achieved with the two laminations of 3/32-inch plywood that we used to sheathe the cap. A larger radius will, of course, be easier to bend.

Use the drawing to make a gluing jig. First draw the exact size and shape of the ribs on a piece of heavy plywood. Use the

plywood as a workbench and gluing jig for each rib. As you glue each rib, align it perfectly with the outlines. Remember to deduct 1/4 inch from the outside edge of the camper cap outline for the thickness of the side and top panel.

Each rib, except for the front and rear one, is made from seven pieces. Three straight pieces of 3/4 × 1 1/2 spruce form the sides and top. The rounds are formed by four 1/4-inch-thick plywood gussets. Two go on each side as shown in *Assembling the*

MAKING A GUSSET PATTERN

PATTERN JIG TO ALIGN GUSSETS AND RIBS FOR GLUING

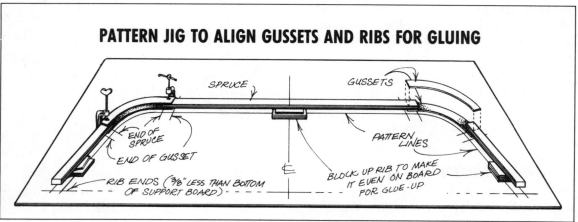

Ribs. Each gusset overlaps the solid spruce straight pieces by at least 2 inches at the top and bottom.

The ribs at the front and back have three additional ¼-inch plywood pieces. These fit around the gussets on one side of the rear rib and one side of the front rib to make a continuous flush surface, on which the front and rear panels are attached. They also provide the material you'll need to create the large rear bevel that you will make after the cap is assembled.

In addition, fill the inside space between the gussets with solid spruce on the front and rear ribs only. Each in-fill should consist of two pieces of solid stock that have been cut to fit the radius as shown in *Assembling the Ribs.* These pieces are for the front and rear panel attachment and for beveling.

Cover your patterned plywood with waxed paper or plastic to prevent the epoxy from gluing a rib to the pattern. Glue the components together as described in "Epoxy as a Glue," page 131. Remember, you don't need a lot of pressure when you glue with epoxy. Small clamps and lead weights will give you enough pressure.

Let each rib cure at least four hours in a warm shop or overnight in an unheated shop. Clean up any epoxy-glue drips on the ribs with a chisel or block plane.

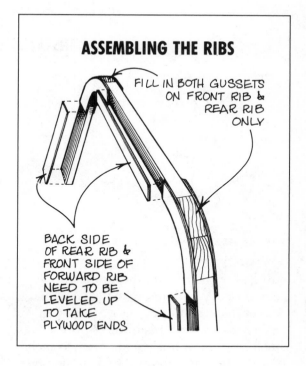

ASSEMBLING THE RIBS

FILL IN BOTH GUSSETS ON FRONT RIB & REAR RIB ONLY

BACK SIDE OF REAR RIB & FRONT SIDE OF FORWARD RIB NEED TO BE LEVELED UP TO TAKE PLYWOOD ENDS

6. **NOTCH THE SUPPORT BOARDS FOR THE RIBS.** Lay out ¾-inch-wide × 1½-inch-deep notches for a rib every 10 to 16 inches along the length of the truck bed. Space the notches evenly. Where spacing allows, plan to install a rib against a vertical stud for extra support. Our 8-foot cap used seven ribs on each side. The ribs were spaced on approximately 13½-inch centers. Chop the notches out with a chisel. The ribs do not have to fit snugly into the notches because the epoxy will flow into any gaps and create strong joints.

7. **INSTALL THE RIBS.** First, saturate the notches and the edges of the support board with epoxy to seal all the edge grain. The ribs are then glued and filleted into the notches in the support boards as shown in *Assembling the Ribs.* Start with a rib that will go against studs. Later, you will clamp it to the stud and then use that rib to hold the others in position until the epoxy has cured. Saturate the adjoining

INSTALLING THE RIBS

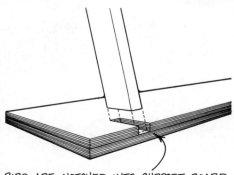

RIBS ARE NOTCHED INTO SUPPORT BOARD & EPOXY GLUED INTO PLACE

TONGUE DEPRESSORS ARE JUST THE RIGHT SIZE HERE

BEVEL SUPPORT BOARD TO MATCH ANGLE OF TRUCK SIDES & FILLET AROUND RIBS

surfaces of the rib and the studs with a coat of epoxy and follow that coat with a coat of thickened epoxy as described in "Epoxy as a Glue," page 131. Apply a small amount of thickened epoxy to each notch to fill any gaps and seal all the plywood edge grain. Clamp the rib to the studs on each side. Apply epoxy in the same manner until all the other ribs have been installed. Clamp thin rips of ½- or ¾-inch stock between the ribs to hold them in position until the epoxy has cured. Then apply a small fillet at the base of each rib. Enough epoxy may squeeze out to make the fillet. If not, add a bit more.

8. TRIM THE STUDS AND SUPPORT BOARDS. With a hand saw, trim the vertical studs to match the angle of the ribs. If necessary, clean up the cuts with a block plane.

The outside edges of the support boards need to be beveled slightly to continue the angle of the ribs. Measure this angle with a bevel gauge and transfer it to the support boards. To avoid scratching the truck, remove the cap and cut the angle with a block plane.

9. SHEATHE THE ROUNDED PORTION OF THE CAP. The rounded portions of the cap are sheathed with two layers of ³⁄₃₂-inch plywood. If you are using metrically sized plywood, 3 millimeters is close enough. It's much easier to make the bend with two laminations of ³⁄₃₂-inch than with a single piece of ¼-inch plywood. The two laminations and the two epoxy glue lines will bring you very close to the ¼-inch thickness of the plywood that is used to sheathe the flat portions of the cap. The difference can be sanded flush later. It won't matter if you sand through the top lamination because the joint will be painted.

Cut four pieces of ³⁄₃₂-inch plywood to width so that the edges will be centered on the joints between the gussets and the spruce portions of the ribs as shown in *Sheathing the Rounds*. If your cap is 8 feet long, use full 8-foot panels. If it is shorter, cut the panels to length.

Start with a dry run. Clamp the plywood in place over the ribs. Put pads of scrap plywood under the C-clamps to protect the sheathing. Place a clamp every 3 inches where the edges of the plywood meet the butt blocks and the front and rear ribs. If you have deep-throated clamps that will reach further into the plywood, use those, too. Check that the plywood is parallel to the sides of the truck bed and perpendicular to the ribs. When everything is lined up, mark the position of the plywood on the ribs and remove the clamps, but leave them adjusted and in reach.

The areas that can't be reached with clamps will be stapled temporarily with ½-inch-long chisel-point staples. You'll shoot the staples through the 1-inch-square pads of ⅛-inch-thick plywood and into both of the sheathing laminations. The pads make it easy to remove the staples later without

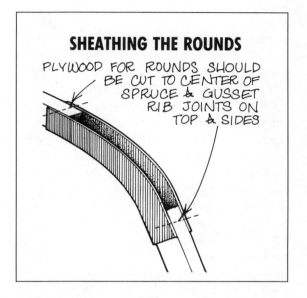

SHEATHING THE ROUNDS

PLYWOOD FOR ROUNDS SHOULD BE CUT TO CENTER OF SPRUCE & GUSSET RIB JOINTS ON TOP & SIDES

damaging the sheathing. So prepare a few dozen pads. An electric stapler will make the job easier.

The job can be done alone, but it will be much easier if you have a helper to hold the plywood in place while you clamp. Equip yourself and your helper with rubber gloves and old clothes. You can attach one sheet of plywood and wait for the epoxy to cure before you attach another on top, but that almost doubles the amount of work and time needed. Even though the epoxy is slippery, we found it easy to put two layers on at once. Your dry run will help you decide how to go.

As described in "Epoxy as a Glue," page 131, roll or squeegee a liberal coat of epoxy onto the mating faces of the two plywood sheathing pieces until they are saturated. Use an acid brush to coat the tops of the gussets and ribs. Then add approximately equal amounts of low-density filler and silica to the epoxy to thicken it to the consistency of catsup. Roll or squeegee the mixture onto the mating surfaces of the two pieces of plywood and laminate the pieces together. Thicken the epoxy a bit more, until it is the consistency of mayonnaise, and then recoat the tops of the ribs and gussets. Finally, roll or squeegee unthickened epoxy onto the sheathing face that will be against the ribs. Clamp the plywood onto the ribs along the bottom edge. Then wrap it carefully and tightly over the round and clamp as you proceed. Work from the middle out to the ends until the plywood is against the ribs along the entire length of the cap. After the round is clamped in place, shoot staples through the 1 × 1-inch pads and both laminations and into the ribs wherever the sheathing is not pressed against the ribs.

Take a look under the ribs. There may be some small gaps between the ribs and the sheathing even after you staple. Thicken the epoxy a bit more to get a peanut butterlike consistency, and then push a little of the mixture into the gaps with a

gloved finger. Use your finger to make small fillets on either side of the rib where it meets the sheathing. You don't need to fillet the whole rib, just where there are gaps. These fillets will add greatly to the strength of the cap.

When the epoxy has cured, remove the clamps and carefully lift the staple pads with a chisel or pliers. Later, when you coat the cap with epoxy, the tiny holes that are left by the staples will be filled. After the cap weathers for a few months, the holes will become virtually invisible.

Use a rabbet plane to clean any epoxy drips off the top and bottom edges of the sheathing and to ensure a good mating between the flat side and top panels. A perfect fit is not necessary since the seam will be filled and sealed with epoxy and then painted, but it should be close. If necessary, use a block plane to trim the front and back edges of the plywood flush with the sides of the front and back ribs.

Repeat the process for the rounded portion on the other side of the cap. Congratulations! You've just completed the toughest part of the job.

---

10. INSTALL THE RIB BLOCKING. Four blocks of ¾ × 1½-inch spruce are glued with epoxy into each bay that is formed by the ribs. As *Installing Blocking* shows, the blocks are centered on the seams that are between the rounds and the flat top and side pieces. These blocks provide additional structural support at the seams and

a solid attachment for the ¼-inch plywood sheathing.

Measure and cut each block for a snug fit between the ribs. Use epoxy to glue the blocks to the inside edges of the rounds, as illustrated, and then clamp them in place.

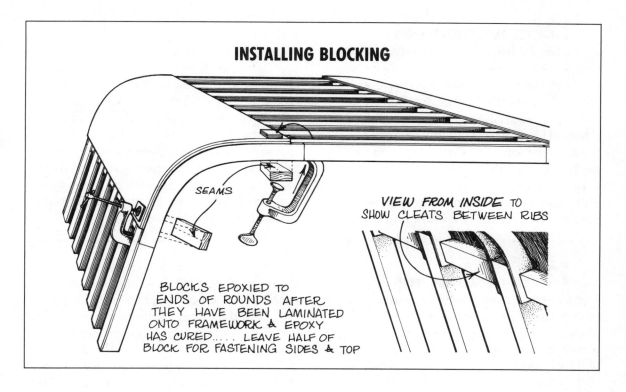

INSTALLING BLOCKING

SEAMS

VIEW FROM INSIDE TO SHOW CLEATS BETWEEN RIBS

BLOCKS EPOXIED TO ENDS OF ROUNDS AFTER THEY HAVE BEEN LAMINATED ONTO FRAMEWORK & EPOXY HAS CURED..... LEAVE HALF OF BLOCK FOR FASTENING SIDES & TOP

11. CUT AND ATTACH THE TOP PANEL.

The top is easy to cut and attach because it's flat and gravity is with you. Measure across the top of the cap between the two rounds to determine the width you need for the ¼-inch plywood top panel. Measure at the front and at the back. Hopefully, the measurements will be the same. If there is a slight difference, you can taper the width of the top panel to compensate. Rip the panel to width and, if necessary, cut it to length. Then saturate the bottom of the panel and the tops of the ribs and gussets with epoxy. Thicken the epoxy to a mayonnaiselike consistency and apply it to the top edges of the ribs and gussets. Lay

the panel in place. Clamp it along the front and back and, using the little pads, staple it in the middle. Again, you can fill small gaps underneath the top panel with small finger fillets.

After the epoxy has cured, remove the clamps and staples. Wrap #80 grit sandpaper around a block and sand the joint between the top and the rounds. Blow out the dust and then use a putty knife to fill the joint flush with epoxy that has been mixed with low-density filler. After the epoxy has cured, lightly sand the area again. If necessary, use a block plane to trim the edges of the plywood flush to the sides of the front and rear ribs.

12. CUT AND ATTACH THE SIDE PANELS.

The sides are the most visible areas on the camper cap. If you plan to use a clear finish, pick the best sides of the plywood pieces for the outside face and be careful not to bruise it when you staple and clamp. The sides are cut and attached by the same procedures that were used for the top, except that gravity is no longer in your favor. So, the side panels may take a little more effort. Again, be sure to measure for the width at the front and back so you can taper slightly the top edges of the panels, if necessary.

After the epoxy has cured, remove the clamps and staples. As with the joint between the top and the rounds, sand the joint between the sides and the rounds. Blow out the dust. Thicken the epoxy to a mayonnaiselike consistency and fill the joint. Let it cure and then lightly sand the area again. Finally, use a block plane to trim the edges of the plywood flush to the sides of the front and rear ribs.

13. CUT THE BACK AND FRONT PANELS.

The front and back panels are each made from a single piece of ⅜-inch hardwood plywood. If you plan to use a clear finish, use your best panel for the back, which will be highly visible. The front panel will lay against the cab and be virtually invisible except from inside the truck cab.

Later, after the front and rear panels have been attached, you will make wide chamfers, cutting off the front and rear edges of the cap. As a result, the front and rear panels do not have to fit precisely along the profile of the cap.

Measure the portion of the rear panel that extends below the cap to get a precise fit in the tailgate opening. Then subtract ¼ inch from the width to allow for weather-stripping. Next, cut the panels to manageable rectangles that are 2 or 3 inches larger than the final height and width. Put the cap on the truck. Carefully measure the height and width of the tailgate opening and use a jigsaw to notch out the bottom of the rear panel so that it fits snugly in place. Cut the bottom of the rear panel.

Tack the edges of the rear panel to the ribs with a few 1-inch drywall screws. There is no need to predrill. The screw holes will be removed when you chamfer. Run a pencil along the sides and top of the cap so that you scribe the camper profile onto the rear panel. Remove the screws and take the panel off the truck.

Cut along your scribe line with a jigsaw. Lay out the door opening. As mentioned, you can make one door or two and you can make the opening any size you want so long as it meets your needs. Make a radius of at least 2 inches on the top corners of the door. This will make the corners more durable. It also will make it possible to cut the door opening out in one jigsaw cut so that you can save the cutout to make the door.

Remove the cap from the truck. Temporarily attach the front panel with a few screws, scribe it, and cut it out.

14. **FRAME THE OPENINGS FOR REAR DOORS AND FRONT WINDOW OR ACCESS HOLE.** It's easiest to do this work on the workbench before the front and back panels are installed. Frame the opening in the rear panel on the inside with 2-inch-wide strips of 1-inch-thick plywood. Glue with epoxy and clamp the plywood flush to the edges of the openings. To accommodate the 2-inch radii at the top of the door opening, you'll need to cut the piece that goes over the door from a 4-inch-wide strip of plywood, as indicated by the dotted line in *Cutting and Attaching Front and Back Panels.*

If your truck has a rear window that slides open, you can make a hole in the front panel of the cap and install a weather tight rubber boot between the cab and the cap (see "Sources," page 295, for the boot). The boot is handy because you can heat the cap with the truck heater.

Installation procedures will depend on the boot you buy, so buy the boot before you make the hole in the cap. Then follow the manufacturer's instructions. When you decide on the final size of the hole, the perimeter of the cutout can be framed with plywood like the door opening, if necessary. However you install the boot, don't put it in yet. Later, after all the openings are cut, you'll coat the cap with epoxy and seal all the plywood edges to prevent water leaks that may discolor and rot the plywood.

Instead of the access port and boot, you can make a simple sealed window in the front of the cap. This allows an unrestricted view through the cap from the rear-view mirror. Make the window out of a clear piece of ¼-inch-thick acrylic such as Lexan. Cut the opening so that the window will overlap the outside of the opening by at least 1 inch on all sides.

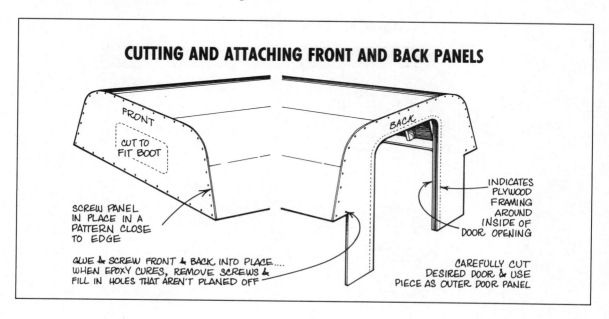

CUTTING AND ATTACHING FRONT AND BACK PANELS

FRONT

CUT TO FIT BOOT

BACK

SCREW PANEL IN PLACE IN A PATTERN CLOSE TO EDGE

GLUE & SCREW FRONT & BACK INTO PLACE.... WHEN EPOXY CURES, REMOVE SCREWS & FILL IN HOLES THAT AREN'T PLANED OFF

INDICATES PLYWOOD FRAMING AROUND INSIDE OF DOOR OPENING

CAREFULLY CUT DESIRED DOOR & USE PIECE AS OUTER DOOR PANEL

15. ATTACH THE FRONT AND REAR PANELS.

Roll a saturating coat of epoxy onto the outsides of the back ribs, the sheathing edges, and the inside of the rear panel. Then, thicken the epoxy to a mayonnaise-like consistency and brush the mixture onto the outside of the back ribs and the sheathing edges. Position the back panel with the screw holes you made when you scribed the panel. Insert additional plywood screws close to the edge. Use as many screws as you need to clamp the panel firmly to the ribs. Again, there is no need to predrill because the screw holes will be planed off when you chamfer the edges. Wipe up any epoxy that may have squeezed out. Repeat the process for the front panel.

---

16. CHAMFER THE FRONT AND REAR EDGES.

When the epoxy has cured, remove all the screws. With a jack plane, make a 1¼- to 1½-inch-wide 45-degree chamfer along the front and rear edges of the cap. As *Chamfering Outside Edges* shows, you'll be planing through the sheathing and the gussets and into the spruce ribs and gus-set infills. Use the plywood and lamination glue lines as a guide when you cut the bevel. If the lines run straight, you know the bevel is flat. Finish the bevel with a block plane or Surform tool followed by a file and, finally, a piece of #60 grit sandpaper that has been wrapped around a block of wood.

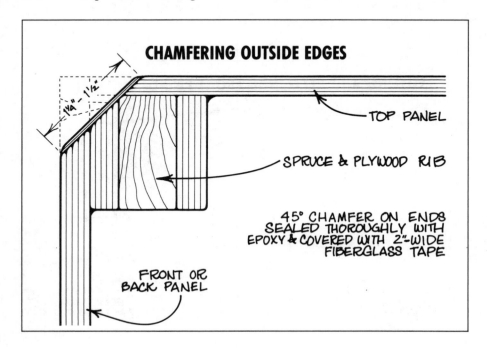

CHAMFERING OUTSIDE EDGES

1¼" – 1½"

TOP PANEL

SPRUCE & PLYWOOD RIB

45° CHAMFER ON ENDS SEALED THOROUGHLY WITH EPOXY & COVERED WITH 2"-WIDE FIBERGLASS TAPE

FRONT OR BACK PANEL

17. **INSTALL THE SIDE WINDOWS.** The window scheme you choose is a real opportunity for you to customize your cap. You could choose to have no windows at all or, at the other extreme, you could use several operable boat windows or ports on each side. We took a relatively simple approach and installed a fixed ¼-inch-thick, 1-foot-square smokey Lexan panel on each side of the cap. We used the same procedure that was described for the front window.

The window width we chose was the maximum we could use without cutting through any ribs. We used ¾ × 1½ framing. We used epoxy to glue the framing to the ribs and made fillets in the corners as shown in *Installing Side Windows.* Install the Lexan windows with screws and caulk as described for the front window. If you intend to paint around the windows, paint before you install the Lexan.

If you choose to use boat-type fixed ports or windows or operable RV windows, make sure that they fit between the ribs before you buy them. Most windows come with flanges that simplify installation. As with the boot, buy the windows before you cut the holes. The Beckson boat-type windows (see "Sources," page 295) come sealed or operable. RV windows usually have sliding or louvered glass, removable screens, and aluminum frames that allow easy installation without interior framing.

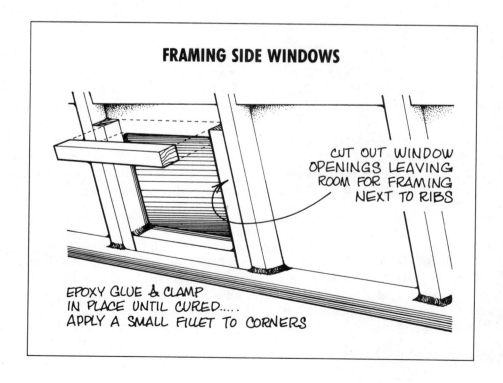

FRAMING SIDE WINDOWS

CUT OUT WINDOW OPENINGS LEAVING ROOM FOR FRAMING NEXT TO RIBS

EPOXY GLUE & CLAMP IN PLACE UNTIL CURED.....
APPLY A SMALL FILLET TO CORNERS

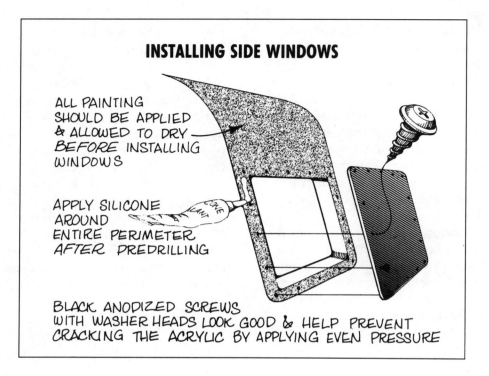

INSTALLING SIDE WINDOWS

ALL PAINTING
SHOULD BE APPLIED
& ALLOWED TO DRY
BEFORE INSTALLING
WINDOWS

APPLY SILICONE
AROUND
ENTIRE PERIMETER
AFTER PREDRILLING

BLACK ANODIZED SCREWS
WITH WASHER HEADS LOOK GOOD & HELP PREVENT
CRACKING THE ACRYLIC BY APPLYING EVEN PRESSURE

18. **COAT THE CAP WITH EPOXY AND FI-BERGLASS THE CHAMFERS.** Saturate the entire outside of the cap with epoxy (see "Epoxy as a Coating," page 132), including the pieces you cut out for the doors and the exposed plywood edges of all the openings. Apply a layer of 2-inch-wide fiberglass tape to the chamfers on the front and rear edges as described in "Reinforcing Epoxy with Fiberglass Mesh Tape," page 137. Apply two more layers of epoxy to the entire cap. Later, to hide the exposed plywood laminations at the edges, we painted the bevel to match the color of the truck. We also painted the seams between the rounds and the sides.

19. **MAKE THE REAR DOOR(S).** As mentioned earlier, we installed two doors in the rear of our cap. Our doors consist of 1-inch-thick foam insulation that is sandwiched between the rear panel cutout on the outside and a ⅛-inch-thick mahogany plywood panel on the inside. The perimeter framing or blocking for the doors is laminated from four layers of ¼-inch plywood scrap, which matches the thickness of the foam insulation. If you don't want to bother laminating scraps together, you can make the framing from 1-inch-thick marine plywood or you could even use 1-inch-thick rips of solid wood. We made the laminations 1½ inches wide. You may have to make yours wider to accommodate the hinge and hasp hardware you've chosen.

Stainless steel, brass, or even aluminum piano hinges add a lot of support to a door, but you may decide other types of hinges look better. A wide variety of hasps and locking bolts are available. We used a safety hasp with a padlock and handle for the outside, a sliding bolt and a knob on the inside, and 2-inch-wide piano hinges. Marine grade hardware works especially well because it's usually bronze, brass, or chrome plated to withstand the elements. Whatever hardware you choose, remember that it has to fit inside the closed tailgate of the truck.

If you choose to include nonopening rear windows in the doors, you can make your own plexiglass windows or you can use Beckson ports that come with their own window framing (see "Sources," page

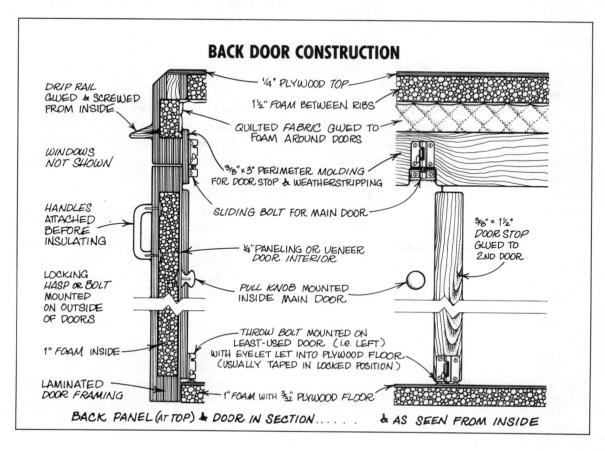

BACK DOOR CONSTRUCTION

- DRIP RAIL GLUED & SCREWED FROM INSIDE
- WINDOWS NOT SHOWN
- HANDLES ATTACHED BEFORE INSULATING
- LOCKING HASP OR BOLT MOUNTED ON OUTSIDE OF DOORS
- 1" FOAM INSIDE
- LAMINATED DOOR FRAMING

- ¼" PLYWOOD TOP
- 1½" FOAM BETWEEN RIBS
- QUILTED FABRIC GLUED TO FOAM AROUND DOORS
- ³/₈" x 3" PERIMETER MOLDING FOR DOOR STOP & WEATHERSTRIPPING
- SLIDING BOLT FOR MAIN DOOR
- ¼" PANELING OR VENEER DOOR INTERIOR
- PULL KNOB MOUNTED INSIDE MAIN DOOR
- THROW BOLT MOUNTED ON LEAST-USED DOOR (i.e. LEFT) WITH EYELET LET INTO PLYWOOD FLOOR (USUALLY TAPED IN LOCKED POSITION)
- 1" FOAM WITH ³/₃₂" PLYWOOD FLOOR

- ³/₈" x 1½" DOOR STOP GLUED TO 2ND DOOR

BACK PANEL (AT TOP) & DOOR IN SECTION . . . . . . & AS SEEN FROM INSIDE

295). The ports come in various thicknesses. If the port you buy is slightly thicker than the door, it can protrude slightly on the outside without looking bad or being difficult to seal. Another option is to skip the rear windows altogether. In any case, the rear windows should be well-sealed and inoperable to keep dust and fumes out of the truck.

After you laminate the scraps for the perimeter framing and window, cut the top radii on the band saw or with a jigsaw. If you will be using nonopening windows in the doors, lay out the openings on the outside door panel and cut the openings with a jigsaw. We made our window opening 10 inches square. Then use the outside panel as a template to lay out the door perimeter and window openings on the inside paneling. Cut the inside panel.

Glue and/or screw the door handles and/or knobs through the inside and outside panels as shown in *Back Door Construction.* Use large washers as reinforcement under the heads of the screws inside the door. Glue with epoxy and clamp the window and perimeter framing to the inside of the outside door panel. When the epoxy has cured, remove the clamps and cut and fit the rigid sheet insulation so that it fits snugly inside the framing. Then glue it with epoxy and clamp the inside panel of the door to the framing.

---

20. **HANG THE DOOR(S) AND ATTACH THE DOOR STOPS.** The saw kerf that was removed when you cut out the door or doors should give you just about the right clearance between the door and the opening. Still, you may want to use your block plane to chamfer slightly the inside edges of the door. To hang the door, use shims to center it in the opening and to hold it in place while you install the piano hinge or butt hinges.

Glue a 1½-inch-wide strip of ⅜-inch plywood onto the edge of one door as shown in *Back Door Construction.* If you use two doors, this stop strip will close on the other door. If you use one door, the strip will close on the back panel. Glue a 3-inch-wide strip of ⅜-inch plywood to the top and sides of the door framing as shown in *Back Door Construction.* Note that you'll have to cut out a notch for the sliding bolt catch. Then you'll have to mount the catch on a ⅜-inch-thick plywood pad.

---

21. **ATTACH THE DRIP RAIL AND PROFILE BLOCKS.** To keep water from running into the door openings, we attach a drip rail just above the doors. The rail, which we made from ¾-inch-thick spruce, protrudes 1½ inches from the back panel. It is glued

PROFILE BLOCKS

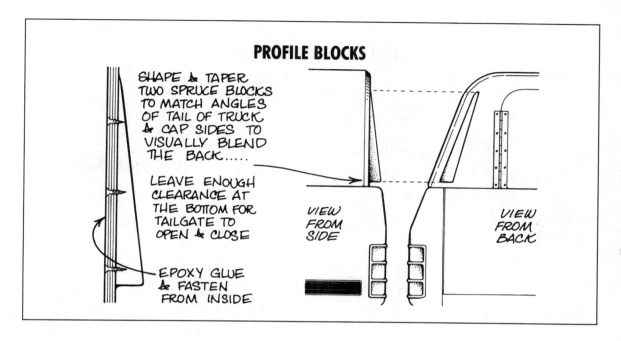

SHAPE & TAPER TWO SPRUCE BLOCKS TO MATCH ANGLES OF TAIL OF TRUCK & CAP SIDES TO VISUALLY BLEND THE BACK.....

LEAVE ENOUGH CLEARANCE AT THE BOTTOM FOR TAILGATE TO OPEN & CLOSE

EPOXY GLUE & FASTEN FROM INSIDE

VIEW FROM SIDE

VIEW FROM BACK

in place with epoxy and attached with three or four small screws that were inserted from inside the cap to hold it in position until the epoxy could cure. Just plane the rail down to a pleasing profile.

After finishing our cap, we thought it looked a bit awkward when it was viewed from the side because the cap ended inside the tailgate. So we made two profile blocks from 1½-inch-thick spruce. The width of the blocks is equal to the distance between the outside of the cap and the outside of the tailgate. Shape the blocks to follow the profile of the truck as shown in *Profile Blocks*. Leave enough clearance at the bottom for the tailgate to open. Glue the blocks to the back panel with epoxy and insert the screws from the inside to hold the blocks until the epoxy cures.

We coated the drip rail and profile blocks with epoxy. Later, we painted them the same color as the accent strips that are over the windows.

22. INSTALL THE WEATHERSTRIPPING.

Weatherstripping is needed on the bottom of the support boards and around the doors to make the cap dust-free and watertight. Use closed-cell weatherstripping, which comes with adhesive on one side. You can find it at home centers and RV dealers. Be particularly careful when you

INSTALLING WEATHERSTRIPPING

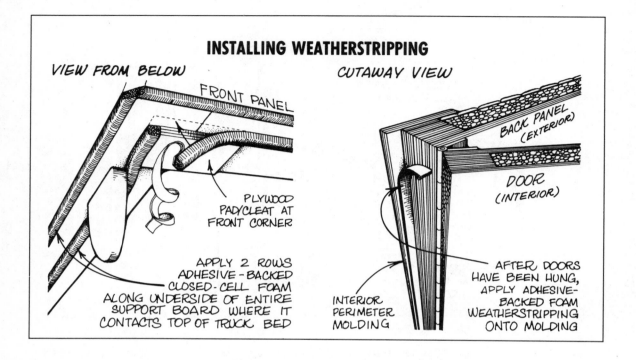

VIEW FROM BELOW

FRONT PANEL

PLYWOOD
PAD/CLEAT AT
FRONT CORNER

APPLY 2 ROWS
ADHESIVE - BACKED
CLOSED- CELL FOAM
ALONG UNDERSIDE OF ENTIRE
SUPPORT BOARD WHERE IT
CONTACTS TOP OF TRUCK BED

CUTAWAY VIEW

BACK PANEL
(EXTERIOR)

DOOR
(INTERIOR)

AFTER DOORS
HAVE BEEN HUNG,
APPLY ADHESIVE-
BACKED FOAM
WEATHERSTRIPPING
ONTO MOLDING

INTERIOR
PERIMETER
MOLDING

weatherstrip the doors because when you travel, a slight vacuum is created at the back of the truck. This vacuum will draw fumes and dust toward the doors. The weatherstripping in this area should be removed and replaced if dust or fumes start to find their way into the cap. To fight dust and drafts, place a double row of 1-inch-wide gasket material underneath the support boards. Put one strip on each side of the studs. We usually replace this weatherstripping about every six months or whenever the cap is removed from the truck.

23. **INSTALL THE TOP HATCH.** The top hatch is important for ventilation, especially during hot weather. Unless you intend to use your cap for cargo only, we strongly suggest that you install a top hatch. When we travel in hot weather, we open the truck windows and the hatch to let air flow into the cab windows and out the cap. The hatch admits light and makes the small cap seem less claustrophobic. And, it's nice to see the stars and have a source of fresh air when you lie down to sleep.

We used a 1-foot-square, plastic RV-type hatch with screening and a transparent acrylic top. It was inexpensive, but the frame is not very strong and the thumbscrew that raises and lowers the top is flimsy. Another problem is that we didn't anticipate the way that it protrudes above the cap. As a result, we have to be careful when we put things on the top rack.

If we did it again, we would use a large boat-type hatch that is stronger, watertight, and fits almost flush to the top of the cap (see "Sources," page 295).

24. BUILD AND INSTALL THE CARRYING RACKS.

The two carrying racks are 2 inches thick and built from two laminations of 1 × 6 mahogany. Laminate the stock with epoxy. Cut the racks so that they are 48 inches long and put 2-inch radii on the top edges as shown in *Building the Racks*. Set the racks on top of the cap and scribe the bottom cuts as shown. Make the bottom cut. Lay out and cut three tie-down slots in each rack. Round the top edges and the inside of the slots with a ¼-inch roundover bit in the router.

Prefinish each rack by sanding and applying three coats of unthickened epoxy to all surfaces. After the epoxy has cured, place the rack in position and lightly draw its outline on the top. Remove the rack and predrill for one 1½-inch-long #12 screw at each end. Put the rack back in place and have someone hold it in position while you go into the cap and predrill through the holes and into the rack.

Saturate the bottoms of the racks and the gluing surface on the top of the cap with unthickened epoxy. Then thicken the epoxy to a peanut butterlike consistency and apply a generous coat to the top of the cap and the bottom of the rack. Put the rack in position and screw it in place

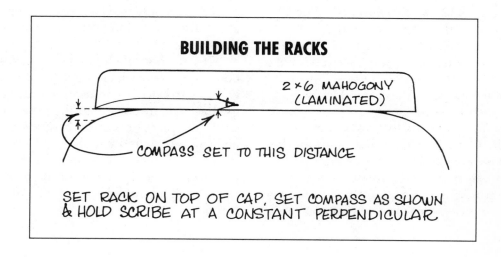

BUILDING THE RACKS

2 × 6 MAHOGONY (LAMINATED)

COMPASS SET TO THIS DISTANCE

SET RACK ON TOP OF CAP, SET COMPASS AS SHOWN & HOLD SCRIBE AT A CONSTANT PERPENDICULAR

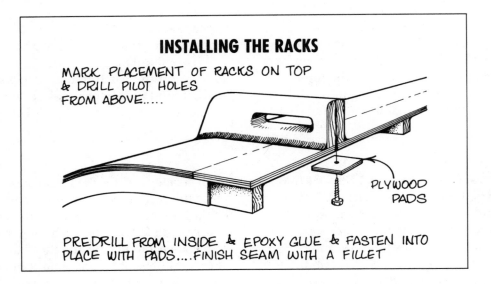

INSTALLING THE RACKS

MARK PLACEMENT OF RACKS ON TOP
& DRILL PILOT HOLES
FROM ABOVE.....

PLYWOOD
PADS

PREDRILL FROM INSIDE & EPOXY GLUE & FASTEN INTO
PLACE WITH PADS....FINISH SEAM WITH A FILLET

from inside the cap. Use large washers or ¼-inch pads of plywood under the screw heads. Tighten the screws until you get a continuous line of squeezed-out glue. Form the squeezed-out glue into small fillets all around the base of each rack. Add more thickened epoxy, if necessary.

When we haul material, we use plastic slip-tie straps to hold pieces of indoor-outdoor carpet on the racks. This protects the racks and the objects that are tied on top.

25. INSULATE THE CAP AND BED. The cap is insulated with Styrofoam, which comes in 4 × 8 sheets. We used 1½-inch-thick insulation in the ceiling so that it fits flush with the bottom of the ribs. For the front and back panels and the floor, we used 1-inch-thick insulation.

The foam cuts easily with a sharp utility knife. Cut pieces for a friction fit for the flat areas between the ribs. For the rounded areas between the gussets, cut 2- or 3-inch-wide strips and fit them in place. Do the rounded areas last so that you can use up your scraps. Use panel adhesive to attach the insulation to the front and back panels.

If you choose to insulate the sides and bottom of the truck bed, cut ⅜-inch plywood panels to fit and use panel adhesive to attach the insulation to the plywood. Later, the pieces for the side of the truck bed can be covered with fabric. Don't attach these pieces to the inside of the bed, however. Instead, friction fit them so you can take them out when you take the cap off.

INSULATING THE CAP

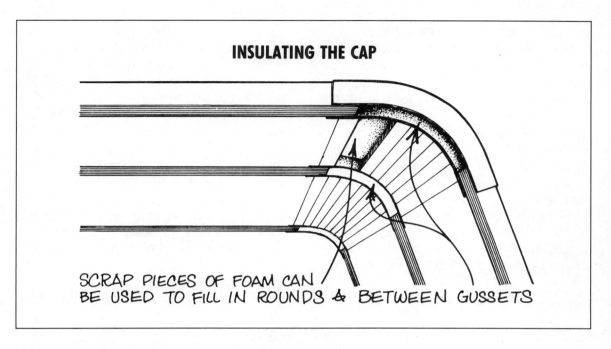

SCRAP PIECES OF FOAM CAN
BE USED TO FILL IN ROUNDS & BETWEEN GUSSETS

INSULATING THE BED

5 INDIVIDUAL PIECES OF 1"-THICK FOAM
COVERED WITH FABRIC

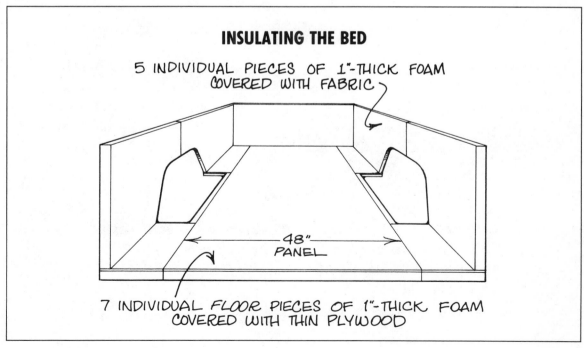

48"
PANEL

7 INDIVIDUAL FLOOR PIECES OF 1"-THICK FOAM
COVERED WITH THIN PLYWOOD

26. **INSTALL THE FABRIC LINER.** We chose to line the inside of the cap with a quilted fabric for a number of reasons. The fabric is easy to work with, easy to apply, inexpensive, and looks and feels great. It also keeps outside noise out and inside noise in. A trip to your local fabric store will provide lots of ideas for designs and colors. Light colors brighten up the interior and make it seem larger, but they are also harder to keep clean. A small patterned print makes it easier to match pieces. Quilted fabric is the easiest to work with, adds a little more insulation, and has just enough stiffness to help hold its

shape without stretching.

Apply the fabric in sections, as shown in *Fabric Layout*. Start with the large overhead pieces, which are labeled 6 and 7. You'll probably have to sew these pieces together, perpendicular to the ribs, to cover the ceiling. Cut the fabric a little larger than the area that is to be covered. Use thumbtacks of a matching or complementary color in a neat pattern to attach the fabric to the ribs overhead. Stretch the fabric tight as you put in each thumbtack. Trim off the excess fabric as you work your way to the ends and corners.

FABRIC LAYOUT

(45" WIDE)

13 YARDS OF QUILTED FABRIC WILL LEAVE PLENTY OF YARDAGE (SHADED AREAS) FOR PIECING AROUND BACK PANEL / DOOR

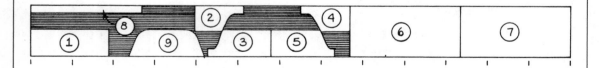

1 • FRONT TRUCK BED

2 & 3 • SIDE TRUCK BED

4 & 5 • SIDE TRUCK BED

6 & 7 • OVERHEAD CAP

8 • EXTRA (6") TO SEW BETWEEN 6 & 7 PIECES (SMALLER CAPS MAY NOT NEED THIS EXTRA WIDTH)

9 • FRONT PANEL CAP

INSTALLING FABRIC LINER

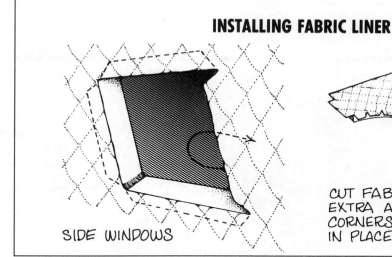

SIDE WINDOWS

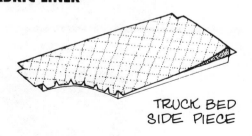

TRUCK BED
SIDE PIECE

CUT FABRIC TO FIT WITH 1"
EXTRA ALL AROUND — TRIM
CORNERS FOR FOLDING & GLUE
IN PLACE WITH PANEL ADHESIVE

27. APPLY FINISH. Epoxy is an excellent undercoating for exterior paint. A good paint job should last for years and when the paint does show wear, you can just paint it again. If you want a clear finish, then you must coat the epoxy with a spar varnish that includes a sunscreen that will protect the epoxy from the sun. The varnish will probably need a touch-up every year or so.

We used paint and varnish. We painted a wide border on all the edges and along the bottom seam of the rounds to hide the joint. We also painted a black stripe to match the smoked-Lexan windows from the top of one side window to the top of the other. We painted the top of the cap with reflective aluminum paint to keep it cooler in hot weather. You can see the aluminum paint only from above. The rest of the cap is varnished.

This bench, which is made from half a sheet of plywood, is handy and comfortable in front of a fireplace, as a foot rest in front of your favorite easy chair, or even as a coffee table. It works well in a hall or entryway as a place to sit when you remove or put on your shoes. Our daughter sometimes uses it as a homework desk when she sits on the floor. She extends her legs under the bench and spreads her books over the top. The bench is rugged and sturdy. It is intended for carefree use in a variety of situations.

This bench uses no moldings. It celebrates the fact that it is made of Appleply, a brand of multi-ply that is similar to a European product known as baltic birch. Both products are extremely high-quality plywood and are made of about twice as many laminations as typical plywood. They both expose voidless edges when they are cut, which makes them ideal for

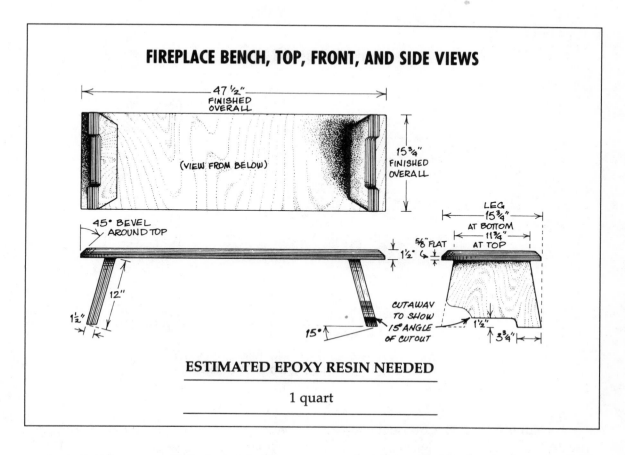

FIREPLACE BENCH, TOP, FRONT, AND SIDE VIEWS

47 ½"
FINISHED
OVERALL

(VIEW FROM BELOW)

15¾"
FINISHED
OVERALL

LEG
15¾"
AT BOTTOM
11¾"
AT TOP

45° BEVEL
AROUND TOP

⅝" FLAT
1½"

CUTAWAY
TO SHOW
15° ANGLE
OF CUTOUT

12"

1½"

1½"

3¾"

15°

ESTIMATED EPOXY RESIN NEEDED

1 quart

projects that have exposed plywood edges. Adding to the spare, clean look of the bench is an absence of braces, cleats, or screws. The legs are simply attached with epoxy. The legs and top of this bench are 1½ inches thick, made of two layers of ¾-inch-thick plywood. The maple face veneer finishes beautifully with varnish or oil.

1. LAMINATE THE PIECES. Cut the half sheet of plywood into three 16 × 48-inch pieces. Laminate two of these pieces together. Cut the remaining piece into four 12 × 16-inch pieces. Laminate these pieces into two pairs. As you make the laminations, expose the best faces of the plywood.

Make the laminations by spreading epoxy on the mating faces and then clamping them or using weights (see "Epoxy as a Glue," page 131).

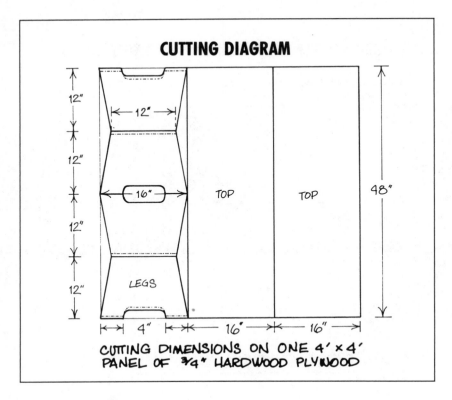

CUTTING DIAGRAM

CUTTING DIMENSIONS ON ONE 4' x 4'
PANEL OF 3/4" HARDWOOD PLYWOOD

2. CUT OUT THE LEGS. Choose the most attractive faces of the two leg laminations for the outside of the legs. Cut the sides of the legs with a band saw or jigsaw and clean up the saw cuts with a block plane that has been set for a very thin cut. Slightly break the edges with two or three passes of the plane. Set the blade of your circular saw to 15 degrees and cut a 15-degree angle on the top and bottom of the legs. (See page 158 for tips on cutting bevels with a circular saw.) Use a jigsaw to cut the 15-degree angle on the indentations that form the feet.

3. CHAMFER THE BENCHTOP. Cut the chamfer on the top of the bench with a 7/8-inch chamfering bit in the router. If you don't have the bit, use a straightedge-guided circular saw. Mark a line around the bench that is 7/8 inch in from each edge. Set the saw blade at 45 degrees and cut along the lines. This will produce a 7/8-inch-deep chamfer.

4. **ASSEMBLE THE BENCH.** Flip the top upside down and place it on a workbench. A scrap of carpeting under the bench will protect the face veneer. Mark the position of each leg on the bottom of the bench. Apply epoxy to the mating surfaces. Use weights, a bevel gauge, and a heavy box to hold each leg in position at the 15-degree angle, as shown in *Bracing the Legs*. This is the only pressure required to achieve the epoxy bond. Once both legs are positioned and braced in place, leave the whole affair overnight to allow the epoxy to cure. After the epoxy has cured, remove the weights and sand or chisel away any excess epoxy at the joints.

---

5. **APPLY FINISH.** Our favorite finish for this maple veneer is hand-rubbed Watco Danish Oil followed by furniture wax. For this finish, start by sanding the edges of the plywood with #60 grit sandpaper. Sand the entire bench with #80, #120, and then #220 grit sandpaper. Wet sand with #600 grit sandpaper as described in the instructions on the can.

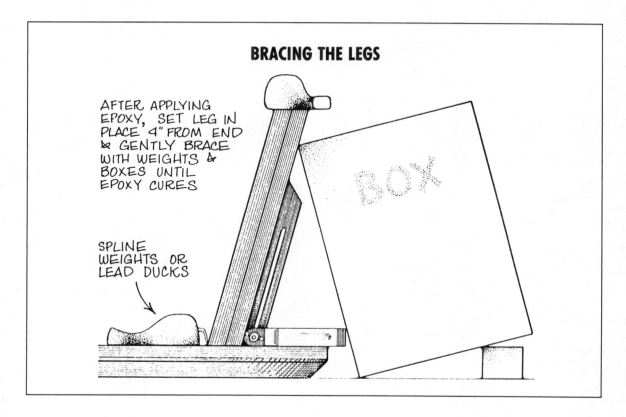

BRACING THE LEGS

AFTER APPLYING EPOXY, SET LEG IN PLACE 4" FROM END & GENTLY BRACE WITH WEIGHTS & BOXES UNTIL EPOXY CURES

SPLINE WEIGHTS OR LEAD DUCKS

BOX

CHAPTER SIX
MORE
OUTDOOR
PROJECTS

FOLDING
PICNIC
TABLE

Big enough for a game of Ping-Pong, yet portable enough to put in the back of a station wagon, this folding table is just the ticket for family picnics. The top uses a full 4 × 8 sheet of 1-inch Marine plywood. The table is not lightweight, but each piece of the two-piece top has an attached folding leg, so it's easy to move around. Attach a couple of optional metal handles and transportation becomes even easier.

While constructed with the outdoors in mind, this table is bound to be pressed into indoor service as well. It's great for the recreation room or workshop. It can be just what you need when all the cousins are expected for Thanksgiving dinner.

FOLDING PICNIC TABLE EXPLODED VIEW

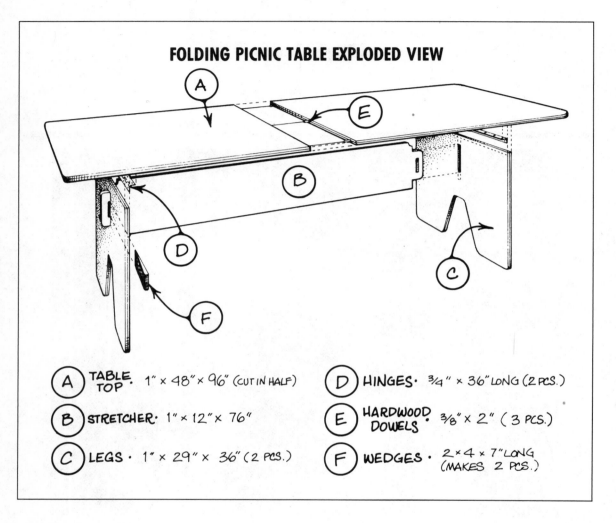

A TABLE TOP · 1" × 48" × 96" (CUT IN HALF)

B STRETCHER · 1" × 12" × 76"

C LEGS · 1" × 29" × 36" (2 PCS.)

D HINGES · ¾" × 36" LONG (2 PCS.)

E HARDWOOD DOWELS · ⅜" × 2" (3 PCS.)

F WEDGES · 2 × 4 × 7" LONG (MAKES 2 PCS.)

1. CUT THE PLYWOOD PARTS. Cut all of the parts to the dimensions in the materials list. Lay out the large V-shaped cut on the bottom of one leg and cut it out with a jigsaw. Sand the sawn edge. Use one leg as a pattern for the other. Lay out the 3-inch radii at the corners of the table and cut them with a jigsaw. Also lay out the tenons on the ends of the stretcher and the 1-inch radius notches in the stretchers, which make room for the hinges as shown in *Hinge Detail*. Make these cuts with the jigsaw.

2. CUT THE SLOTS. Lay out the mortise slots in the legs and the wedge slots in the stretcher tenons. Cut each slot with a jigsaw after you have drilled a hole in the slot for the jigsaw blade. Put scrap behind the pieces so that the plywood doesn't splinter when the drill bit exits. Use a scrap of 1-inch plywood to test the width of the mortise slots in the legs. Adjust as necessary with a rasp and sandpaper. The stretcher tenons should slip easily into place, but not be so loose that they make the table unstable. After all the components have been cut out, break all the edges by cutting a slight chamfer with the block plane. Sand the chamfer to create a soft edge.

3. INSTALL THE DOWELS IN THE TABLETOP. With a doweling jig, drill holes for three dowels. Locate one dowel 2 inches from each side and one in the middle.

If the dowels aren't tapered at the ends, you can slightly taper them with a pencil sharpener so they will find the holes easier. Glue the dowels into one side of the table. You may need to wax the protruding part of the dowels so they will slide easily into the other half of the tabletop.

4. ATTACH THE PIANO HINGES TO THE TABLE. Position the hinges on the bottom of the tabletop, as illustrated. Make sure that they are square to the sides of the table. Attach them with ⅞-inch Phillips-head wood screws.

5. ATTACH THE LEGS TO THE PIANO HINGES. Screw the legs to the piano hinges. With a block plane, bevel the top edge of one leg as shown in *Hinge Detail*. This is to let the leg swing open a little more than 90 degrees so that you have room to insert the stretcher. After you slightly bevel the leg, swing it up to see if you can insert the stretcher. Remove a few shavings at a time until the tenon can be inserted without straining the piano hinge. If the hinge is repeatedly strained, the screws will eventually strip.

BOTTOM, FRONT, AND SIDE VIEWS

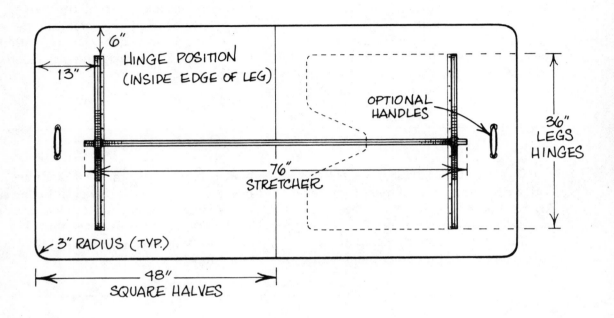

6"

13"

HINGE POSITION
(INSIDE EDGE OF LEG)

OPTIONAL
HANDLES

36"
LEGS
HINGES

76"
STRETCHER

3" RADIUS (TYP.)

48"
SQUARE HALVES

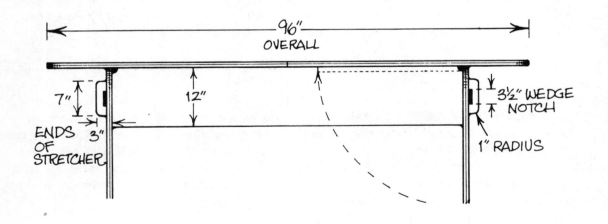

96"
OVERALL

7"

12"

3½" WEDGE
NOTCH

ENDS
OF
STRETCHER

3"

1" RADIUS

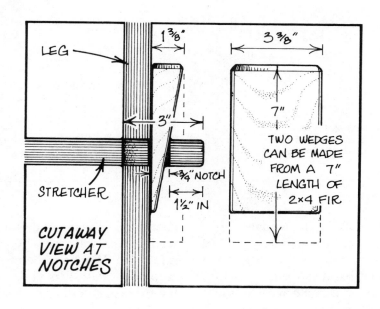

LEG

1 3⁄8"

3 3⁄8"

3"

7"

TWO WEDGES
CAN BE MADE
FROM A 7"
LENGTH OF
2×4 FIR

3⁄4" NOTCH

1 1⁄2" IN

STRETCHER

CUTAWAY
VIEW AT
NOTCHES

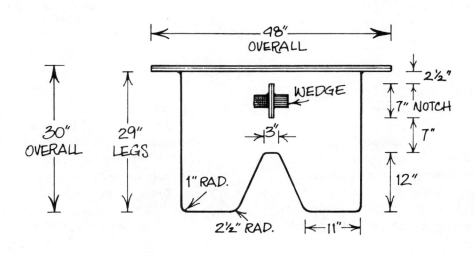

48"
OVERALL

WEDGE

2 1⁄2"

7" NOTCH

7"

3"

30"
OVERALL

29"
LEGS

12"

1" RAD.

2 1⁄2" RAD.

11"

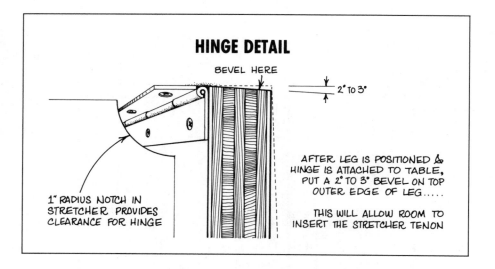

HINGE DETAIL

BEVEL HERE

2° TO 3°

1" RADIUS NOTCH IN STRETCHER PROVIDES CLEARANCE FOR HINGE

AFTER LEG IS POSITIONED & HINGE IS ATTACHED TO TABLE, PUT A 2° TO 3° BEVEL ON TOP OUTER EDGE OF LEG.....

THIS WILL ALLOW ROOM TO INSERT THE STRETCHER TENON

6. MAKE THE WEDGES. The wedges can be hardwood or a tight-grained softwood such as Douglas fir. Start with a 1½ × 3⅜ × 7-inch block and band saw it diagonally into two wedges. You can accomplish the same thing with a hand saw after you secure the block in a vise.

Remove any saw marks and chamfer the edges with a block plane. A large chamfer on the big end will prevent the wedge from splitting when it is tapped into place. Don't sharpen the small end to a point because a small flat is required to tap the wedge out of the slot.

Soak the wedges overnight in boiled linseed oil and buff them dry with a soft cloth. This will prevent the wedges from splitting.

7. APPLY FINISH. Before you finish the table, do a trial assembly to ensure that you have the proper clearances and fit. Assemble the table upside down if you are working alone. Tap the wedges in just enough to draw the tenon shoulders snugly against the legs. Carefully flip the table upright. Support the tabletop firmly against the support board until the table is upright.

We finished our table with Watco Marine Oil followed by three coats of spar varnish. This shows off the wood and is durable enough for a table that may be subjected to an occasional rain shower, but isn't left outside. However, varnish breaks down under constant exposure to sunlight. For a table that will see constant exposure, exterior enamel paint would be a more durable finish.

SOLAR SHOWER

Instead of hitting you with an icy blast, this shower soaks you with water that has been gently warmed by the sun. We are sure you'll find it very convenient for a quick rinse after a swim in the pool or for just cooling off after a hot day. During warm weather, when there is gardening, mowing, wood cutting, landscaping, and other dirty work, this outside shower can also help keep the house clean. Exposed as it is to the sun and fresh air, the shower will always smell delightfully clean and healthy.

This shower uses a 42-gallon steel tank that is lined with fiberglass. The tank can be purchased from Sears for less than $100. Since it uses only solar energy, the shower can reduce your electrical use during hot weather. You can make it even more efficient by enclosing the tank in a plywood box that is insulated on the north side and the bottom and covered with plexiglass or

SOLAR SHOWER

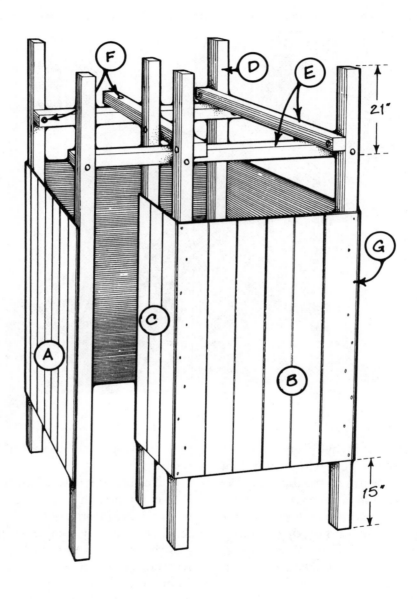

21"

15"

(A) **PLYWOOD SIDES** • 3 PCS. 48" × 48"

(B) **PLYWOOD SIDE** • 1 PC. 30" × 48"

(C) **PLYWOOD SIDE** • 1 PC. 18" × 48"

(D) **TIMBER POSTS** • 6 PCS. 4" × 4" × 96"

(E) **TIMBER BEAMS** • 4 PCS. 4" × 4" × 48"
(TWO 8' POSTS CUT IN HALF)

(F) **CARRAIGE BOLTS** • 10 PCS. 5/16" × 7½"
WITH WASHERS & NUTS

(G) **DRYWALL SCREWS** • BOX OF 100 - 2" LONG

BOLT PATTERN IN 4×4's

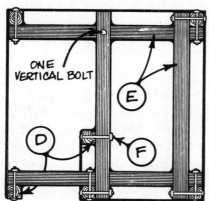

ONE VERTICAL BOLT

CUTTING LAYOUT ON
TWO 5/8" × 4' × 8' PANELS

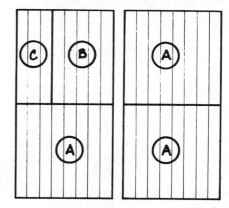

glass on the top and sides. The free-standing shower is quick and easy to build because there are no holes to dig. It also gives you the option of building the shower in the shop, although if you have electricity available on-site, you'll probably want to build it there. The shower is heavy and unwieldy after it is built.

Location is important when you plan your solar shower, especially in the northern climates. If you live in Arizona, New Mexico, or Florida, you can place the shower almost anywhere and use it almost year-round, but farther north it must receive as much sunshine as possible to keep the water comfortably warm for perhaps six months of the year. An ideal location is a southern exposure that is not shaded by trees or the landscape from dawn till sunset. It also helps if the location is sheltered by a windbreak on one or two sides. It's not crucial that the shower be perfectly level, but you should place it on a fairly level spot so all the posts firmly contact the ground.

The shower is constructed of pressure-treated 4 × 4 posts and rough sawn, grooved exterior siding. If you want to paint the posts a different color than the siding, paint them before you assemble the shower. There are several styles of plywood siding from which you can choose, but make sure you get exterior siding, not sheathing. Sheathing, such as CDX, is designed to hold up for short periods of exposure to the weather until it can be covered with siding. The X stands for exposure, not exterior. Only plywood designated as siding is designed for permanent exposure.

---

1. CUT THE PLYWOOD. The shower uses two full sheets of plywood. Cut them as shown in the diagram.

---

2. ASSEMBLE THE WALLS. You can fasten the plywood to the posts with 2-inch galvanized drywall screws or galvanized 8d nails. Roundhead nails look nice with plywood siding and you can sink them flush without a nail set. Unfortunately, the roundhead nail and the extra resistance that is created by the rough, galvanized surface, make the nails a little tricky to drive without bending them. In any case, there's no need to predrill. Attach ½ of a sheet of plywood to two posts to form one wall. Prop the piece in place. Attach another ½ of a sheet to another post and then attach this assembly to the first wall. Work your way around until all the walls are assembled.

3. ASSEMBLE THE BEAMS. Put the shower in position and make sure all the posts have firm footing. Level the shower by slipping large flat stones under appropriate posts, if necessary. Measure 21 inches down from the top of the posts and strike lines for the bottom of the two lower beams. On each mark, just below the line, tap in a nail about halfway. Put a beam up on the nails. Level the beam by tapping up on the nails or down on the beam. When the beam is level, drill ⁵⁄₁₆-inch-diameter holes for the carriage bolts. Take the beam down, pull the nails, then put the beam back up and bolt it in place. Do the same with the other beam.

When both lower beams have been bolted in place, lay the upper beams on them and drill and bolt them in place. You'll probably have to retighten the bolts in a year or so as the lumber dries out.

4. APPLY FINISH. You can paint your shower, but plywood siding is specifically designed to work well with all types of stain—solid color, semitransparent, or transparent. We used a heavy coat of solid brown oil stain to blend in with a wooded environment.

5. INSTALL THE TANK. Paint the tank flat black so it will absorb the sun's warmth. Our tank has three outlets—two on top and one on the bottom. All three are threaded to accept a garden hose. We punched a little hole in the plastic plug in one of the top outlets to allow air to enter when the water flows out. The other top outlet is fitted with a coupling that will accept the threaded end of a garden hose. This outlet is used to fill the tank. We screwed a plastic valve onto the bottom outlet so that we can turn the water on and off. For a shower head, we attached the kind that has a rubber hose with a rubber connector on the end—the type designed to hook up to a bathtub faucet.

Carefully hoist the tank in place and fill it with clean water. A couple of days of direct sunlight will bring the water up to a comfortable temperature. You can check the temperature of the water by placing your hand on the bottom of the tank. Remember to add water after you shower or as necessary. With a few hours of sunlight each day, the shower will remain warm. If the water gets too hot, you can throw a white towel over the tank and give it time to cool.

6. **PROVIDE DRAINAGE.** In some locations, such as a sandy beach house, you may not need to provide drainage. But in most places, you'll need to prevent the floor of the shower from becoming a mud puddle. We used four, round, precast paving stones inside the shower and filled in around them with gravel. We found that this provided the most comfortable footing. Pavers and gravel are available at masonry-supply stores.

---

7. **ADD OPTIONAL ACCESSORIES.** A variety of hooks can be arranged around the outside or inside of the shower to hold clothes and towels.

PATIO
BOX

Get your yard organized with this handy outdoor storage bin. Use it to store the garden hose, sprinklers, rubber boots, garden tools, and other items that tend to get left out in the garden or on the patio or deck. You also could keep it near the barbecue to store lighter fluid, charcoal, or even a hibachi. The bin can double as a bench and, if you make the sides longer, you can use it to store long-handled garden tools such as shovels and rakes.

The bin is very simple to make. It is held together with 2-inch #12 Phillips-head wood screws. We made ours from high density overlay (HDO) plywood,

which is an extremely tough, waterproof material. We also painted ours to further protect it from the weather. If you don't mind the look of the HDO, you could just give the exposed plywood edges a few heavy coats of oil. If you do paint the HDO, be sure to rough up the surface with #80 grit sandpaper. Otherwise, the surface will be too smooth to take the paint. Other options include the use of medium density overlay (MDO) plywood, which must be painted if it is to be used outdoors, but doesn't need to be sanded. Or, you could make the bin of marine plywood and paint or stain it.

PATIO BOX EXPLODED VIEW

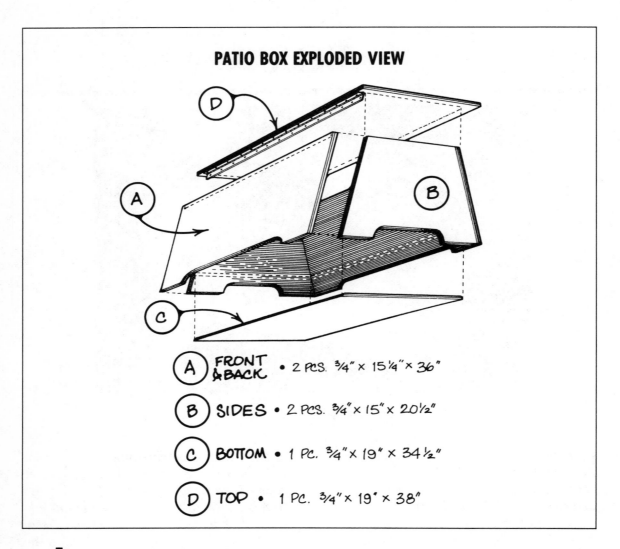

(A) **FRONT & BACK** • 2 PCS. ¾" × 15¼" × 36"

(B) **SIDES** • 2 PCS. ¾" × 15" × 20½"

(C) **BOTTOM** • 1 PC. ¾" × 19" × 34½"

(D) **TOP** • 1 PC. ¾" × 19" × 38"

1. CUT THE PIECES. Cut all the pieces to overall dimensions on the table saw. Note that the sides taper 10 degrees from 20½ inches at the bottom to 15 inches at top. Make these cuts with a straightedge-guided circular saw. In addition, the front and back edges of the bottom and the top and the bottom edges of the front and back are beveled to conform to the tapered sides. Rip these bevels on the table saw with the blade tilted 10 degrees. After all the cuts are made, clean up any saw marks with a block plane.

TOP, FRONT, AND SIDE VIEWS

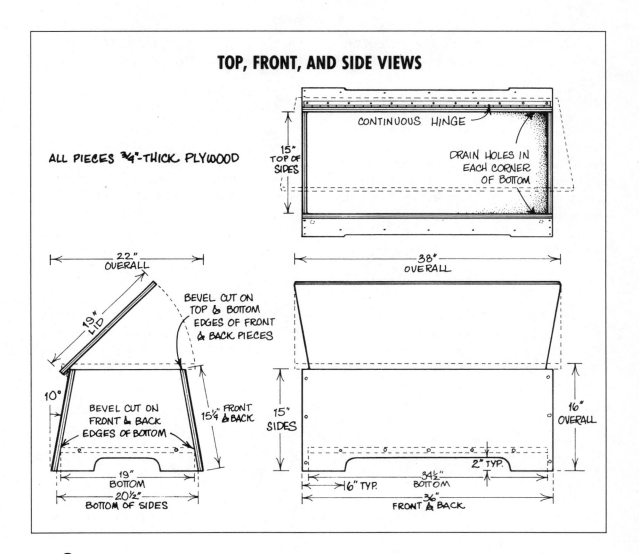

ALL PIECES ¾"-THICK PLYWOOD

15" TOP OF SIDES

CONTINUOUS HINGE

DRAIN HOLES IN EACH CORNER OF BOTTOM

22" OVERALL

38" OVERALL

19" LID

BEVEL CUT ON TOP & BOTTOM EDGES OF FRONT & BACK PIECES

10°

BEVEL CUT ON FRONT & BACK EDGES OF BOTTOM

15¼" FRONT & BACK

15" SIDES

16" OVERALL

19" BOTTOM

20½" BOTTOM OF SIDES

6" TYP.

2" TYP.

34½" BOTTOM

36" FRONT & BACK

2. ASSEMBLE THE SIDES TO THE FRONT AND BACK. *Top, Front, and Side Views* shows the approximate spacing for the 2-inch #12 galvanized Phillips-head wood screws that are used to assemble the bin. Predrill and countersink the screws carefully through a light pencil line that is ⅜ inch in from the edges of all the faces that are to be screwed. Hold the drill as square as possible. A small square held near the bit can be a useful guide. If you don't plan to plug or seal the screws, put a few drops of linseed oil in each screw hole to protect the screws from rust.

3. **INSERT THE BOTTOM.** Flip the bin upside down and drop in the bottom. Tap it snugly in place, then predrill and insert the screws along the ends and sides.

---

4. **DRILL DRAIN HOLES AND ATTACH THE LID.** Drill ½-inch drain holes in each corner of the bottom. The lid is attached with a piano hinge on the outside. Center the lid on the bin, put the hinge in position, and mark the location of the hinge on the bottom of the lid. Remove the lid and screw the hinge to it. Then attach the hinge to the back of the bin. If small children will have access to the bin, you may want to add a chest lid support. These inexpensive devices, which are used on toy boxes, prevent the lid from slamming shut. You can get one from Constantine's (see "Sources," page 295).

---

5. **ROUND-OVER THE EDGES.** Paint won't stick to sharp edges, so round them with #80 grit sandpaper. If you used HDO, the edges will be sharp enough to rip through the sandpaper, so break them first with a block plane. Sand the entire outside with #80 grit sandpaper.

---

6. **APPLY FINISH.** As mentioned, the HDO can be painted or you can apply just a few coats of Watco Exterior Oil to the exposed plywood edges. A bin of marine plywood can be painted or oiled. An MDO bin must be painted.

BOAT OR GARDEN CART

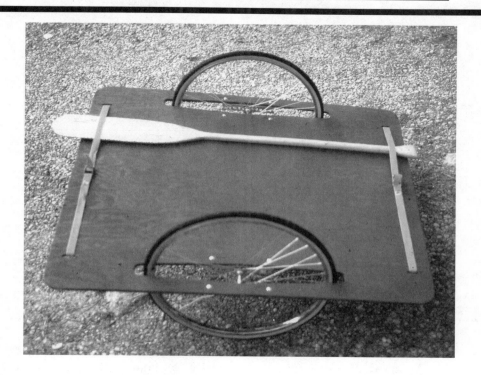

Half of a sheet of plywood, a couple of bicycle wheels, a few pieces of hardware, and an afternoon are all it takes to build this versatile little cart. We designed it to haul our boat to the water from our trailer or backyard. However, it's proven to be equally handy around the shop and garden. We've used it to haul sacks of compost, trays of seedlings, firewood, and 2 × 6s and metal roofing for a building we constructed.

The cart will work for a kayak, canoe, rowing shell, or any other boat that will fit in the 36-inch space between the wheels. The nice thing about its simple design is that you easily can adapt it to your needs. Ours is 4 × 4 feet square. Yours could be narrower and/or longer.

We made ours from ½-inch Marine plywood. This makes a very handy, lightweight cart that can handle loads up to 100 pounds. Use ¾- or 1-inch plywood for

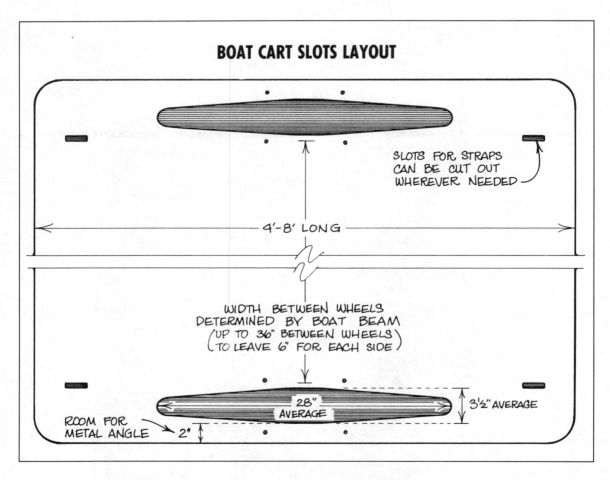

BOAT CART SLOTS LAYOUT

SLOTS FOR STRAPS CAN BE CUT OUT WHEREVER NEEDED

4'-8' LONG

WIDTH BETWEEN WHEELS DETERMINED BY BOAT BEAM (UP TO 36" BETWEEN WHEELS TO LEAVE 6" FOR EACH SIDE)

28" AVERAGE

3½" AVERAGE

ROOM FOR METAL ANGLE 2"

heavier loads. We used 26-inch front bicycle wheels that are available at any bike store. For heavier loads, you might want to use mountain bike tires. Of course, you easily can change the location of the strap slots to suit the shape of your boat. The 1-inch-wide tie-down straps are available from boating supply stores.

1. CUT THE PLYWOOD TO SIZE. To make the cart as shown, cut a sheet of plywood in half so that you have two 4 × 4-foot sheets. To customize the cart to your boat, measure the boat's beam at the widest point and add 5 inches to get the width. Then cut a 3-inch radius at each corner with a jigsaw.

2. CUT THE SLOTS. The exact dimensions of the slots you cut for the tie-down straps and the wheels will depend on the straps and wheels you use. *Boat Cart Slots Layout* provides guidelines. Drill starter holes and cut the slots with a jigsaw. Clean up the cuts with sandpaper.

---

3. APPLY FINISH. Sand the cart with #80 grit sandpaper and slightly break all the edges so that they will hold paint. Prime and paint the cart with exterior paint. You can staple indoor/outdoor carpeting to the cart to protect the finish of your boat and make it easier to slide the boat on and off.

---

4. INSTALL THE WHEELS. Attach the wheels to the underside of the plywood with 12-inch sections of aluminum angle or steel angle iron as shown in *Section View.* You can purchase a 48-inch section at a building-supply store and cut it into four pieces with a hacksaw. Predrill the angle iron and the plywood for ¼-inch carriage bolts that are about ½ inch longer than the thickness of plywood you use. Use two bolts on each side of each wheel for a total of 8 bolts. Also drill through the iron for the wheel hub bolts. Attach the pieces of angle iron to the wheels with the nuts that come with the wheels. Then attach the irons to the cart. Now, you are ready to roll!

One word of caution! Unsealed bicycle wheel bearings will corrode if they are immersed in salt water. Use sealed bearings or be careful to keep the hub out of the water.

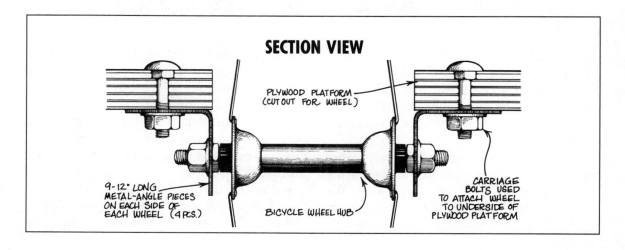

SECTION VIEW

PLYWOOD PLATFORM
(CUT OUT FOR WHEEL)

9-12" LONG
METAL-ANGLE PIECES
ON EACH SIDE OF
EACH WHEEL (4 PCS.)

BICYCLE WHEEL HUB

CARRIAGE
BOLTS USED
TO ATTACH WHEEL
TO UNDERSIDE OF
PLYWOOD PLATFORM

FLOATING
BAIT
TANK

This plywood tank floats almost sub-merged, alongside or behind a boat, or tied to a dock to keep bait fish and/or your catch alive. It has an angled bow and a keel so you can tow it behind a slow-moving boat.

The 45-degree angle of the front does more than facilitate towing. It causes the front flat to automatically close when the tank is towed. This protects the bait or catch. The door floats open when the tank is at rest, which allows the water to circu-late through the screens that are installed behind the door and at the back of the tank.

The tank has two hinged hatches on the top. These hatches are large enough for you to use a dip net to scoop bait. They also provide easy access to the entire interior and shade the fish on hot days when the surface of the water is warm. In addition, the two hatches let you use screening to di-

BAIT TANK

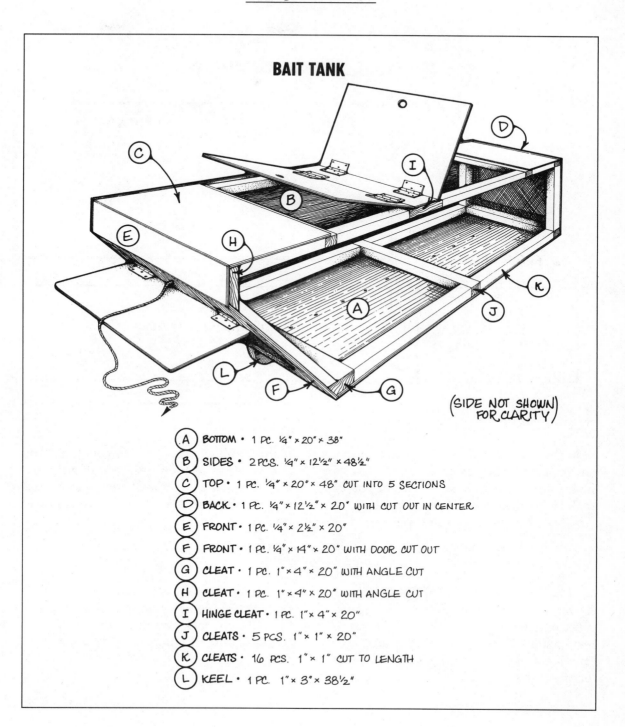

(SIDE NOT SHOWN) FOR CLARITY)

(A) BOTTOM • 1 PC. ¼" × 20" × 38"

(B) SIDES • 2 PCS. ¼" × 12½" × 48½"

(C) TOP • 1 PC. ¼" × 20" × 48" CUT INTO 5 SECTIONS

(D) BACK • 1 PC. ¼" × 12½" × 20" WITH CUT OUT IN CENTER

(E) FRONT • 1 PC. ¼" × 2½" × 20"

(F) FRONT • 1 PC. ¼" × 14" × 20" WITH DOOR CUT OUT

(G) CLEAT • 1 PC. 1" × 4" × 20" WITH ANGLE CUT

(H) CLEAT • 1 PC. 1" × 4" × 20" WITH ANGLE CUT

(I) HINGE CLEAT • 1 PC. 1" × 4" × 20"

(J) CLEATS • 5 PCS. 1" × 1" × 20"

(K) CLEATS • 16 PCS. 1" × 1" CUT TO LENGTH

(L) KEEL • 1 PC. 1" × 3" × 38½"

TOP, FRONT, SIDE, AND BACK VIEWS

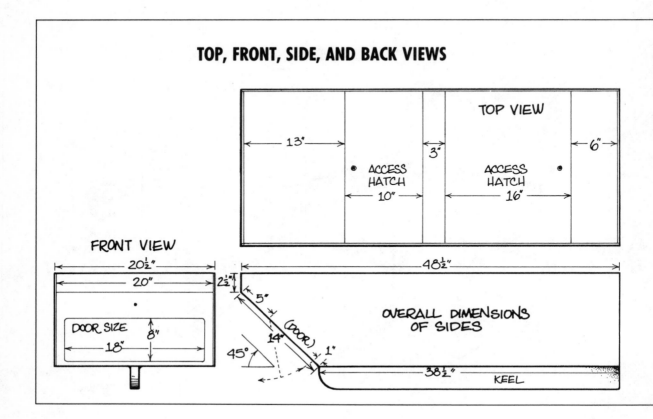

vide the tank in half so that you can store separately the live catch and bait. You can just tack the partition screen in, or you can make it removable for more versatility.

The tank is essentially a ¼-inch-thick marine plywood box. Since the tank doesn't need to be watertight, none of the measurements are critical and you may use screws, nails, staples, or waterproof glue to hold it together.

---

1. PREPARE THE CLEAT STOCK. The cleats form the frame of the tank and provide a place to nail the plywood. Rip 30 linear feet of stock to ¾ × 1 inch. Also rip 6 linear feet to ¾ × 4 inch. Cut off a 20-inch length of the ¾ × 4-inch stock and put it aside. You'll use it as cross cleat I. Now rip a 45-degree bevel on the remaining ¾ × 4-inch stock and then cut it into pieces G and H, which are each 20 inches long.

3. **CUT AND ATTACH THE BACK AND ITS CLEATS.** Attach the back to the rear bottom cleat. Cut and attach the top cross cleat. Keep it down ¼ inch so that the top will butt the plywood back. Then cut and attach the two vertical cleats in between.

4. **CUT THE PLYWOOD FOR THE FRONT.** Cut the plywood pieces E and F and bevel the edges as indicated in the drawing.

5. **ASSEMBLE THE FRONT.** Attach the plywood front piece F to the beveled cleat on the bottom. Attach plywood front E to the remaining beveled cleat H. Make the plywood ¼ inch proud of the cleat so that the top will butt against it. Attach that assembly to the top of the front piece F. Fit and attach the two vertical cleats between the beveled cleat as shown in *Bait Tank*. Note on the drawing that the ends of these cleats are installed at opposing 45-degree angles.

6. **CUT AND ATTACH THE SIDES.** Cut the sides and attach them to the tank. Use a block plane, if necessary, to plane all the cleats and plywood edges flush.

BACK VIEW

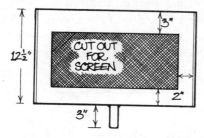

2. **CUT THE PLYWOOD BOTTOM AND ATTACH THE CLEATS.** Cut the plywood bottom to size with a 45-degree bevel on the front edge so it will be flush with the beveled cleat G. It's easier to cut the cleats to fit as you assemble the bait tank. Start by positioning cleat G with a couple of small C-clamps. Then fit and cut the remaining bottom cleats and clamp them as you go. Keep the cleats flush with the outside edges of the bottom so you have a place to attach the sides. Now flip the bottom over and screw, staple, or nail the cleats in place.

7. CUT AND INSTALL THE TOP AND HATCHES.

Begin by cutting the entire top C to the dimensions in the material list. Start assembling the top by fitting the front piece in place on the tank. Install the cross cleats and then the filler cleats between them. Note that the plywood covers only half of the cross cleat. The other half is a lip on which the hatch will close. Center the 3-inch plywood strip on cleat I and fasten them together. Now lay the front hatch in position and use it to locate where the screws should go through the sides and into cleat I. Leave a $\frac{1}{16}$-inch gap so the hatch will open easily. Attach the remaining cross cleat and the rear top piece of plywood. Again, leave a lip for the rear hatch.

8. MAKE THE FRONT AND REAR CUTOUTS.

With a jigsaw, make the cutouts in the front and rear plywood panels. Use the front cutout as a door and attach it to the front with two small butt hinges. The rear cutout is scrap. You can cover the front and rear openings with thin plastic screening, which is available at home-supply centers and hardware stores. Just staple the screening to the inside of the front and rear panels. Or, if you anticipate catching big, aggressive fish, you can use heavier metal grillwork and nail it in place.

9. INSTALL OPTIONAL PARTITION SCREEN.

If you want to install a partition that will isolate bait fish from your catch, cut a piece of screening about 2 inches larger than the tank's inside measurements and bend the edges of the screen back 90 degrees. Staple the screen to the inside of the tank wherever you choose. You might want to partition a small area for the bait fish so they'll be easy to catch.

10. CUT AND ATTACH THE KEEL.

The keel is made from a $\frac{3}{4} \times 3$-inch piece of solid wood. Cut a 3-inch radius or a 45-degree angle on the front. The keel must be squarely attached down the center of the tank if it's to do its job of making the tank tow in a straight line.

With the tank upside down, hold the keel in position and draw around it with a pencil. Remove the keel and drill four fastening holes in the bottom of the tank in the middle of the keel outline. Hold the keel in position and then reach inside the tank and predrill for 1-inch galvanized drywall screws. Insert the screws through the bottom of the tank and into the top of the keel.

11. INSTALL THE TOWLINE AND BALLAST.

Drill a ⅜-inch hole that is centered just over the front flap. Thread the towline through the hole and tie a large stopper knot inside. Remember, the tank is not designed for high-speed towing, but for very slow trolling or to float alongside you while you fish. You might have to put a ballast weight inside the tank to make it float deeper in the water so that it provides more cover for the fish. The tank should float so that 2 to 4 inches of the top project above the water. Temporary weights, such as small flat rocks, can be used or small weights of any kind can be permanently attached to the inside bottom of the tank.

CAMP ROCKER

Perfect for car or RV camping, around the campfire, or on the backyard patio, this portable rocker stores flat and assembles and disassembles in seconds. Two hardwood wedges lock it together. The chair consists of four small pieces. You might want to make two chairs. You can get them both out of one full sheet of plywood.

Because we wanted to paint our rocker, we built it of medium density overlay (MDO) plywood. MDO takes paint beautifully without any preparation, and it's designed to hold up to outdoor use. Marine grade plywood would be a good choice if you want to give the rocker a natural finish.

CAMP ROCKER EXPLODED VIEW

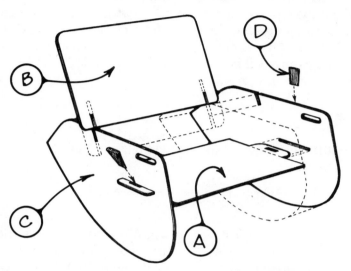

(A)	PLYWOOD SEAT	• 1 PC. ¾" × 16" × 22"
(B)	PLYWOOD BACK	• 1 PC. ¾" × 16" × 22"
(C)	PLYWOOD SIDES	• 2 PCS. ¾" × 18" × 36"
(D)	HARDWOOD WEDGES	• 2 PCS. ¾" × 3" × 5"

CUTTING DIAGRAM

1 SQUARE = 2 INCHES

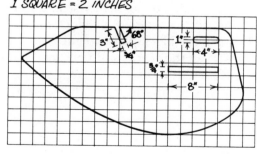

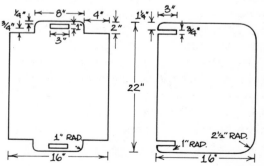

1. LAY OUT AND CUT THE PARTS. Lay out the back, seat, and one side as shown in the *Cutting Diagram.* Take particular care when you mark and cut the shape of the rocker since a rounded bottom profile will make the rocking action smooth and effortless, but even a small bump will be evident each time you rock back and forth.

Cut the three pieces with a jigsaw. Then use the side piece as a pattern for the other side. It's a good idea to change to a new blade halfway through the cutting phase because the MDO dulls blades quickly. Don't force the blade or you may chip the overlay.

---

2. MAKE THE CUTOUTS AND SLOTS. Cut the slots with a router as described in "Cutting Slots with a Router," page 14.

---

3. PREPARE THE EDGES. After you cut out the parts, slightly bevel all the edges with a sharp block plane to prevent the MDO from chipping. Use a fine-toothed rasp or file to bevel the slots and corners.

Lightly sand the edges with #80 grit sandpaper and then fill all the voids in the plywood edges with wood filler. If you choose to cut a logo, design, or initials into the back, do it now.

---

4. MAKE THE WEDGES. The wedges can be oak or mahogany. A light tapping should be all that is required to securely set them in place. Make the wedges from a ¾-inch-thick piece of wood. Each wedge should be 3 inches wide and 5 inches long. The taper is from the full ¾ inch at the top to ¼ inch at the bottom.

It's easier to rough-cut the taper on a band saw. Mark the taper with a ballpoint pen and leave the line when you rough-cut the taper. Start the cut from the ¾-inch end and use a push stick. When the cut

blade is about halfway through, reach around to the back of the blade and pull the wedge through. Keep the push stick in place to guide the cut. Keep your hands away from the blade at all times. Next, secure the wedge in a bench vise and finish cutting it to the line with a block plane. Then use the block plane to cut a small bevel on all the corners. If you don't have a band saw, you can cut the wedges with a jigsaw or even do the whole job with a block plane.

SHOOTING BENCH

This portable, folding shooting bench and stool make it easy to sight in a new rifle or scope. They also are handy for recreational shooting. They are much more comfortable than lying on the ground or draping yourself over a log for a steady position. The bench comes apart in minutes and lays flat in the trunk of your car or behind the seat of your truck. One sheet of plywood is all you need to build both the bench and the stool.

Most shooters sight in their rifles at various known distances. With this portable bench, you can leave the target in position and carry the bench away from the tar-

get to the measured distances. You'll find the bench equally useful for handguns or rifles and a handy platform for ammunition, sandbags, a spotting scope, and other gear. The three-legged design makes it stable on uneven ground. It becomes even more stable under the weight of sandbags and guns. At home, it can double as a handy table in the garage or shop.

The bench rest and stool are built of ¾-inch ABX or AB Marine Grade plywood. ABX will have a few small voids in the laminations, but will cost less than the marine plywood, which will be almost free of voids.

SHOOTING BENCH EXPLODED VIEW

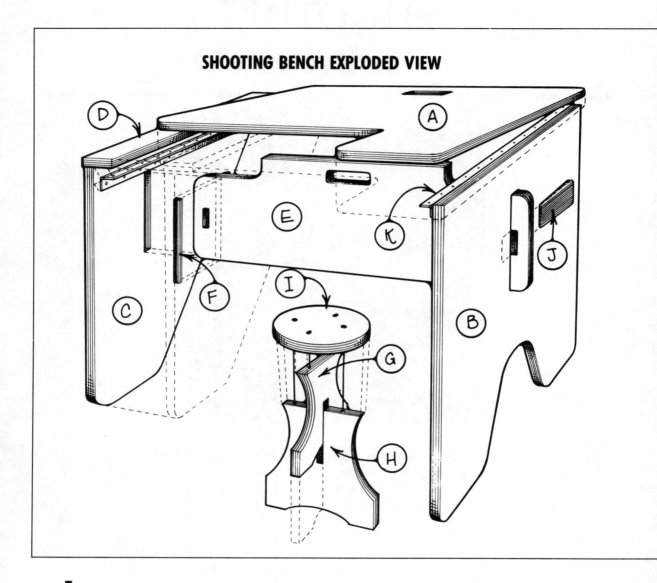

1. LAY OUT AND CUT ALL THE PIECES. Lay out all the pieces for both the bench and the stool on a sheet of plywood as shown in the *Cutting Diagram*. Use a ballpoint pen and a framing square. All of the 2-inch ra-

dii can be scribed from the 4-inch-diameter lid of a 1-pound coffee can. You'll need a compass for the other radii. Cut out the pieces with a jigsaw.

(A) TABLE TOP • 1 PC. ¾" × 34" × 40"

(B) RIGHT LEG • 1 PC. ¾" × 29" × 32"

(C) LEFT LEG • 1 PC. ¾" × 22" × 28¼"

(D) SHIM • 1 PC. ¾" × 2" × 22"

(E) SUPPORT BOARD • 1 PC. ¾" × 14" × 36"

(F) SUPPORT BOARD CLEATS • 4 PCS. ¾" × ¾" × 11"

(G) STOOL LEG (TOP) • 1 PC. ¾" × 12" × 14"

(H) STOOL LEG (BOTTOM) • 1 PC. ¾" × 12" × 14"

(I) STOOL SEAT • 1 PC. ¾" × 13" DIAMETER

(J) HARDWOOD WEDGE • 2 PCS. ¾-1" × 2" × 6-7"

(K) CONTINUOUS HINGE • 1 PC 22" LONG + 1 PC. 32" LONG

2. SMOOTH THE EDGES. Run a block plane over the straight edges to smooth any saw marks and bumps. Clean up the curves with files and sandpaper and then cut a very slight bevel on all the edges with the block plane. Later, you'll sand the edges with #60 grit sandpaper to produce a small round on all the edges.

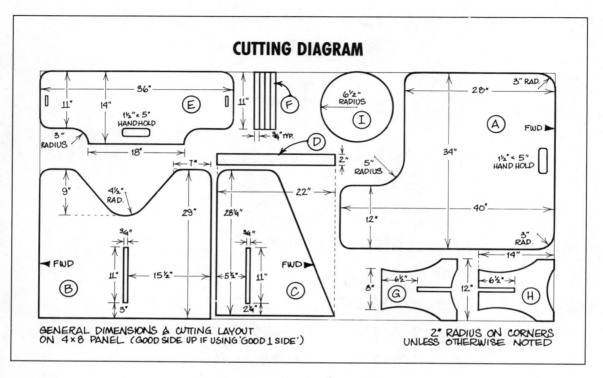

CUTTING DIAGRAM

GENERAL DIMENSIONS & CUTTING LAYOUT
ON 4×8 PANEL (GOOD SIDE UP IF USING 'GOOD 1 SIDE')

2" RADIUS ON CORNERS
UNLESS OTHERWISE NOTED

3. CUT THE SLOTS AND HAND HOLDS. The inside edge of all the slots and hand holds are square to the surface, except for the wedge slots on the support board. Angle these wedge slots as shown in *Support Board Slots* so that the wedges will work better.

Begin by marking all the slot locations. Drill a ¼-inch hole in each slot to start the jigsaw blade. Clamp a scrap of wood under the slot before you drill so that the wood won't splinter when the bit exits. Don't force the bit.

Use a scrap of ¾-inch plywood to check the width of the leg slots. Adjust the fit as necessary by rasping and sanding. Then put the support board into the slot to make sure the slot is the right length. You shouldn't have to force the plywood in and out of the leg slots, but a sloppy fit will make the bench rest unstable.

4. SAND THE EDGES. Sand a slight round over on all the edges, including the slots and hand holds.

SUPPORT BOARD SLOTS

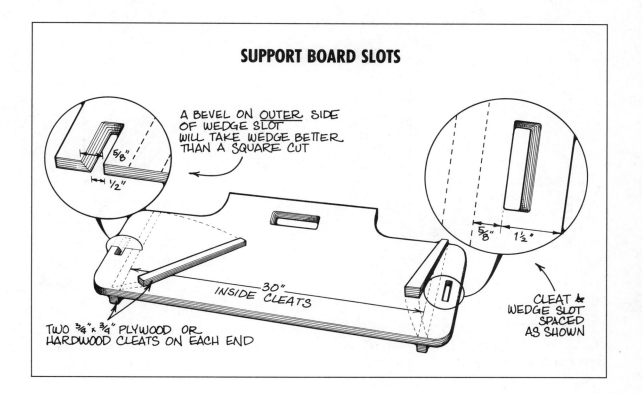

A BEVEL ON OUTER SIDE OF WEDGE SLOT WILL TAKE WEDGE BETTER THAN A SQUARE CUT

5/8"

1/2"

5/8"   1½"

30" INSIDE CLEATS

CLEAT & WEDGE SLOT SPACED AS SHOWN

TWO ¾" x ¾" PLYWOOD OR HARDWOOD CLEATS ON EACH END

5. ATTACH THE CLEATS. The support-board cleats provide stops against which the legs are wedged. Glue and screw them securely to each side of the support board as illustrated.

---

6. ASSEMBLE THE LEGS. The legs are attached to the top with piano hinges, which allow them to fold in. Glue and screw a shim to the bottom of the table as shown in *Attaching the Legs*. This shim, which is located under the left leg, lets the left leg fold over the right leg.

Attach the piano hinges to the bottom of the table and then attach the legs to the hinges. Use Phillips-head wood screws because the limited clearance may not let you hold the screwdriver exactly vertical as required for slotted screws.

After the legs are attached, plane a 2- or 3-degree bevel on the outside, top edge of the left leg as shown in *Attaching the Legs*. This is to allow the leg to bend outward so you can insert the support board.

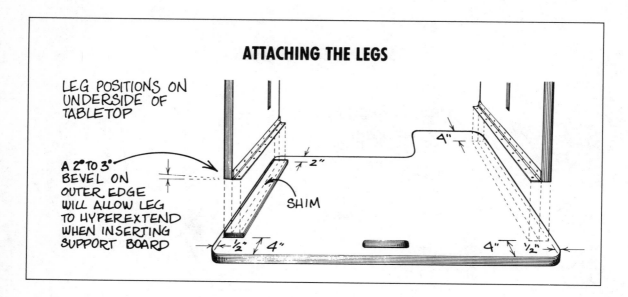

ATTACHING THE LEGS

LEG POSITIONS ON UNDERSIDE OF TABLETOP

A 2° TO 3° BEVEL ON OUTER EDGE WILL ALLOW LEG TO HYPEREXTEND WHEN INSERTING SUPPORT BOARD

SHIM

2"

4"

½"   4"

4"   ½"

7. INSERT THE SUPPORT BOARD. Put one end of the board into the right slot. If you have trouble clearing the inside of the left leg to get to the left slot, don't force the hinge. Plane a little more off the bevel on the top of the left leg.

8. MAKE THE WEDGES. Rip the wedges to the appropriate width on the table saw and do the rough shaping with the band saw or jigsaw. Use a block plane to fine-tune the slope of the wedge and then bevel the top to prevent the wedge from splintering or splitting with use. Assemble the bench rest and test fit the wedges. Fine-tune them with a block plane until they fit.

Soak the wedges overnight in a penetrating oil such as boiled linseed or Watco Marine. You can form a small soaking trough out of aluminum foil for each wedge so that you can pour the oil back into the can later. After the soak, wipe the wedges off and wet sand them with #400 grit sandpaper. Wipe and polish the wedges with a cloth until they're dry. More oil will bleed out of the wood later, so set the wedges aside overnight and polish them one more time before you use them.

9. ASSEMBLE THE STOOL. Slip the two sections of the stool together. The fit can be good and snug since you won't be disassembling it. Make sure the tops of both sections are snug. If not, plane the proud one flush. Put the seat in position and predrill and countersink for 1½-inch wood screws. Take the top off and put glue on the top edge of the base. Replace the seat and screw it in place.

10. APPLY FINISH. Finishing is optional. We sealed our bench and stool with two coats of varnish. Paint or oil are other options.

CHAPTER SEVEN
AROUND
THE
SHOP

WOODWORKING BENCH

Everyone who works with wood knows how much more useful a workbench becomes when you can work around all sides of it. Yet many of us make do with a bench that sits against the wall in order to save space in our small basement or garage shops. The bench we offer here is designed specifically to give you the versatility of a free-standing bench, even if your shop is cramped. At 200 pounds, it's heavy enough to support hand-planing, yet it disassembles in minutes so you can take it apart and stack it against the wall if it's really in your way. And even if you do have the luxury of a spacious shop, this may be just the auxiliary bench you need.

The bench looks similar to a traditional European-style woodworking bench. It is long and narrow and has a sturdy stretcher that doubles as a shelf. A narrow bench is, of course, suited to a small shop. In addition, a narrow bench is much more versatile for clamping and working on all sides of a project. The 84-inch length provides plenty of work surface. Load the handy shelf with tools and the bench becomes even more stable.

While this bench is traditional in form,

WOODWORKING BENCH EXPLODED VIEW

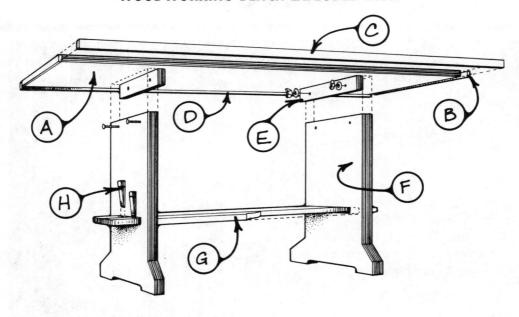

(A)	PLYWOOD TOP	• 1 PC. 2" × 22" × 84" (LAMINATED FROM 2 PCS.)
(B)	END MOLDING	• 2 PCS. ¾" × 2" × 22"
(C)	SIDE MOLDING	• 1 PC. ¾" × 2" × 85½"
(D)	SIDE MOLDING	• 1 PC. ¾" × 3" × 85½"
(E)	PLYWOOD CLEATS	• 2 PCS. 2" × 4" × 14" (LAMINATED FROM 2 PCS.)
(F)	PLYWOOD LEGS	• 2 PCS. 3" × 22" × 31½" (LAMINATED FROM 3 PCS.)
(G)	SHELF	• 2 PCS. 1½" × 5½" × 66"
(H)	WEDGES	• 4 PCS. 1½" × 2" × 8"

its plywood construction is anything but traditional. Old-time woodworkers went to great pains to glue up and hand-plane hardwoods to achieve a flat work surface that would stay flat. Flat and stable are plywood's two greatest attributes. This bench takes advantage of them both.

The benchtop is 34 inches high, a good general woodworking height for the average-sized man. If you do a lot of wood carving, or if you are more than 72 inches tall, consider making the bench a couple of inches higher. If you are 66 inches or shorter, consider a lower bench.

The benchtop and legs are laminated from fir ABX plywood. For this bench, we used two sheets of 1-inch-thick ABX plywood, but unless you live close to a source, 1-inch-thick ABX plywood may be an expensive special order. If so, laminate four sheets of ½-inch-thick ABX instead. Pick the two construction grade 2 × 6 planks for the shelves carefully. They'll really make things tough if they are bowed or warped.

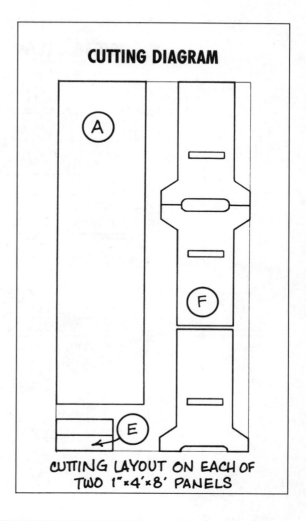

CUTTING DIAGRAM

CUTTING LAYOUT ON EACH OF TWO 1"×4'×8' PANELS

---

1. RIP AND LAMINATE THE PLYWOOD.

Note in *Bottom, Front, and Side Views* that the top is 2 inches thick while the legs are 3 inches thick. Whether you are using two 1-inch-thick panels or four ½-inch-thick panels, rip them all down the middle into pieces that are roughly 24 inches wide.

Cut 32 inches off half of the panels and put these pieces aside. They'll be used in step 3 to make the legs thicker.

Laminate the remaining pieces into two 2-inch-thick stacks by spreading an even coat of yellow glue on every face that is to be laminated. The long stack will be-

BOTTOM, FRONT, AND SIDE VIEWS

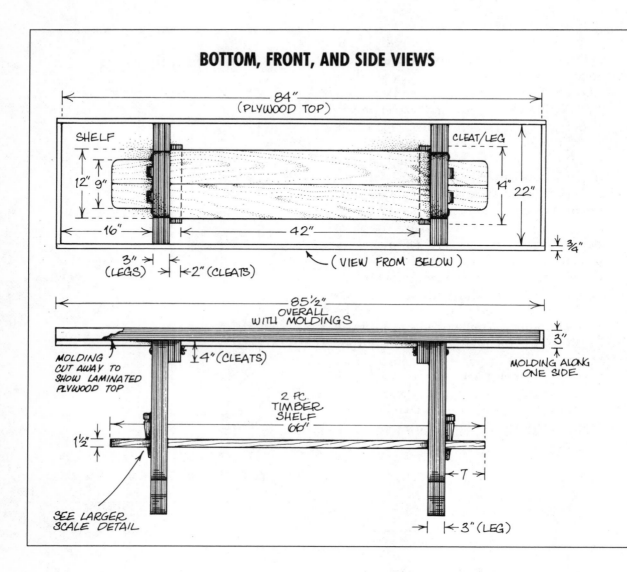

84"
(PLYWOOD TOP)

SHELF

CLEAT/LEG

12" 9"

14" 22"

16"

42"

3/4"

3" (LEGS)

2" (CLEATS)

(VIEW FROM BELOW)

85½" OVERALL WITH MOLDINGS

3"

MOLDING CUT AWAY TO SHOW LAMINATED PLYWOOD TOP

4" (CLEATS)

MOLDING ALONG ONE SIDE

2 PC. TIMBER SHELF 66"

1½"

7

SEE LARGER SCALE DETAIL

3" (LEG)

come the top. Later, the short stack will be crosscut in half after it has been laminated and then laminated to the 32-inch pieces you put aside to become legs. Make sure you have an A face exposed on the top and bottom of both stacks. A scrap of wood about 18 inches long will make a handy glue spreader.

If you have a bunch of deep C-clamps, use them with protective plywood pads to clamp the laminations. If you have only shallow clamps, supplement them

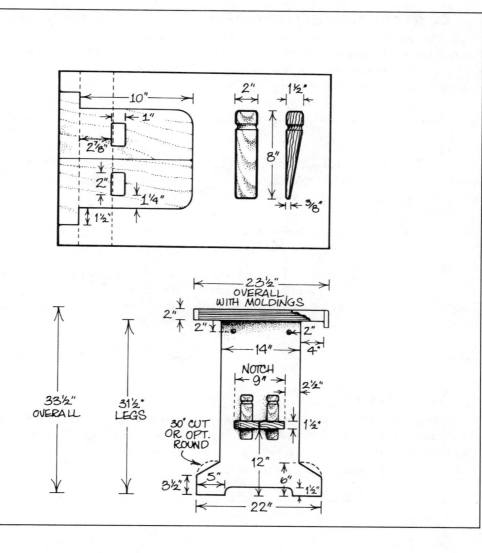

with screws. Decide which face of one lamination will be the underside of the benchtop and place that side of the stack up. Use your shallow C-clamps around the perimeter. Drive a 1½-inch drywall screw into the plywood every couple of feet. The idea is to bite into the plywood at the bottom of the stack without poking through. Use the same procedure for the short stack that will be the legs. The screws in the legs will be covered later by another layer of plywood.

2. **CUT THE TOP AND CLEATS.** Rip the top to its final width on the table saw. Cut it to its final length with a radial arm saw or with a guide and portable circular saw that is equipped with a fine-cutting blade. The top will be too heavy and awkward for a crosscut on most table saws. Make the cleats from the scrap left over from cutting the top.

---

3. **BUILD UP THE LEGS.** Crosscut the leg lamination into two 32-inch-long pieces. Use glue and clamps and/or screws as before to laminate the pieces you put aside so that each piece is built up to a thickness of 3 inches.

---

4. **CUT THE LEGS.** Rip both legs to their final width and crosscut them to their final length. Make sure both legs are the same length and that the tops and bottoms are parallel. Finish shaping the legs with a band saw if you have one or a jigsaw if you don't. Use a block plane to cut a small bevel on all the edges.

---

5. **CUT THE SLOTS.** It is essential that the slots be located exactly in relation to the bottom of the legs. Drill a starter hole and then cut out the slots with a jigsaw. You may need to square up the cuts with a file. Slightly bevel the edges of the slots with a rasp or file to prevent the veneer from chipping when you take the stretcher in and out.

---

6. **ATTACH THE CLEATS.** There are two ways to attach the cleats. We used epoxy as described in "Epoxy as a Glue," page 131. Draw lines on the bottom of the benchtop to locate the cleats and then spread the epoxy on both of the surfaces that are to be glued. Put the cleats in position and hold them down with lead weights. If the cleats slide around on the slippery epoxy, tack a couple of finishing nails into the benchtop on either side of the cleats to hold them in place. Pull the nails when the epoxy cures.

   If you attach the cleats with yellow

glue, clamp the cleats in position with a C-clamp on each end. Predrill and slightly counterbore through the top for four 5-inch-long #10 flathead wood screws. Evenly space these in each cleat. Remove the clamps and put glue on the bottom of the bench and on the cleats. Glue and screw the cleats in place.

7. DRILL THE BOLT HOLES. The benchtop is fastened to the legs with four ⅝ × 6-inch carriage bolts, large washers, and wing nuts. On a flat surface, position the top on the legs. Clamp the legs to the cleats. Making sure that you don't run into the screws that you may have put in the top, drill ⅜-inch holes so the bolts slide in easily.

8. MAKE THE STRETCHER SHELF. As mentioned, it's important to use straight, dry 2 × 6s for the stretcher shelf. Douglas fir is a good choice because it is stable and straight-grained.

The two pieces are not joined together, but they should fit together side by side. Lay them next to each other. Flip them over, if necessary, to find the best fit and then mark the top of each board. You'll get better results if you joint the mating edges, but you can get by without doing this.

Assemble the table and square up the legs. Measure the distance between the inside of the legs and use this measurement to lay out the tenons and wedge slots. Drill starter holes and cut the slots with a jigsaw.

Insert the shelf into the legs to check for fit. Make any necessary adjustments with a block plane and/or chisel. When you are satisfied with the fit, slightly chamfer all the shelf edges with a block plane and then sand the shelf smooth. A slight bevel on the mating edges looks good if the two shelf pieces are jointed for a good fit. Otherwise, it will only accentuate the irregularities.

9. MAKE THE WEDGES. The wedges are made from scraps of 2 × 6s. Cut a piece of 2 × 6 that is 2 inches wide and 8 inches thick. By cutting diagonally with a band saw along the 1½-inch thickness of the stock, you can cut two wedges from a single piece. Cut out two blanks that are 2 inches wide and 8 inches long. On the band saw, rough out the wedges, including shallow Vs for the finger grooves. If you don't have a band saw, clamp a scrap of 2 × 6 in a bench vise and use a hand saw to cut out the two wedges. Clamp the wedges in a vise and use a round rasp to open up the finger grips to a half-round groove. With a block plane, cut a small chamfer on all edges of the wedges. Shape the angle of the wedges with a block plane until they fit snugly into their slots. Sand the wedges with #60 grit sandpaper, soak them in Watco Danish Oil or boiled linseed oil overnight, and then rub them dry with a soft rag. Some oil will bleed out, so rub them down again the next day.

10. INSTALL THE PERIMETER MOLDING.
Rip the Douglas fir moldings to width. The molding on one side of the bench is left 1 inch wider than the 2-inch-thick top. This is to allow you to clamp work to the side of the bench by essentially making a clamp function as a vise.

Cut the end pieces an inch or so longer than the width of the table. Position the molding on the edge with a ½ inch or so extra on each end. Predrill pilot holes and countersinks for 1¼-inch drywall screws. Apply glue to the molding and the plywood edges and screw the molding into place. Use a backsaw to cut the moldings flush to the sides of the bench. Repeat the process with the side moldings. Slightly chamfer the edges of the molding with a block plane and smooth the molding with #80 grit sandpaper.

11. APPLY FINISH. Spot sand the top
as necessary to clean up any rough or splintered areas. Give the entire bench two coats of a penetrating oil such as boiled linseed or Watco Danish.

The bench can be equipped with various woodworking accessories, such as vises, stops, and clamps that will suit just about any project. See "Sources," page 295.

TOOL
CADDY

A good toolbox is as individual as the woodworker who carries it and the selection of tools he chooses to use. The box offered here is the fourth or fifth evolution of our own personal toolbox. Made of ½-inch AB Marine Grade plywood, it's lightweight, weather-resistant, and tough. The overall design is well-suited for any collection of small hand tools, but you'll prob-ably want to change the dividers to suit your tools. So, before we get into the detailed steps of how to build the box, let's look at some things you should consider before you decide how to customize it.

Gather up your favorite hand tools and lay them out as you would want them to go into the box. Start with your longest tool, which is usually a hand saw, level, or fram-

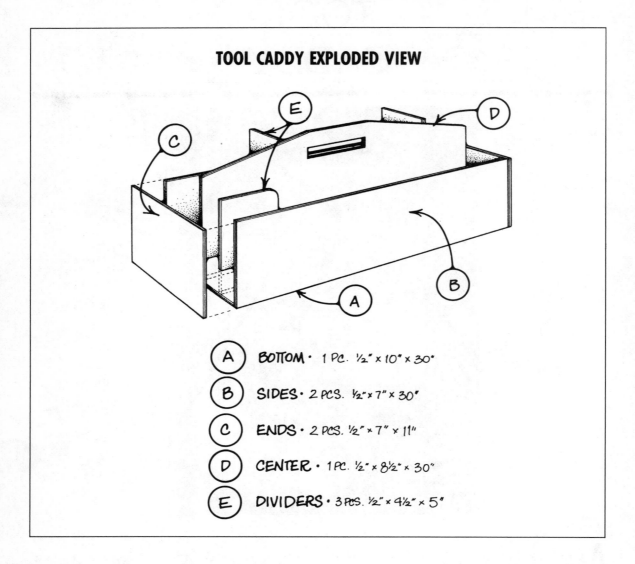

TOOL CADDY EXPLODED VIEW

(A) **BOTTOM** · 1 PC. ½" × 10" × 30"

(B) **SIDES** · 2 PCS. ½" × 7" × 30"

(C) **ENDS** · 2 PCS. ½" × 7" × 11"

(D) **CENTER** · 1 PC. ½" × 8½" × 30"

(E) **DIVIDERS** · 3 PCS. ½" × 4½" × 5"

ing square. This will let you decide if you want to change the length of the box. When you've allocated space for your biggest tools, you may want to go ahead and build the box and center divider. Then you can experiment with the organization of the smaller tools, or even use the box for a

while before you determine the locations of any additional dividers.

Give some thought to the most efficient ways of storing your various tools. You can drill holes in a block of wood to keep your drill bits organized and accessible. Or, you can save space inside the box

TOP, FRONT, AND SIDE VIEWS

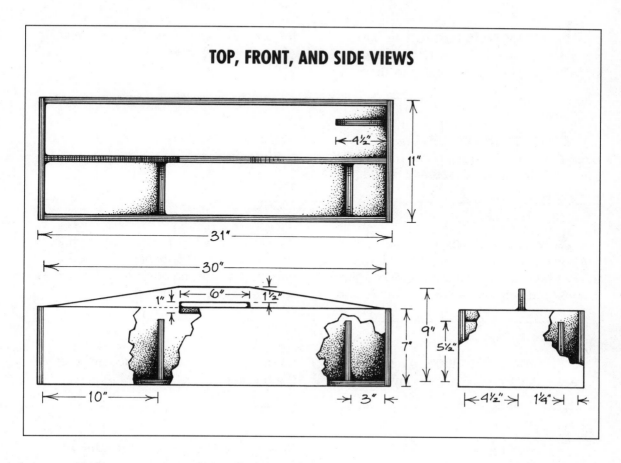

and keep your bits really handy in vertical holes that are drilled into the sides of the box. Chisels need individual compartments to protect their edges. With their irons retracted, hand planes can be laid flat on the bottom of the box. Pencils and pens need a small, deep compartment. A sharpening stone can be wrapped in a towel or put in a wooden box and inserted end up in a deep compartment along with the honing oil. Keep the smallest bins in the tool box large enough for you to insert your hand all the way to the bottom and scratch around as you look for that particular size countersink, drill bit, or Allen wrench.

We put this box together with glue and those excellent square-drive wood screws. These are now common screws in Canada, but you still usually have to get them by mail order in the United States. Why they haven't caught on here is a mystery to us. There are no slots to strip out and the screws stick onto the square driver so you can use one hand to hold the work. If you'd like to order some, see "Sources," page 295.

1. CUT THE PARTS. First, cut all the parts, except the dividers, to the dimensions listed. Then use a jigsaw to shape the handle as shown in *Top, Front, and Side Views*. Sand the sawn edges.

2. CUT THE HANDLE SLOT. Lay out the handle slot. Drill a starter hole for your jigsaw and cut out the slot. Break the edges with a rasp and then sand the slot for a comfortable grip.

3. ASSEMBLE THE BOX. Dry assemble the box with a few 1½-inch screws. Get everything squarely aligned. Remove the screws, put yellow glue on the joints, and then screw the box together. Add more screws every 4 or 5 inches. Attach the handle through the bottom of the box, as well as through the sides.

4. INSTALL THE DIVIDERS. When you have decided on your divider layout, cut the dividers to size and glue and screw them into the box.

5. APPLY FINISH. Of course, you could leave the box unfinished, but a few coats of exterior paint will ensure that the box lasts for many years. A light color will help you find the small items that hide in the corners of the box.

TOOL BENCH/ SAWHORSE

This small, sturdy bench is just 19 inches high, an ideal height for wood-cutting operations in which you want to hold the stock with your knee. A tray underneath the bench keeps your tools handy. It also is a great place to store cans and boxes of nails and screws that you don't want to knock over. The top makes a great surface for clamping. You can slip a clamp through the carrying slot for those really tricky clamp-ups. Although designed as shop furniture, this little unit tends to find other uses. One we made years ago has moved inside as a magazine holder/footrest and occasionally gets used as a writing or reading surface.

Add a receptacle and power will be as handy as your tools. If you work outside, put the receptacle under the top to keep it dry. Make two benches and you'll have a set of sawhorses for working long planks or full plywood sheets. A small clamp-on vise can be attached to the perimeter as needed, and then removed and kept in the tray at other times. Last, but certainly not least, the bench makes a nice seat for lunch and coffee breaks.

TOOL BENCH/SAWHORSE EXPLODED VIEW

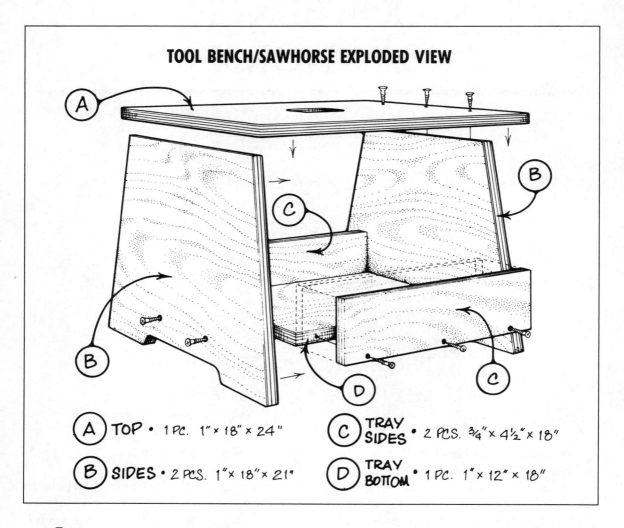

(A) **TOP** • 1 PC. 1" x 18" x 24"

(B) **SIDES** • 2 PCS. 1" x 18" x 21"

(C) **TRAY SIDES** • 2 PCS. ¾" x 4½" x 18"

(D) **TRAY BOTTOM** • 1 PC. 1" x 12" x 18"

1. CUT THE PARTS. Make all of the cuts on the table saw to the size given in the materials list. Cut the angled sides with a straightedge-guided, portable circular saw. Cut the indentations that form the feet with a jigsaw. Sand all the pieces.

2. CUT THE SLOT. Predrill a hole in the top for the blade and then cut the slot with a jigsaw.

3. **ASSEMBLE THE BENCH.** Before you assemble the bench, mark the location of the legs on the underside of the top. Also mark the location of the bottom of the tray on the inside of both legs.

The bench is screwed together with 2-inch #12 Phillips-head wood screws, which are positioned as shown in *Tool Bench/Sawhorse Exploded View.* You can counterbore and plug the screws or, since this is shop furniture, leave them exposed. First screw the legs to the top. Then screw the tray bottom to the legs. Finally, screw the tray sides to the bottom and to the sides.

4. **APPLY FINISH.** You can leave the bench unfinished, but a couple of coats of oil or paint will ensure many years of use.

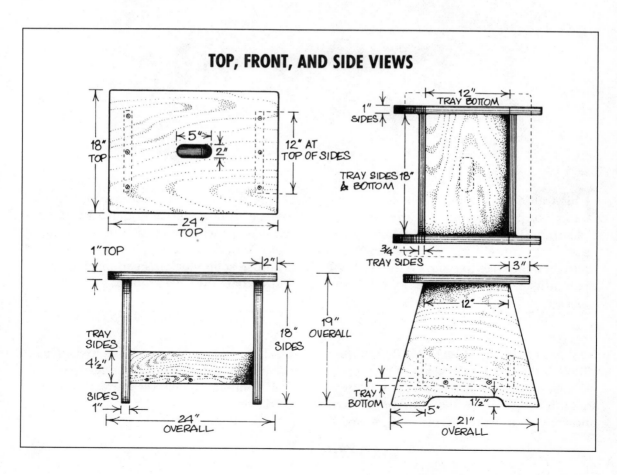

TOP, FRONT, AND SIDE VIEWS

TOOL STRIP

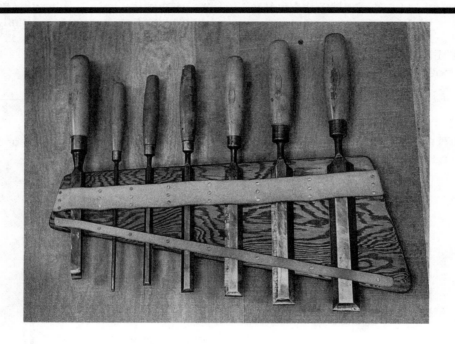

This wall-mounted tool strip consists of a scrap of plywood and a couple of strips of leather. It's a simple idea that easily can be adapted to hold the various hand tools that you might like to hang on the wall. We made ours wider at one end to accommodate a set of chisels. Yours could just as well be rectangular or square. We used a scrap of 1-inch plywood, but anything at least ½ inch thick will work. You could even use solid stock instead of plywood, if that's what you have around.

1. LAY OUT THE TOOLS AND CUT AND FINISH THE PLYWOOD. On the scrap of plywood, arrange and space the tools as you want them to hang. This will determine the size and shape you want the piece of plywood.

Mark the cuts and remove the tools. Cut the plywood and sand the edges to prevent splinters. Finish the surface with oil, paint, or varnish.

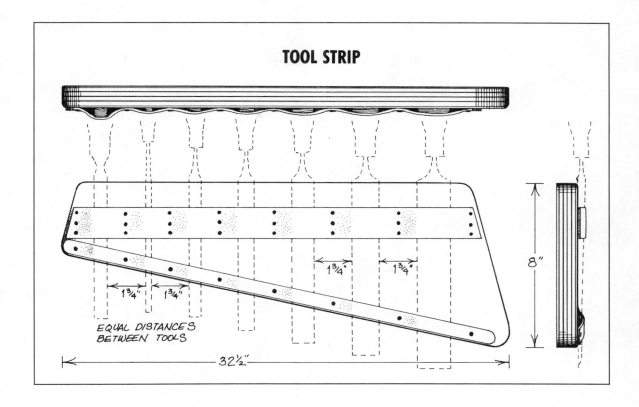

TOOL STRIP

EQUAL DISTANCES
BETWEEN TOOLS

1¾" 1¾"

1¾" 1¾"

32½"

8"

2. **TACK THE LEATHER IN PLACE.** You can buy scraps of leather at a hobby shop. Put the leather over the tools. Tack down one end with copper tacks. Loop the leather over the first tool and adjust it until the tool is held securely, but can be withdrawn. Tack the other end of the loop in place. Repeat the process for each tool. Set the tacks with a nail set. Slice the excess leather off the end with a utility knife. A single strip will suffice for most tools, but two strips of leather will be more secure for larger tools.

3. **ATTACH THE STRIP TO THE WALL.** Screw the strip into the studs in the wall or secure it to drywall or plaster and lathe with molly bolts.

ROCKING MOOSE

Kids can't resist this rocking moose. When we loaned our prototype to a daycare center, he quickly became the most popular toy on the playground. His friendly expression just seems to invite youngsters to climb aboard and gallop away. Constructed of 70 pounds of solid wood and massive plywood laminations, he's designed to befriend generations of little ones.

The moose's rockers, legs, and antlers are made of two sheets of 1-inch-thick AB or AA Marine Grade plywood that has been laminated with epoxy to make it waterproof and, as a result, warp-proof. You can use yellow glue if the moose will only be used indoors. If you do use epoxy, be sure to read "Plywood and Epoxy Projects," which begins on page 127.

We made the head and body staves of

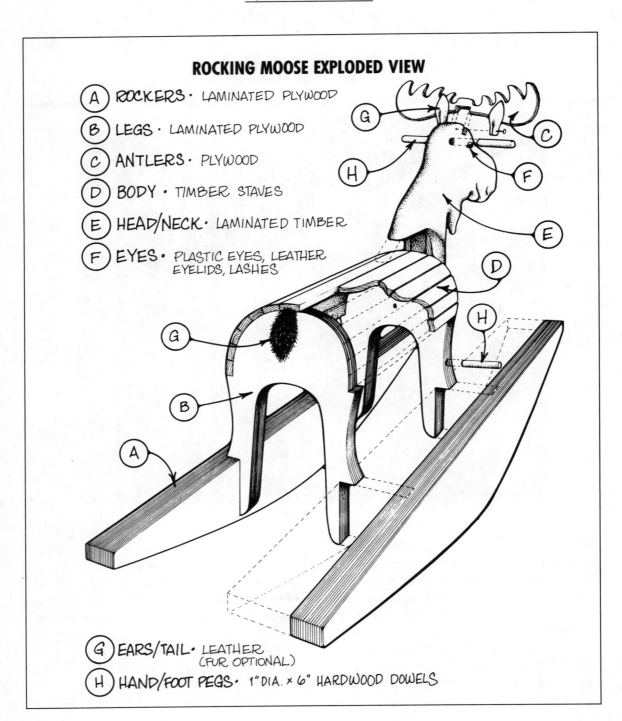

ROCKING MOOSE EXPLODED VIEW

(A) ROCKERS · LAMINATED PLYWOOD

(B) LEGS · LAMINATED PLYWOOD

(C) ANTLERS · PLYWOOD

(D) BODY · TIMBER STAVES

(E) HEAD/NECK · LAMINATED TIMBER

(F) EYES · PLASTIC EYES, LEATHER EYELIDS, LASHES

(G) EARS/TAIL · LEATHER (FUR OPTIONAL)

(H) HAND/FOOT PEGS · 1" DIA. × 6" HARDWOOD DOWELS

kiln-dried Douglas fir. Douglas fir is an affordable, readily available wood that's dimensionally stable, easy to carve, and varnishes to a golden glow. A hardwood such as oak, teak, or walnut would make the moose even more durable, but harder to carve. Or you could even use pine, which is easy to work, but less durable. Whatever wood you choose, select clear, straight-grained pieces for the head and neck. Knots and the tough grain that surrounds them will make carving very difficult.

We laminated two pieces of 1⅛-inch-thick stock for the head and neck piece.

Most lumberyards stock this thickness, which is known as S-2-S six-quarter. This means that a board that was 1½ inches, or six quarters, when it was cut from the tree has been smoothed on two sides (S-2-S). The smoothing process takes the board down to a thickness of about 1⅛ inches.

You can make the moose in standard playground style with the emphasis on durability, or you can approach it like a piece of fine furniture and carefully match the grain, delicately fit the joints, and extensively carve the head and neck.

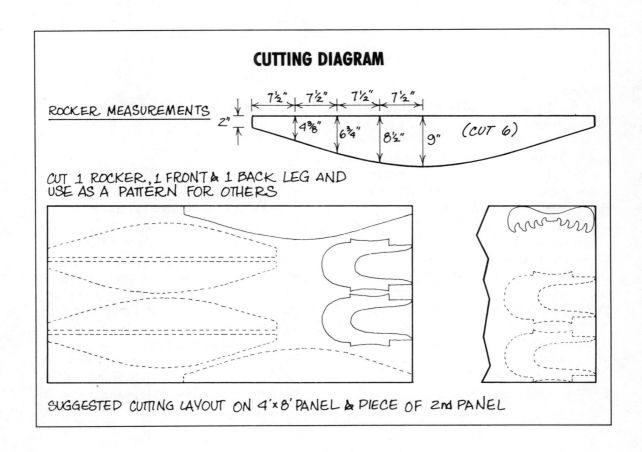

1. **LAY OUT THE ROCKERS.** Each rocker consists of three laminations of plywood. Building the rockers first will give you a sense of the size of the moose. They are heavy so the moose can't tip, and tough enough to stand up to any surface from hardwood floors to gravel.

Lay out the reference points as shown in the *Cutting Diagram.* Then use a flexible batten to lay out the curves as described in "Making and Using a Flexible Layout Batten," page 19. After you cut out the first lamination, use it as a template for the five remaining laminations. You'll use this same template technique for the other plywood components.

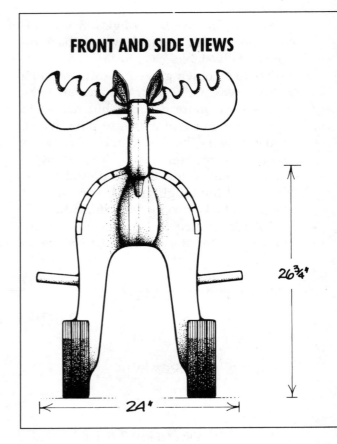

FRONT AND SIDE VIEWS

26¾"

24"

2. **ROUGH-CUT AND GLUE UP THE ROCKERS.** With a jigsaw, cut the first lamination at least ⅛ inch outside the layout line. You'll make the final cut after the laminations are made and the glue has cured, which eliminates the tedious task of cleaning up glue that has squeezed out. Use this first piece as a template to cut five more laminations.

If the moose will see outdoor use, glue up the rockers with epoxy. For indoor use, you can use yellow glue. Now glue up the rockers with epoxy as described in "Epoxy as Glue," page 131. Remember not to bury your final cut lines in the sandwich. If you don't have enough clamps, you can fasten the laminations together with a neat pattern of #10 1½-inch Phillips-head wood screws.

3. **CUT THE ROCKERS TO FINAL FORM.** The rocker curves must be fair to provide a smooth ride. Bumps or flats in the rocker bottom will be very noticeable. To make sure the rockers are identical, use one rocker as a pattern for the other after the glue has cured. First, cut along the original layout lines. Then, use the resulting rocker as a template to draw the final cut on the other rocker. The band saw is best for these cuts. A jigsaw will work too, although it will be more slow and awkward.

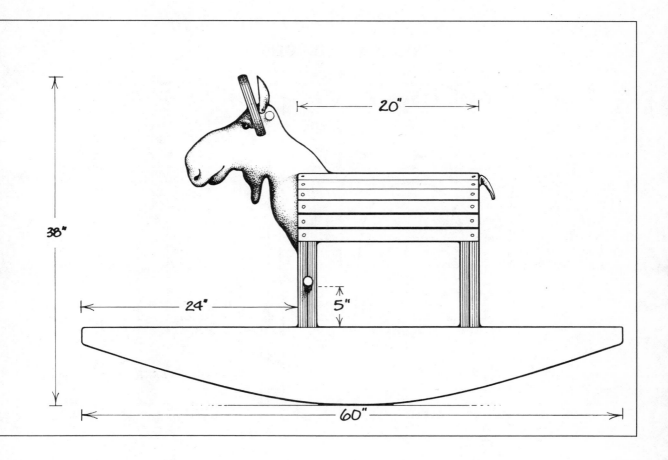

Clean up the bottoms of the rockers with a hand plane or belt sander to make sure they are square and free of irregularities.

After all the rocker surfaces are square, the top is flat and straight, and the bottom of the rocker has a smooth fair surface, cut a small bevel on all the corners with a sharp block plane or a router that is equipped with a 45-degree chamfer bit. Three continuous passes with the plane or one 1/16-inch-deep pass with the router will do the trick. The bevel is primarily for safety because it breaks all the sharp edges, but it also provides a pleasing hand-built look. Sand out any glue strips, clamp marks, or imperfections.

For extra waterproofing, seal the rockers before you assemble the moose by rolling on one or two coats of epoxy with a foam roller, as described in "Epoxy as a Coating," page 132. Scrape away any dust craters and bubbles between the coats of epoxy with a sharp cabinet scraper.

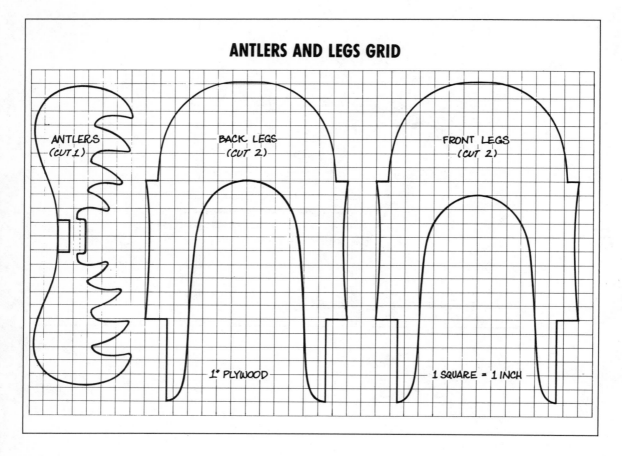

ANTLERS AND LEGS GRID

ANTLERS
(CUT 1)

BACK LEGS
(CUT 2)

FRONT LEGS
(CUT 2)

1" PLYWOOD

1 SQUARE = 1 INCH

4. BUILD THE LEGS AND ATTACH THEM TO THE ROCKERS. The front and back legs each are made of two laminations of plywood. They are identical except for the radius of the lower curve, which is slightly larger on the back legs as shown in *Antlers and Legs Grid*. As with the rockers, layout and cut one lamination for each of the front and back legs and then use it as a pattern for the second lamination. Laminate, cut, and finish as with the rockers. Use the final saw cut to trim the cured glue.

Attach the legs to the rockers with just epoxy or, if necessary, add a wood screw to help locate and clamp the legs. As shown in *Attaching the Legs,* tack or screw a 20-inch-long stave in place across the rockers and behind the front and back legs to help keep the legs aligned while you glue them. Use a square to align the legs at a 90-degree angle to the top of the rockers.

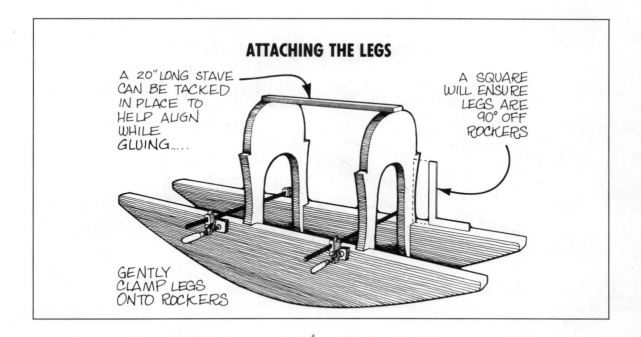

ATTACHING THE LEGS

A 20" LONG STAVE CAN BE TACKED IN PLACE TO HELP ALIGN WHILE GLUING.....

A SQUARE WILL ENSURE LEGS ARE 90° OFF ROCKERS

GENTLY CLAMP LEGS ONTO ROCKERS

5. ATTACH THE STAVES. The 13 staves that form the body are clear, straight-grained fir. Attach them to the legs with 1¼-inch #8 Phillips-head stainless steel wood screws. Countersink and seal the screws with wood plugs that are glued in place. It's not necessary to glue the stave ends to the front and back legs as long as the screws are properly predrilled and tightened.

Make one stave 2½ inches wide and attach it at the top center. The remaining 1¾-inch-wide staves are evenly spaced, with six on each side and a small gap between each stave. After the staves are attached to the legs, fill the screw holes with plugs. Shave the screw plugs flush with a chisel. Round the edges slightly with a block plane. Sand to produce a comfortable, splinter-free seat.

6. CUT THE ANTLERS. Use the illustrated grid to draw the antlers on 1-inch plywood. Make the cut with a jigsaw, but don't cut the notch yet. Round the edges with a ⅜-inch carbide round-over bit in the router, a round rasp, a file, and sandpaper.

GLUING UP THE HEAD AND NECK

CLEAN UP ONE EDGE OF 3' LONG LAMINATED PLANK.
CUT IN HALF & GLUE THIS EDGE TOGETHER TO
MAKE AN 18"
SQUARE BLOCK
(2'4" THICK)

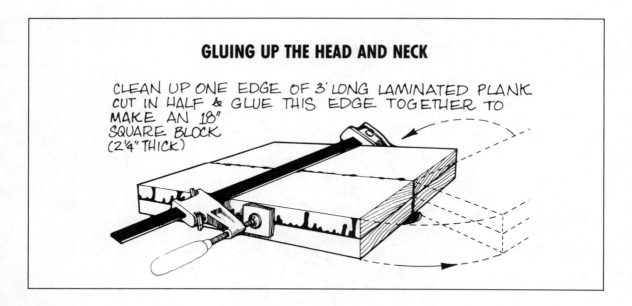

7. GLUE UP THE STOCK FOR THE HEAD AND NECK. Glue up two pieces of six-quarter stock to get a block that is 36 × 9 × 2¼ inches, as shown in *Gluing Up the Head and Neck*. Use epoxy if the moose will be used outdoors or yellow glue if you are building a house moose. When the glue dries, clean up one long edge of the block and then cut it into two 18-inch-long pieces. Glue the two clean edges together to make a block that is 18 inches square and 2¼ inches thick. Make sure the two pieces are clamped together flush and flat because any shape forced into the two pieces by clamping will remain after the glue has cured. If you use epoxy, place two sheets of waxed paper under the joint and clamp the pieces on the flat surface of a workbench. Epoxy is such a tenacious glue that it will stick to waxed paper, so make sure the waxed paper does not glue itself to the workbench surface. Otherwise, you will find yourself tearing apart your bench to remove the glued-up piece.

8. CUT THE HEAD AND NECK PROFILE. After the glue hardens, scrape or plane off any glue drips so that you have a flat surface. Draw the pattern on one side of the head/neck piece. Carefully cut it out with a band saw that has a narrow, sharp blade or use a jigsaw.

9. CUT OUT AND ATTACH THE SHOULDER

PADS. The shoulder pads are optional, but make the moose more realistic and provide a wider gluing surface to which you will attach the front legs. Use the neck portion of the head and neck profile to trace all but the top curve of one shoulder on a piece of six-quarter stock. Freehand draw the top curve, using the *Head and Neck Profile* illustration as a guide. Cut out this one shoulder and use it as a template for the other. Glue the shoulders to the neck.

10. SHAPE THE HEAD, NECK, AND

SHOULDERS. Here comes the fun part. If you are a skilled wood carver, here's your chance to try a realistic moose head. You could even carve the eyes and skip our store-bought version. If carving is not your forte, you can just round-over the edges with a rasp and then sandpaper. You also

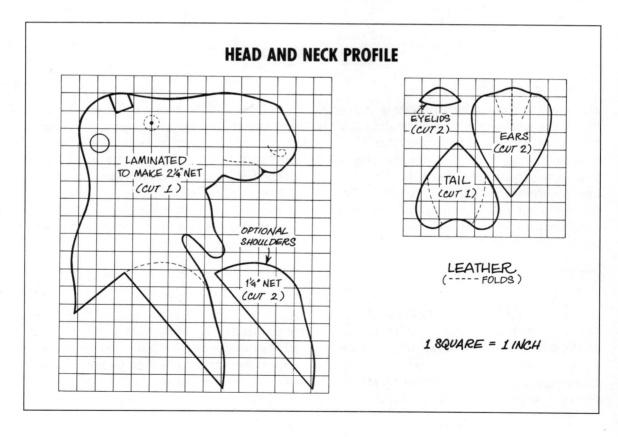

HEAD AND NECK PROFILE

LAMINATED TO MAKE 2¼" NET (CUT 1)

OPTIONAL SHOULDERS

1¼" NET (CUT 2)

EYELIDS (CUT 2)

EARS (CUT 2)

TAIL (CUT 1)

LEATHER (----- FOLDS)

1 SQUARE = 1 INCH

ATTACHING THE ANTLERS

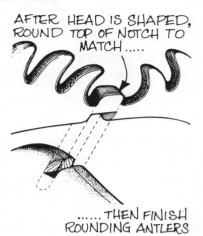

SHAPE ANGLE ON TOP OF NOTCH TO MATCH SLOPE OF FOREHEAD

AFTER HEAD IS SHAPED, ROUND TOP OF NOTCH TO MATCH.....

CUT NOTCH IN HEAD FIRST, SQUARE UP CORNERS & FIT ANTLERS INTO NOTCH - SHOULD BE SNUG, BUT NOT TIGHT.

...... THEN FINISH ROUNDING ANTLERS

may want to carve a little groove to indicate the mouth. As you work, stand back from the piece occasionally and turn it from side to side. Whatever approach you take, it won't matter to the kids. They'll love the moose anyway. Finally, carefully cut the notch in the head for the antlers with a band saw or jigsaw. Trim it as necessary with a rasp or file. Notice that the notch has a slight backward angle. There is no need for an exactly measured angle here, just roughly match the slope of the forehead. Cut the notch in the antlers to fit the head notch and glue the antlers in place. After the glue has cured, finish shaping the base of the antlers so that they match the top of the head, as shown in *Attaching the Antlers*.

11. ATTACH THE HEAD TO THE BODY.

Trim the notch in the neck with a rasp and/or chisel so that it fits snugly over the top stave and front legs. If you're using yellow glue, you need a perfect fit. If you're using epoxy, a small gap is not a problem. Trim the notch to fit with a rasp or paring chisels as necessary. After a final light sanding with #80 or #100 grit sandpaper, the head is ready to be attached to the body of the moose.

Have a helper hold the head and neck